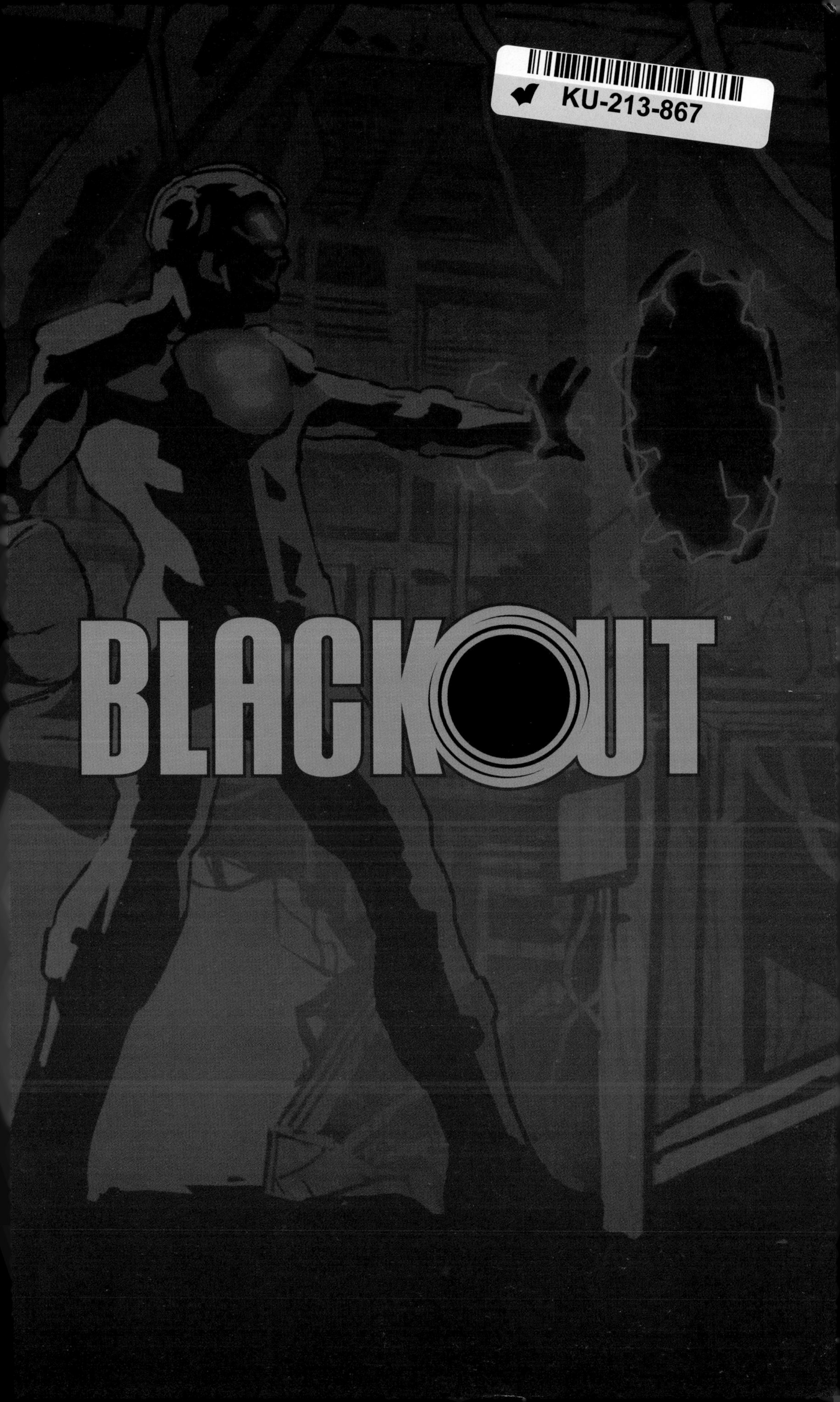
BLACKOUT™

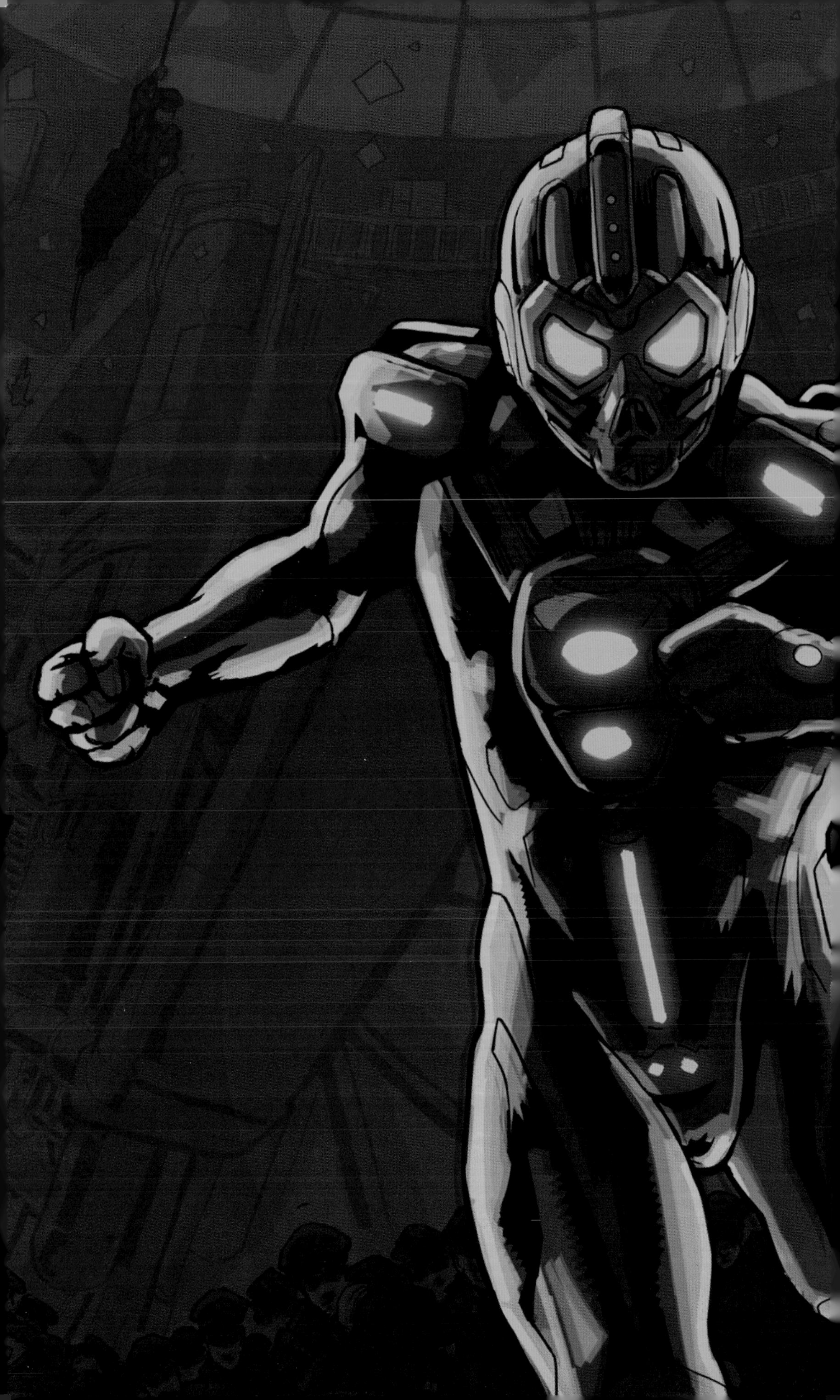

BLACKOUT

VOLUME 1 *INTO THE DARK*

STORY AND LETTERING BY

FRANK J. BARBIERE

ART AND COLOR BY

COLIN LORIMER
(CHAPTERS 1–4)

MICAH KANESHIRO
(CHAPTER 0)

COLOR ASSIST BY

TAMRA BONVILLAIN

COVER BY

RAYMOND SWANLAND

CHAPTER BREAK ART BY

RAYMOND SWANLAND
(CHAPTER 0)

MICAH KANESHIRO
(CHAPTERS 1–4)

PAOLO RIVERA
(PINUP)

DARK HORSE BOOKS

PUBLISHER......................**MIKE RICHARDSON**

EDITOR..................................**CHRIS WARNER**

ASSISTANT EDITORS...**SHANTEL LaROCQUE**
AND **EVERETT PATTERSON**

DIGITAL PRODUCTION.........**ALLYSON HALLER**

COLLECTION DESIGNER.................**NICK JAMES**

BLACKOUT CREATED BY **MIKE RICHARDSON**

Mike Richardson, President and Publisher | Neil Hankerson, Executive Vice President | Tom
Weddle, Chief Financial Officer | Randy Stradley, Vice President of Publishing | Michael
Martens, Vice President of Book Trade Sales | Anita Nelson, Vice President of Business Affairs
| Scott Allie, Editor in Chief | Matt Parkinson, Vice President of Marketing | David Scroggy,
Vice President of Product Development | Dale LaFountain, Vice President of Information
Technology | Darlene Vogel, Senior Director of Print, Design, and Production | Ken Lizzi,
General Counsel | Davey Estrada, Editorial Director | Chris Warner, Senior Books Editor | Diana
Schutz, Executive Editor | Cary Grazzini, Director of Print and Development | Lia Ribacchi, Art
Director | Cara Niece, Director of Scheduling | Mark Bernardi, Director of Digital Publishing

Published by Dark Horse Books
A division of Dark Horse Comics, Inc.
10956 SE Main Street
Milwaukie, OR 97222

First edition: October 2014
ISBN 978-1-61655-555-9

1 3 5 7 9 10 8 6 4 2
Printed in China

International Licensing: (503) 905-2377
Comic Shop Locator Service: (888) 266-4226

BLACKOUT VOLUME 1: INTO THE DARK

This volume collects *Blackout* stories from *Dark Horse Presents* (Volume 2) #24–#26
and from *Blackout* #1–#4, published by Dark Horse Comics.

CHAPTER 0

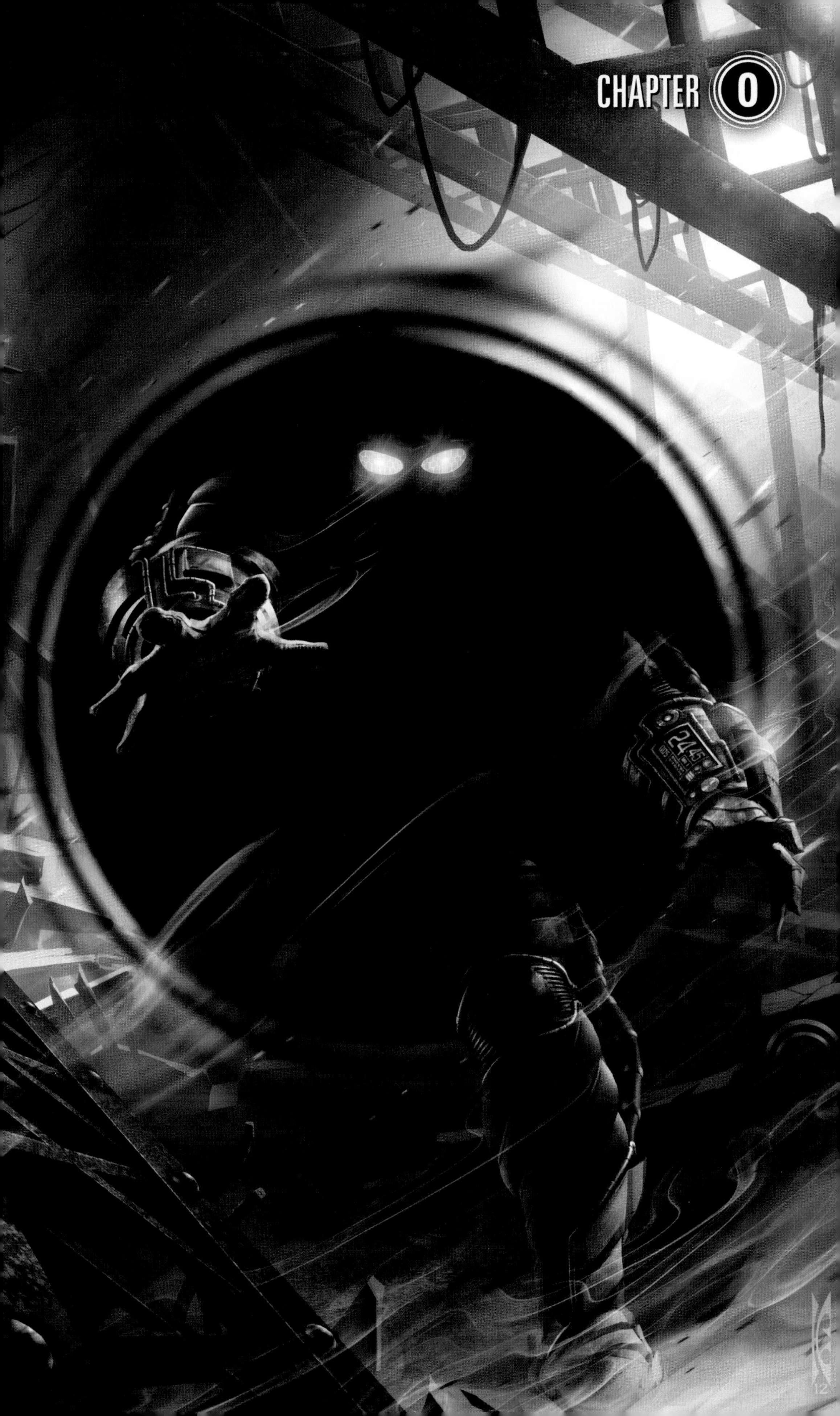

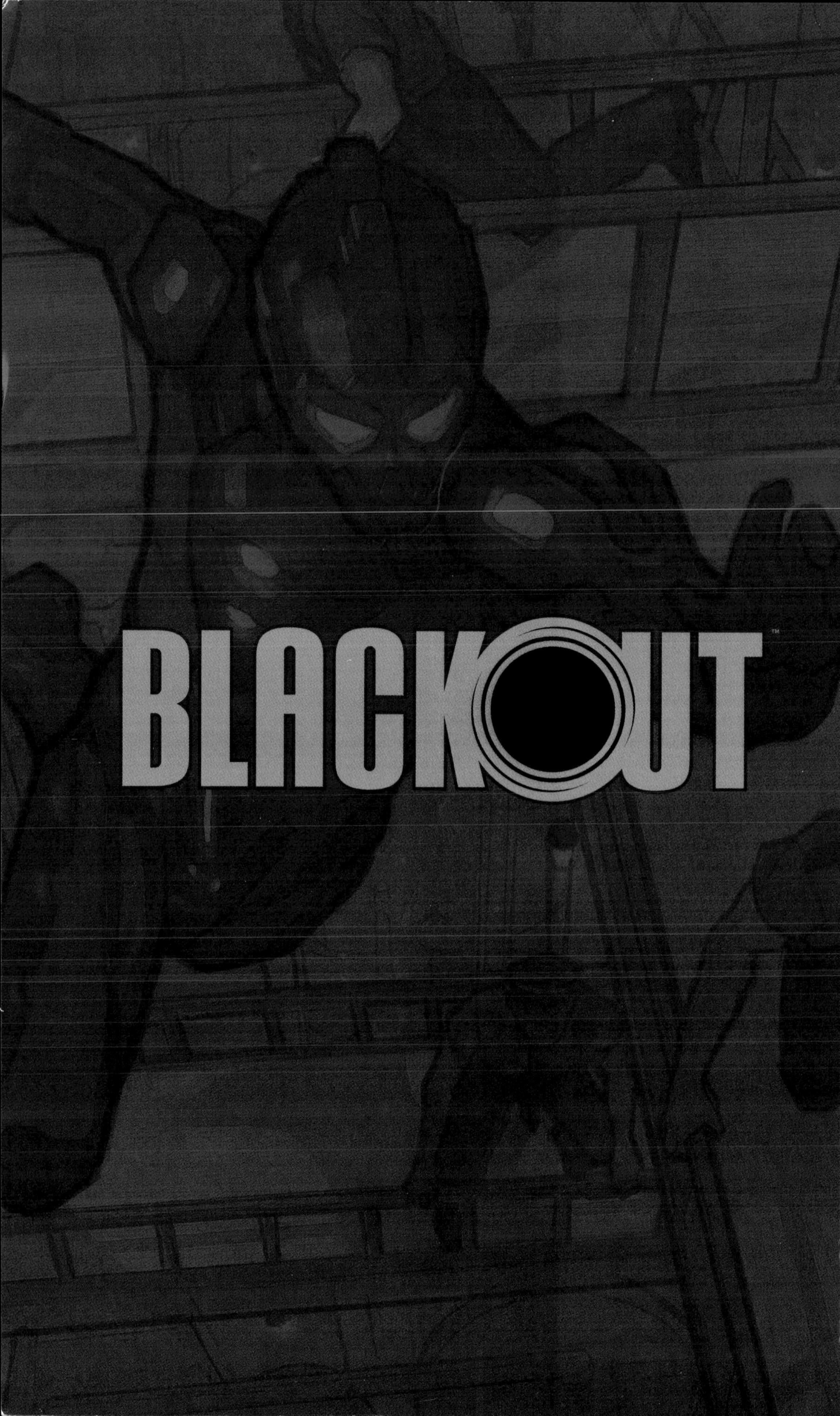
BLACKOUT™

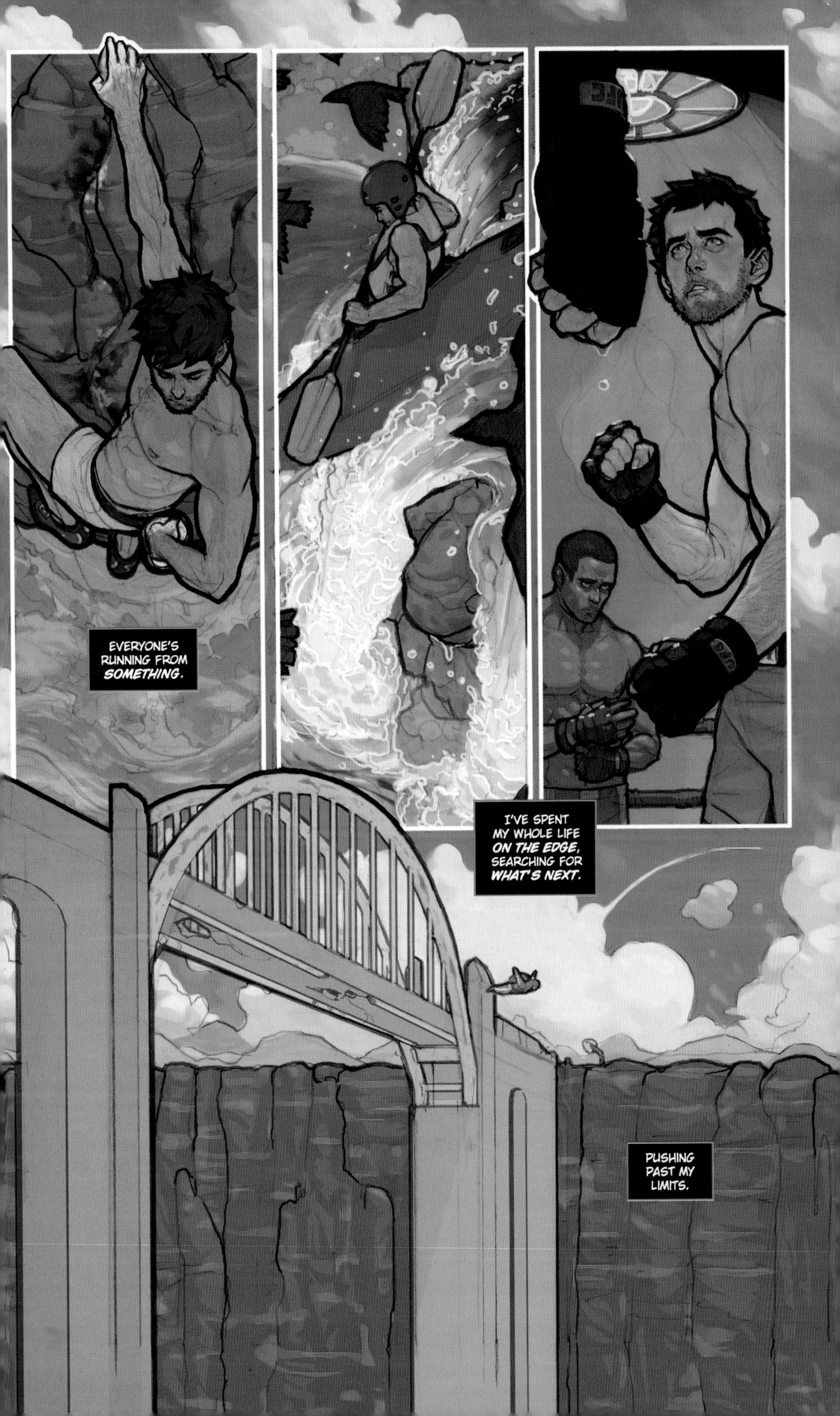
EVERYONE'S RUNNING FROM *SOMETHING*.
I'VE SPENT MY WHOLE LIFE *ON THE EDGE*, SEARCHING FOR *WHAT'S NEXT*.
PUSHING PAST MY LIMITS.

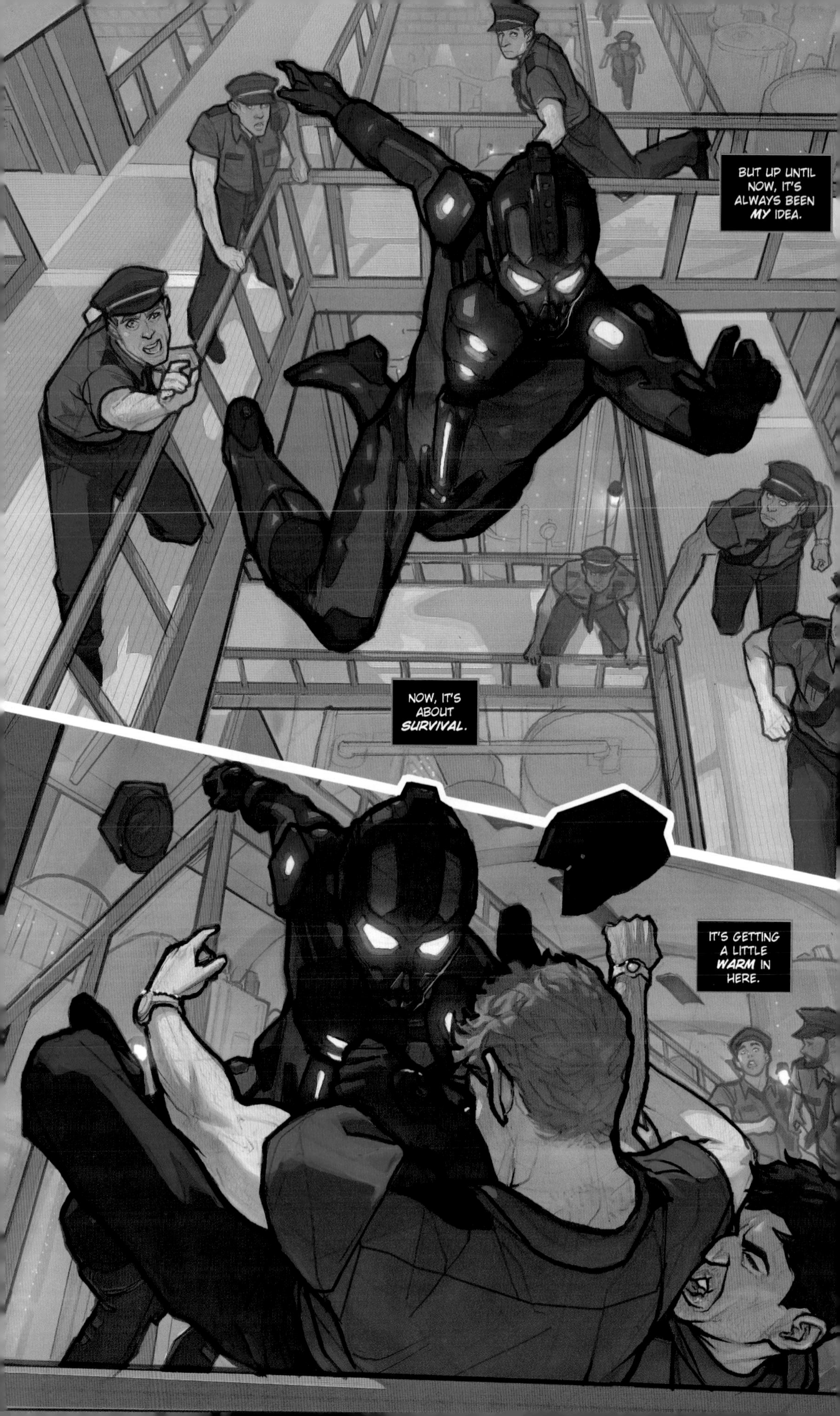
BUT UP UNTIL NOW, IT'S ALWAYS BEEN *MY* IDEA.
NOW, IT'S ABOUT *SURVIVAL*.
IT'S GETTING A LITTLE *WARM* IN HERE.

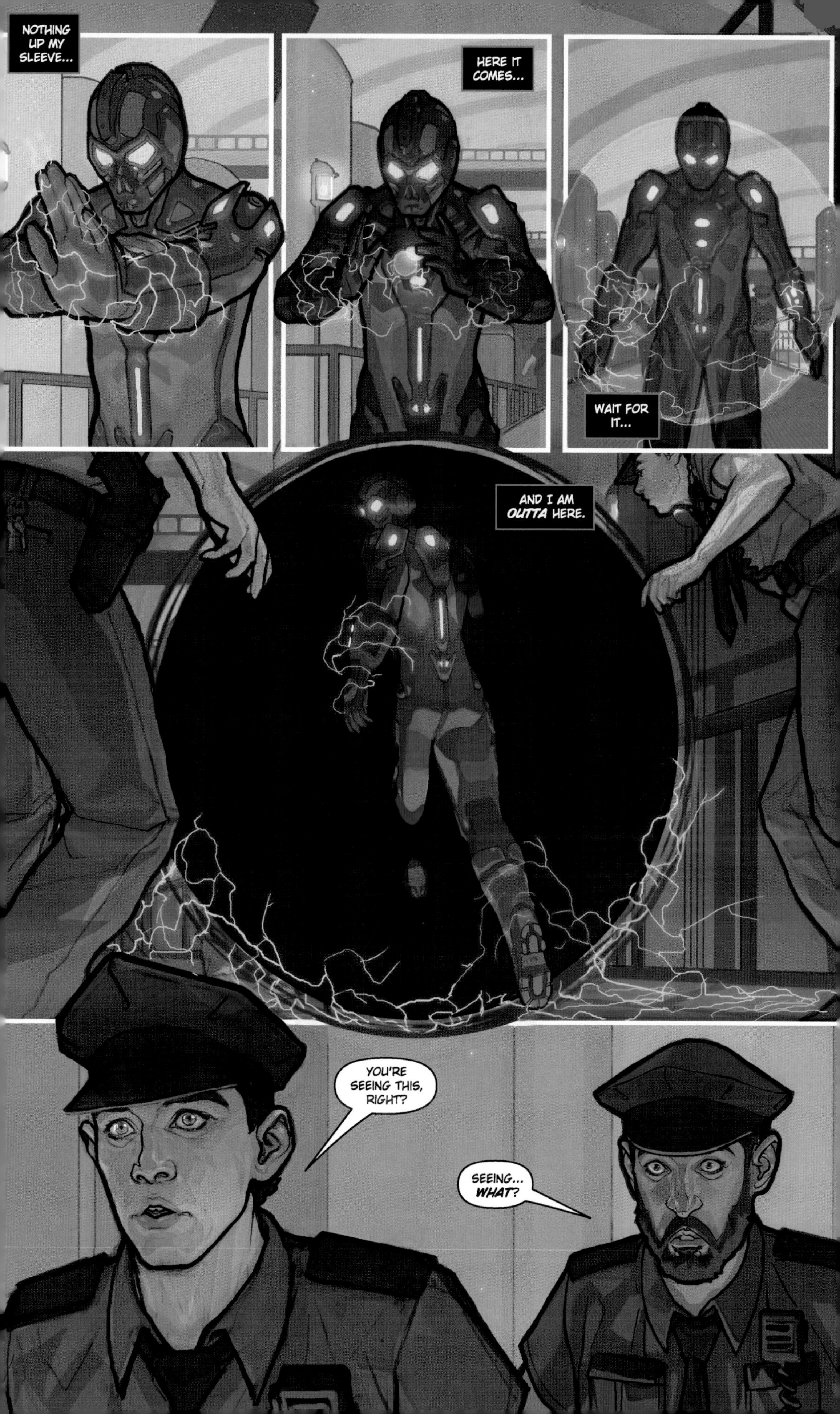
NOTHING UP MY SLEEVE...
HERE IT COMES...
WAIT FOR IT...
AND I AM *OUTTA* HERE.
YOU'RE SEEING THIS, RIGHT?
SEEING... *WHAT?*

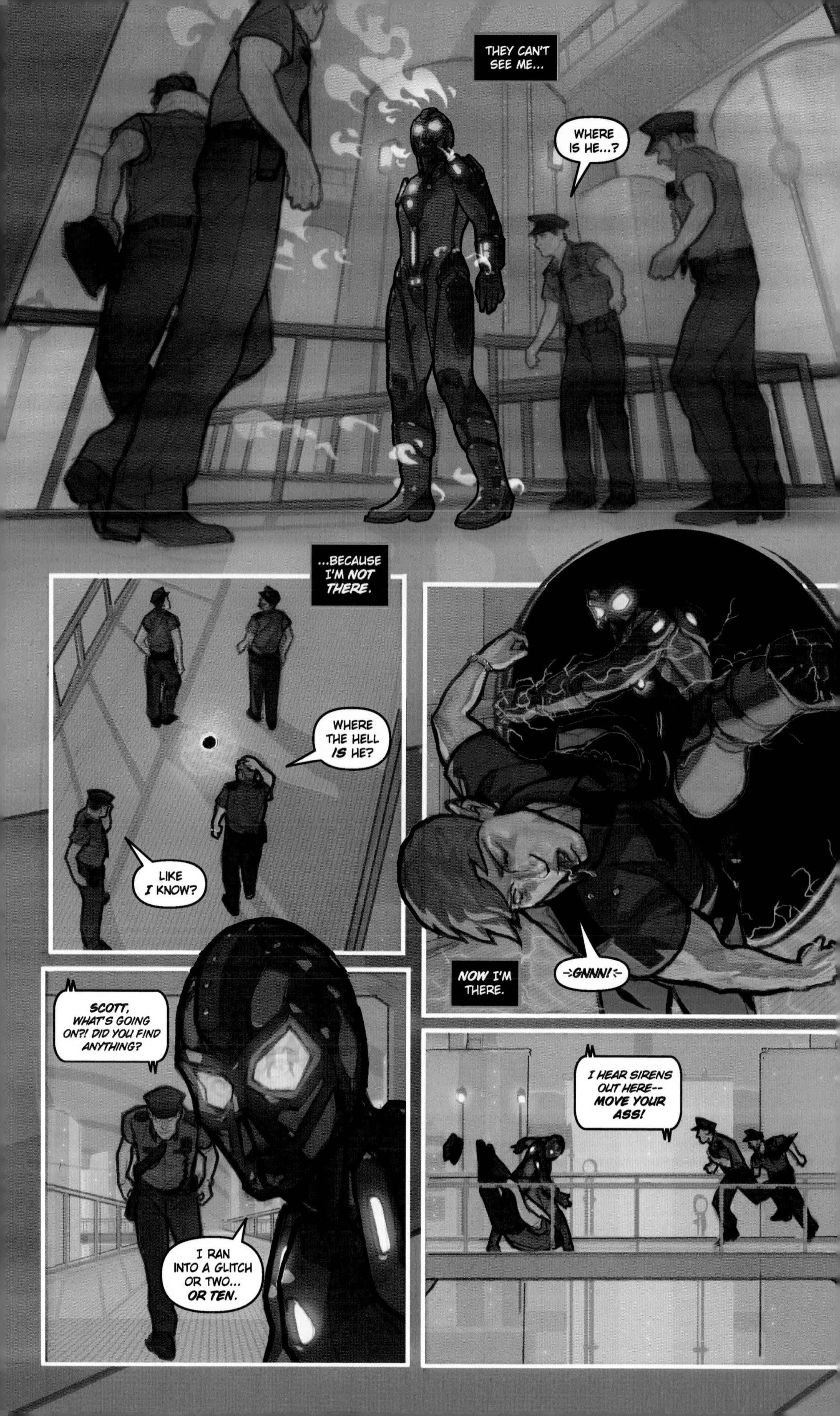
THEY CAN'T SEE ME...
WHERE IS HE...?
...BECAUSE I'M NOT THERE.
WHERE THE HELL IS HE?
LIKE I KNOW?
NOW I'M THERE.
GNNN!
SCOTT, WHAT'S GOING ON?! DID YOU FIND ANYTHING?
I RAN INTO A GLITCH OR TWO... OR TEN.
I HEAR SIRENS OUT HERE-- MOVE YOUR ASS!

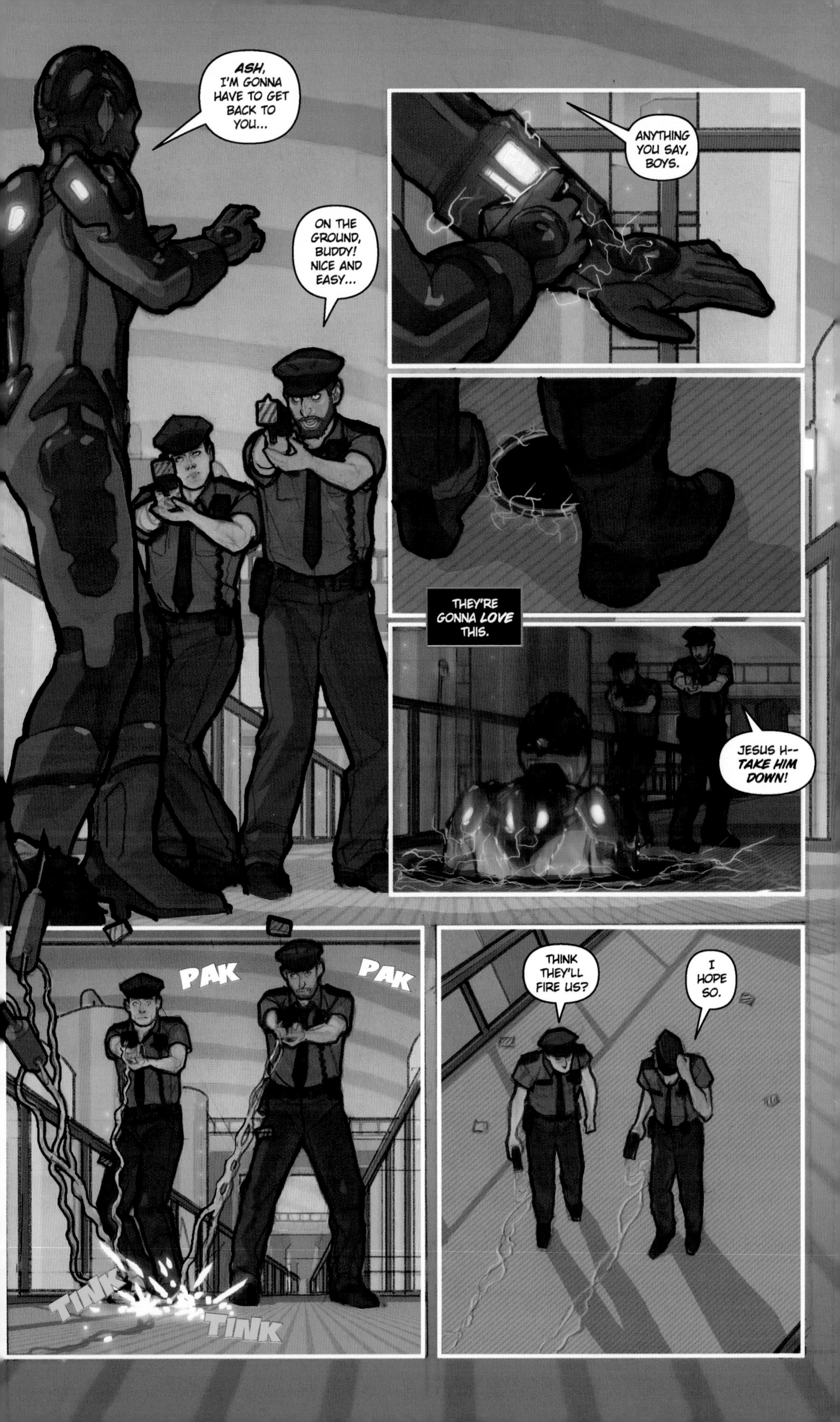
ASH, I'M GONNA HAVE TO GET BACK TO YOU...
ON THE GROUND, BUDDY! NICE AND EASY...
ANYTHING YOU SAY, BOYS.
THEY'RE GONNA LOVE THIS.
JESUS H-- TAKE HIM DOWN!
PAK
PAK
TINK
TINK
THINK THEY'LL FIRE US?
I HOPE SO.

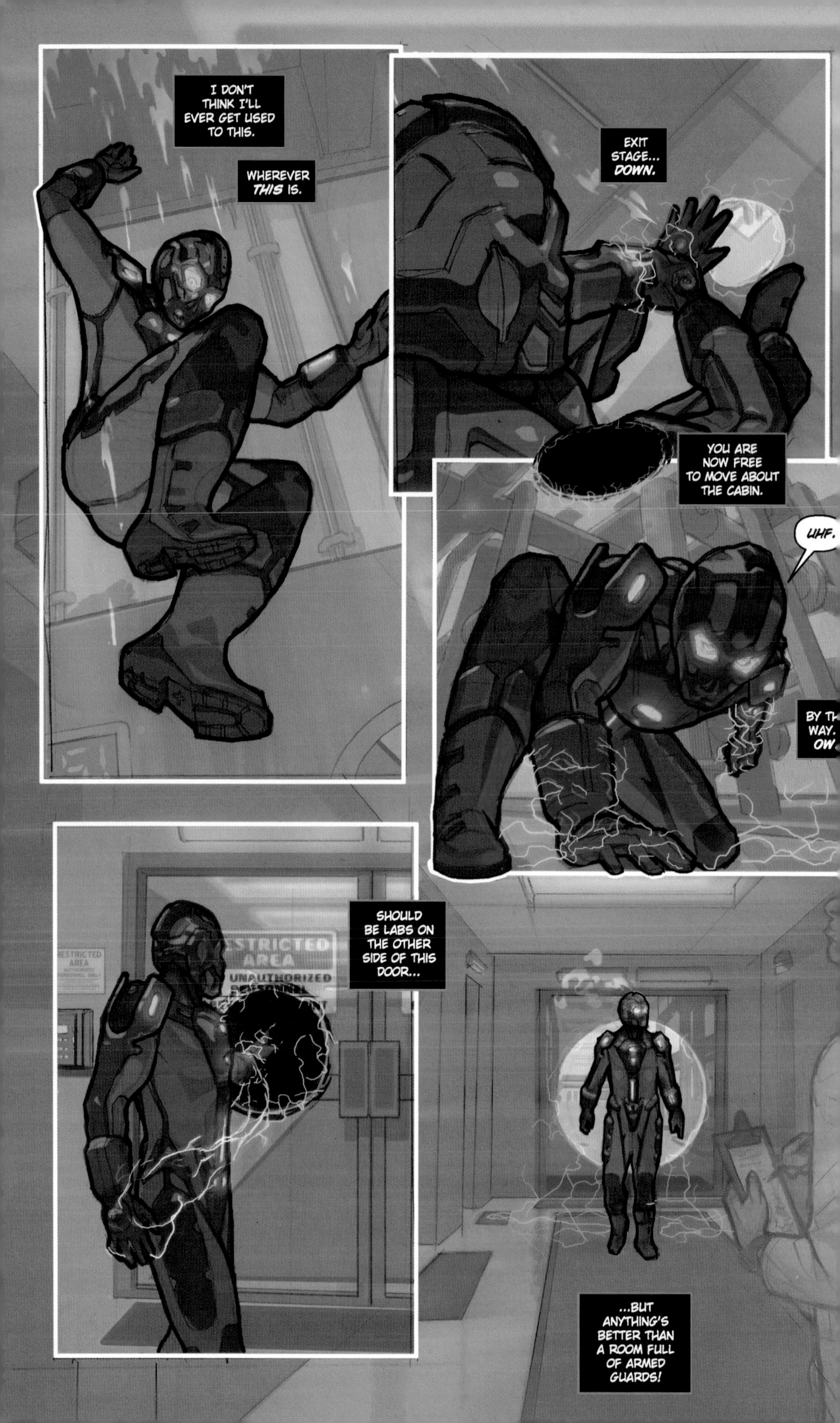
I DON'T THINK I'LL EVER GET USED TO THIS.
WHEREVER *THIS* IS.
EXIT STAGE... *DOWN.*
YOU ARE NOW FREE TO MOVE ABOUT THE CABIN.
UHF.
SHOULD BE LABS ON THE OTHER SIDE OF THIS DOOR...
RESTRICTED AREA
UNAUTHORIZED
...BUT ANYTHING'S BETTER THAN A ROOM FULL OF ARMED GUARDS!

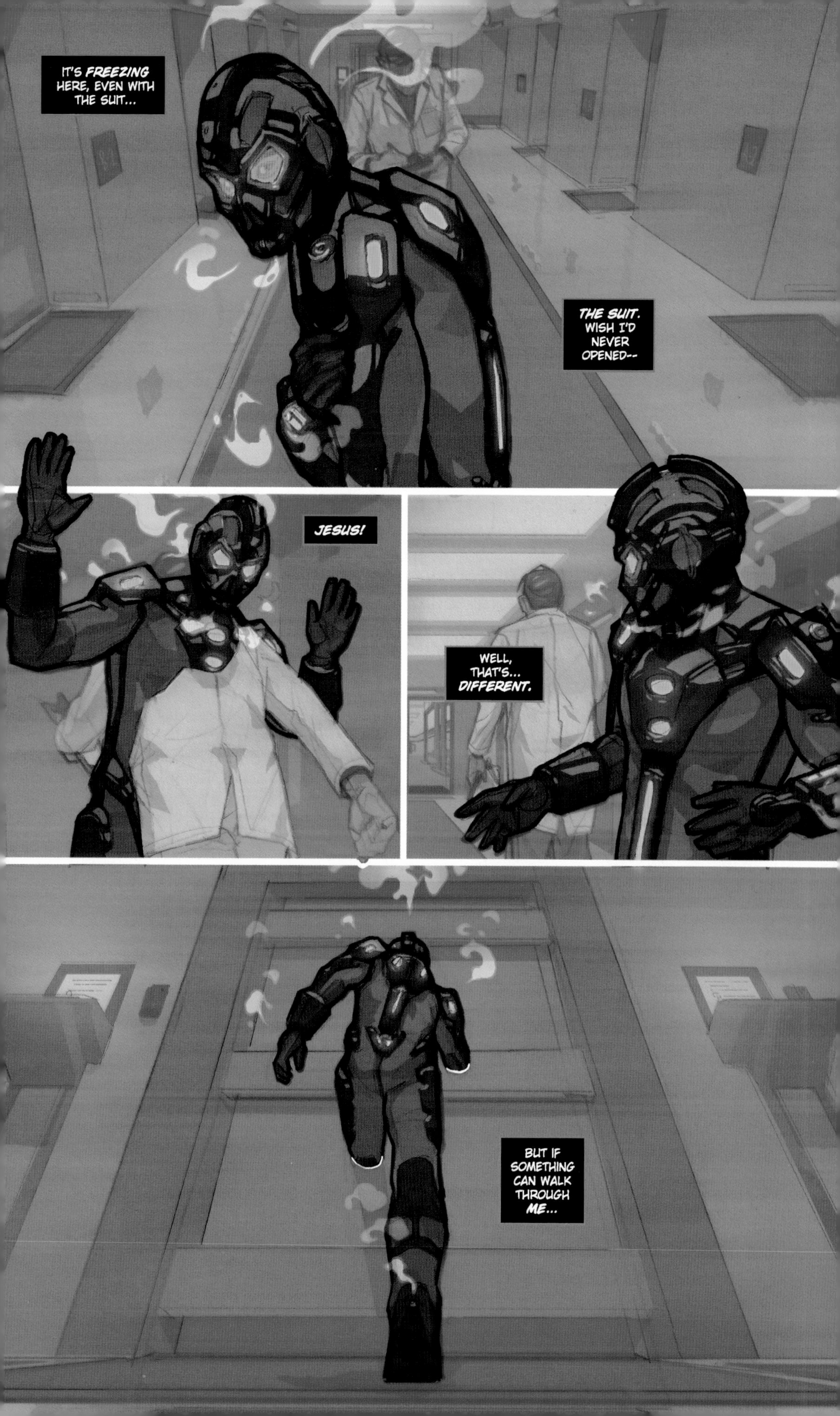
IT'S *FREEZING* HERE, EVEN WITH THE SUIT...
THE SUIT. WISH I'D NEVER OPENED--
JESUS!
WELL, THAT'S... *DIFFERENT*.
BUT IF SOMETHING CAN WALK THROUGH *ME*...

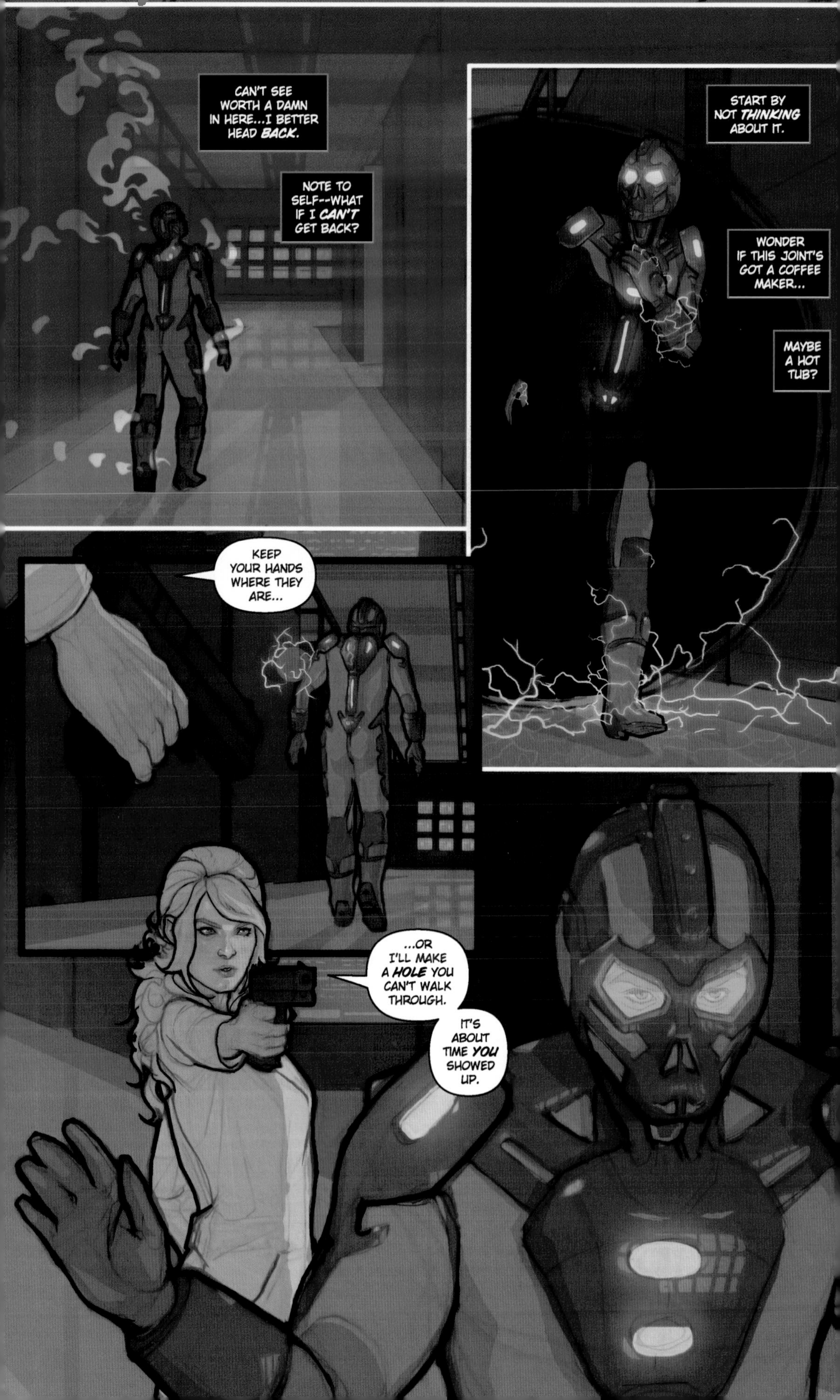
CAN'T SEE WORTH A DAMN IN HERE...I BETTER HEAD BACK.
NOTE TO SELF--WHAT IF I CAN'T GET BACK?
START BY NOT THINKING ABOUT IT.
WONDER IF THIS JOINT'S GOT A COFFEE MAKER...
MAYBE A HOT TUB?
KEEP YOUR HANDS WHERE THEY ARE...
...OR I'LL MAKE A HOLE YOU CAN'T WALK THROUGH.
IT'S ABOUT TIME YOU SHOWED UP.

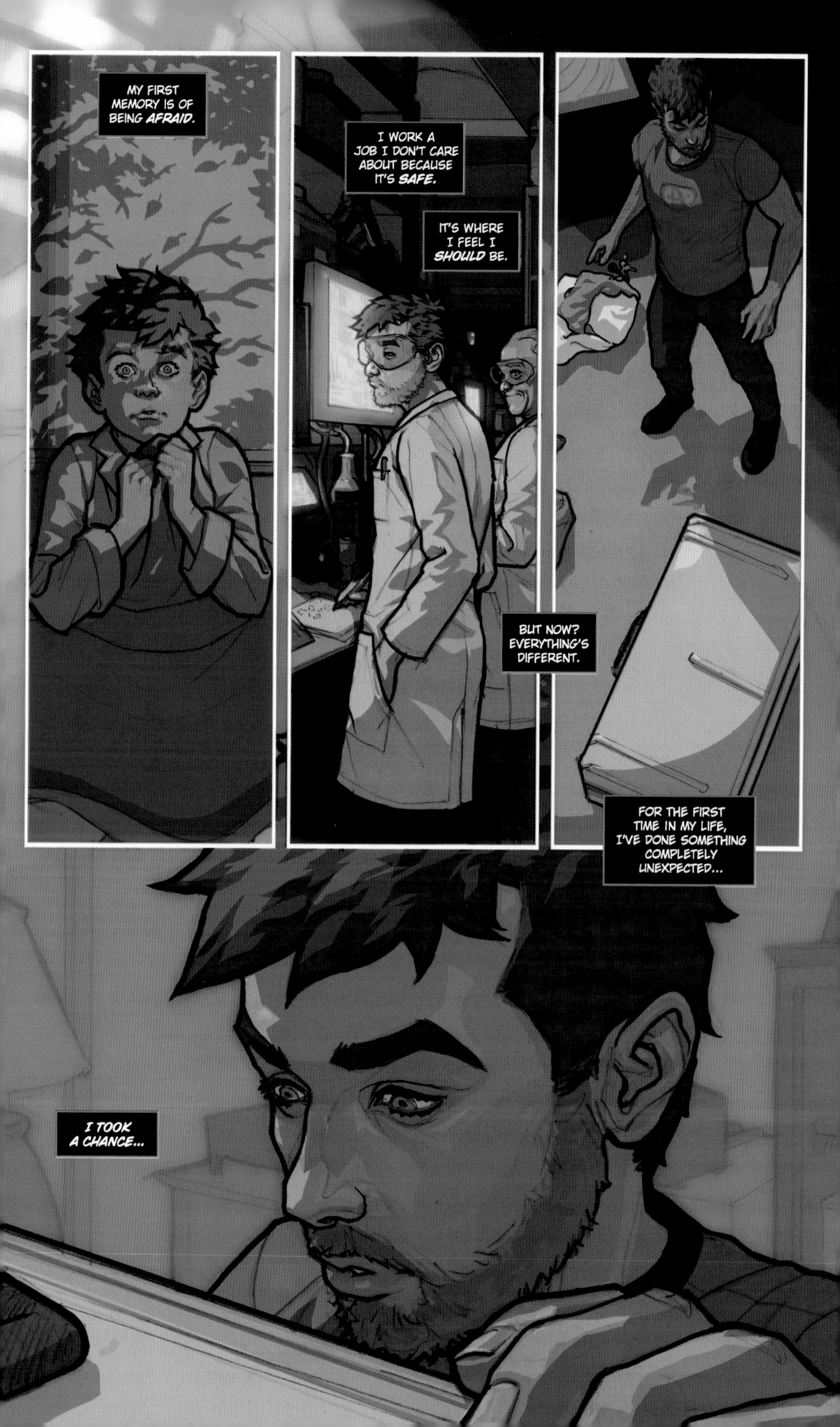
MY FIRST MEMORY IS OF BEING AFRAID.
I WORK A JOB I DON'T CARE ABOUT BECAUSE IT'S SAFE.
IT'S WHERE I FEEL I SHOULD BE.
BUT NOW? EVERYTHING'S DIFFERENT.
FOR THE FIRST TIME IN MY LIFE, I'VE DONE SOMETHING COMPLETELY UNEXPECTED...
I TOOK A CHANCE...

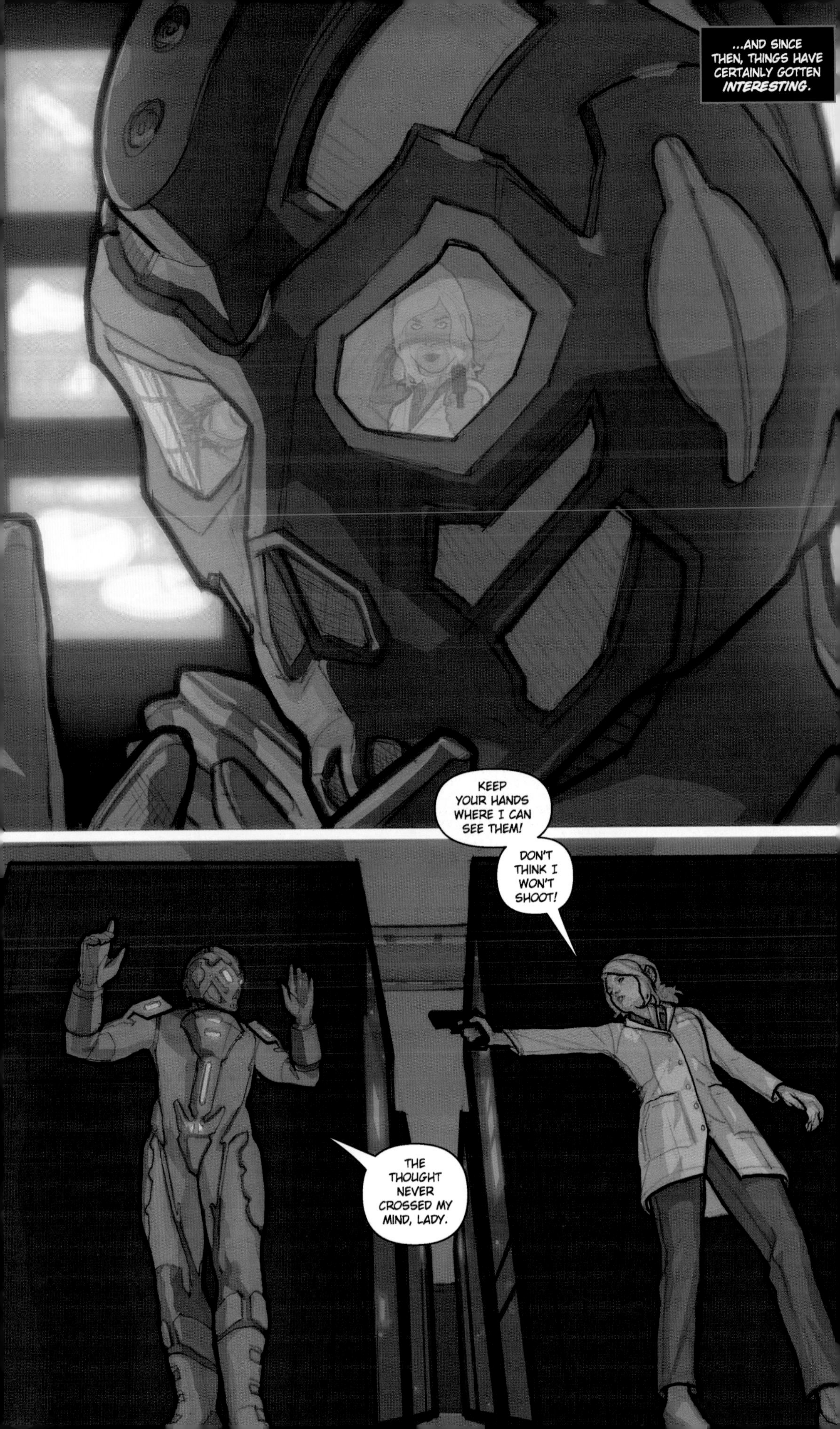
...AND SINCE THEN, THINGS HAVE CERTAINLY GOTTEN *INTERESTING*.
KEEP YOUR HANDS WHERE I CAN SEE THEM!
DON'T THINK I WON'T SHOOT!
THE THOUGHT NEVER CROSSED MY MIND, LADY.

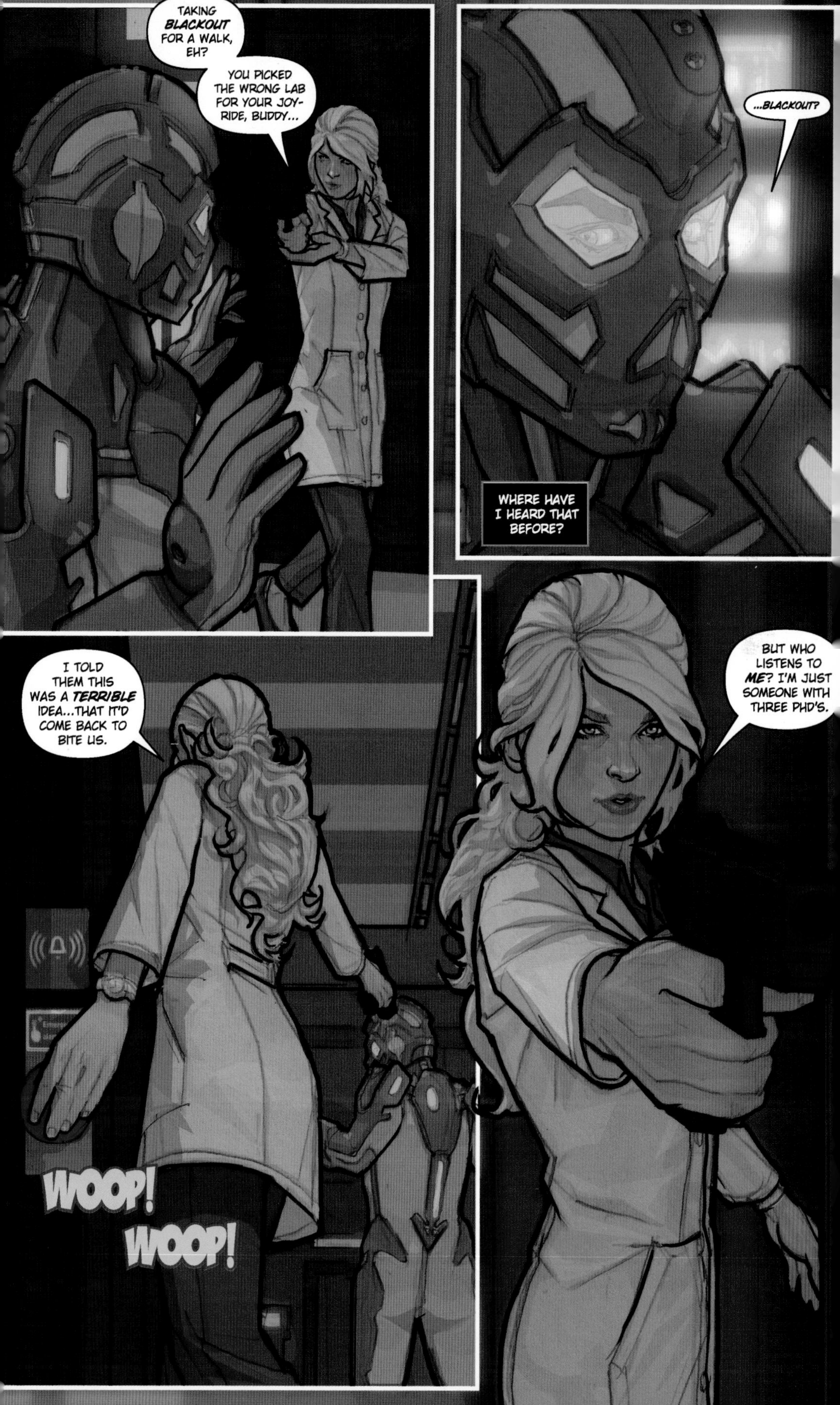
TAKING BLACKOUT FOR A WALK, EH?
YOU PICKED THE WRONG LAB FOR YOUR JOY-RIDE, BUDDY...
...BLACKOUT?
WHERE HAVE I HEARD THAT BEFORE?
I TOLD THEM THIS WAS A TERRIBLE IDEA...THAT IT'D COME BACK TO BITE US.
WOOP!
WOOP!
BUT WHO LISTENS TO ME? I'M JUST SOMEONE WITH THREE PHD'S.

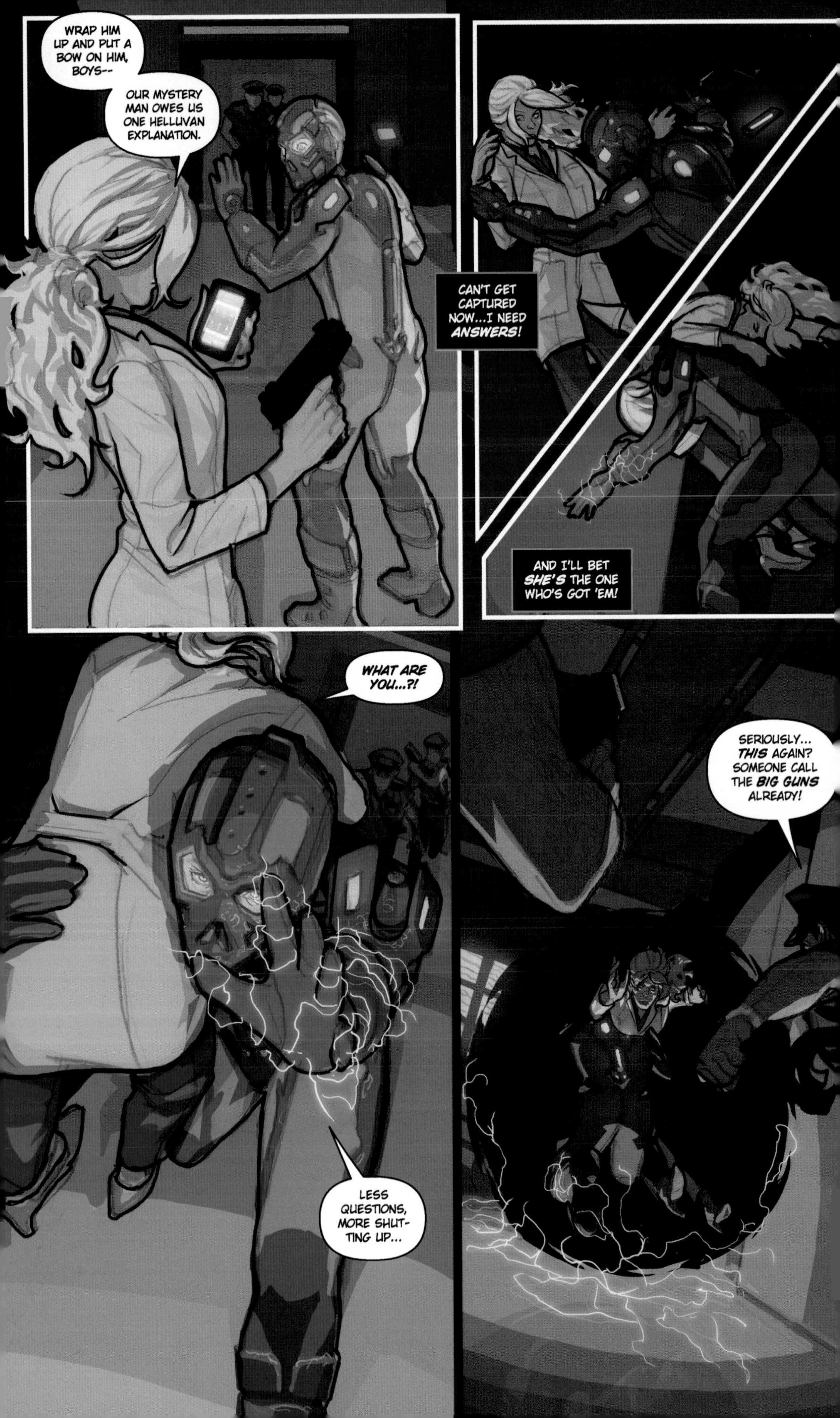

WRAP HIM UP AND PUT A BOW ON HIM, BOYS--
OUR MYSTERY MAN OWES US ONE HELLUVAN EXPLANATION.
CAN'T GET CAPTURED NOW...I NEED *ANSWERS!*
AND I'LL BET *SHE'S* THE ONE WHO'S GOT 'EM!
WHAT ARE YOU...?!
LESS QUESTIONS, MORE SHUT-TING UP...
SERIOUSLY... *THIS* AGAIN? SOMEONE CALL THE *BIG GUNS* ALREADY!

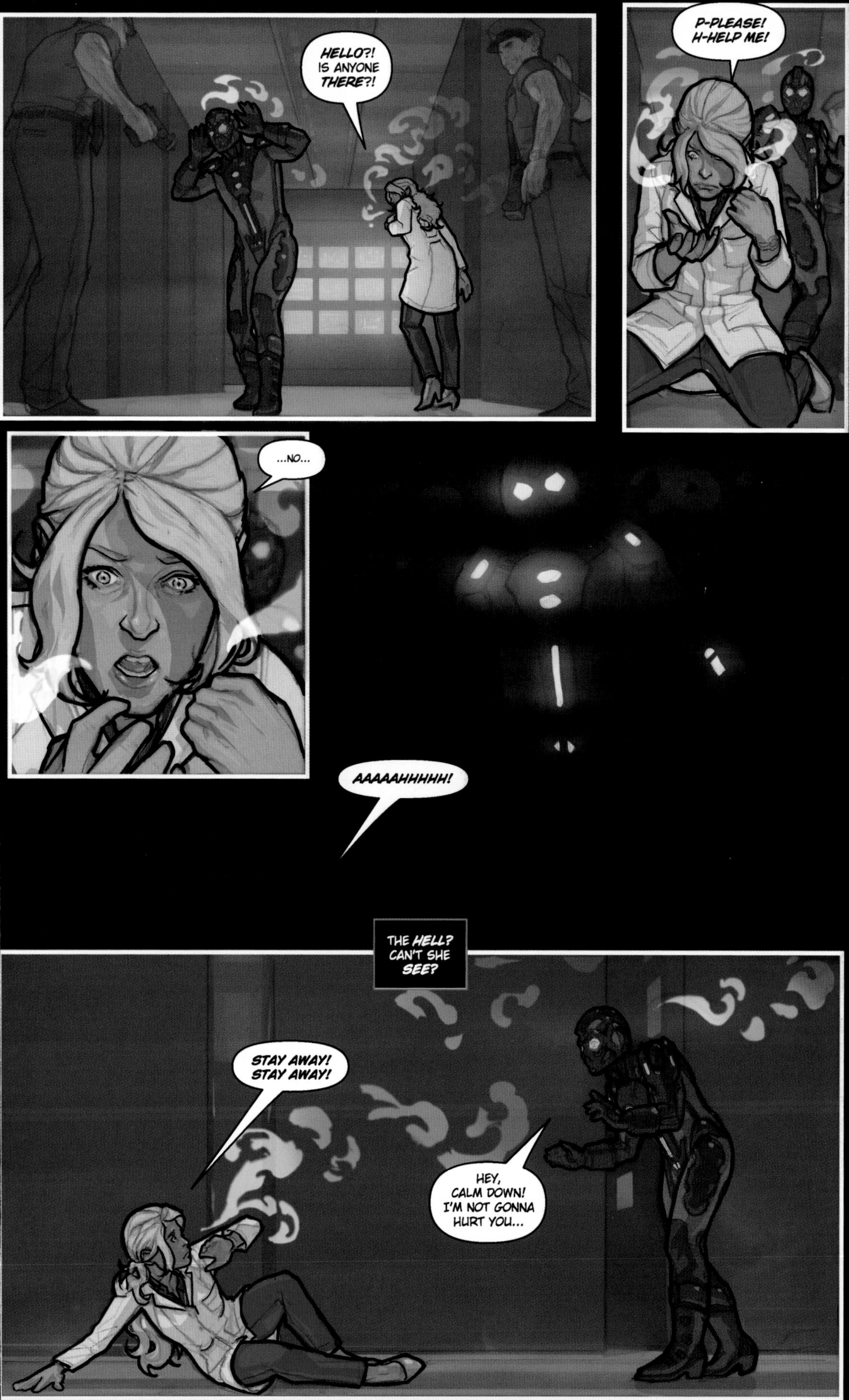
HELLO?! IS ANYONE THERE?!
P-PLEASE! H-HELP ME!
...NO...
AAAAAHHHHH!
THE HELL? CAN'T SHE SEE?
STAY AWAY! STAY AWAY!
HEY, CALM DOWN! I'M NOT GONNA HURT YOU...

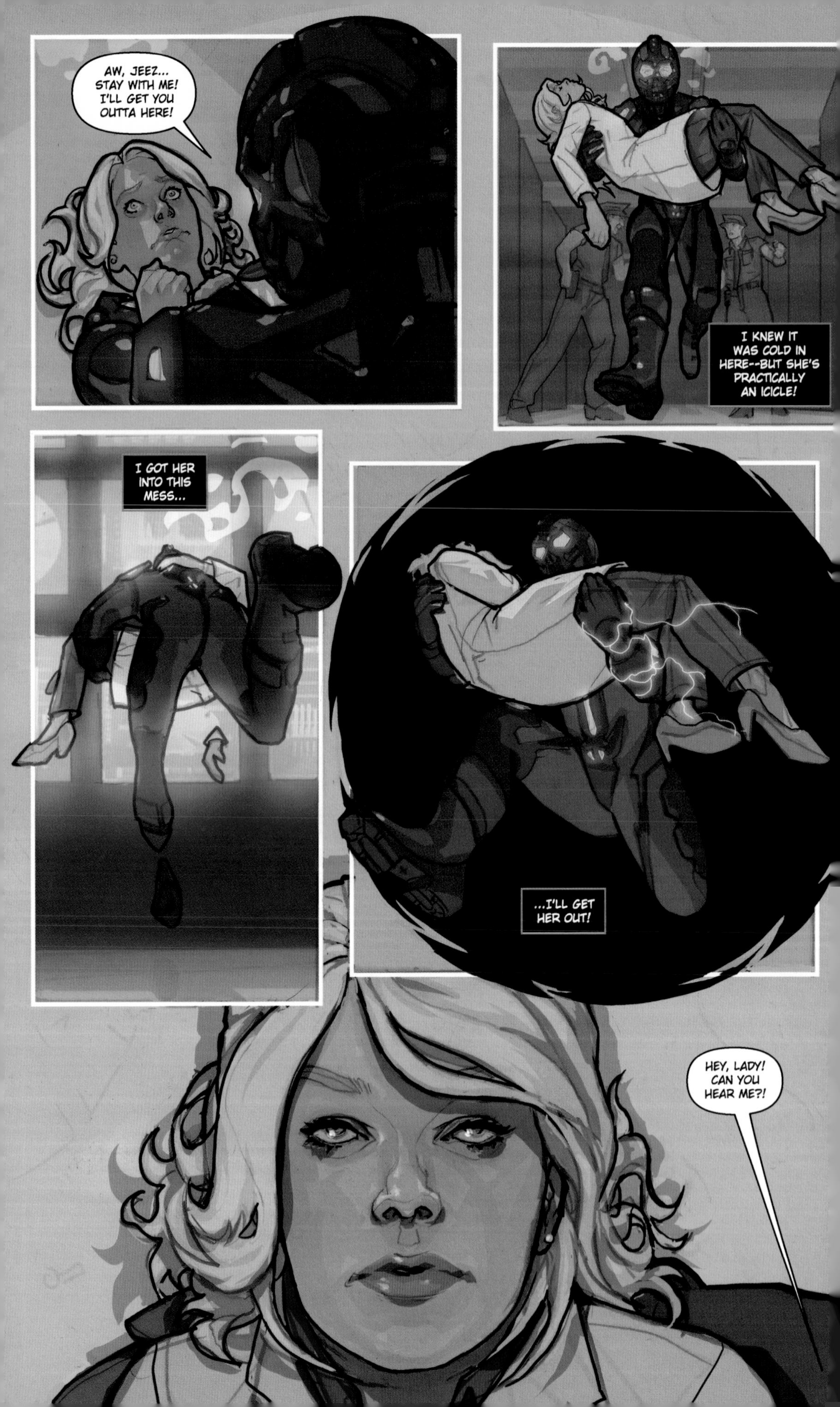
AW, JEEZ... STAY WITH ME! I'LL GET YOU OUTTA HERE!
I KNEW IT WAS COLD IN HERE--BUT SHE'S PRACTICALLY AN ICICLE!
I GOT HER INTO THIS MESS...
...I'LL GET HER OUT!
HEY, LADY! CAN YOU HEAR ME?!

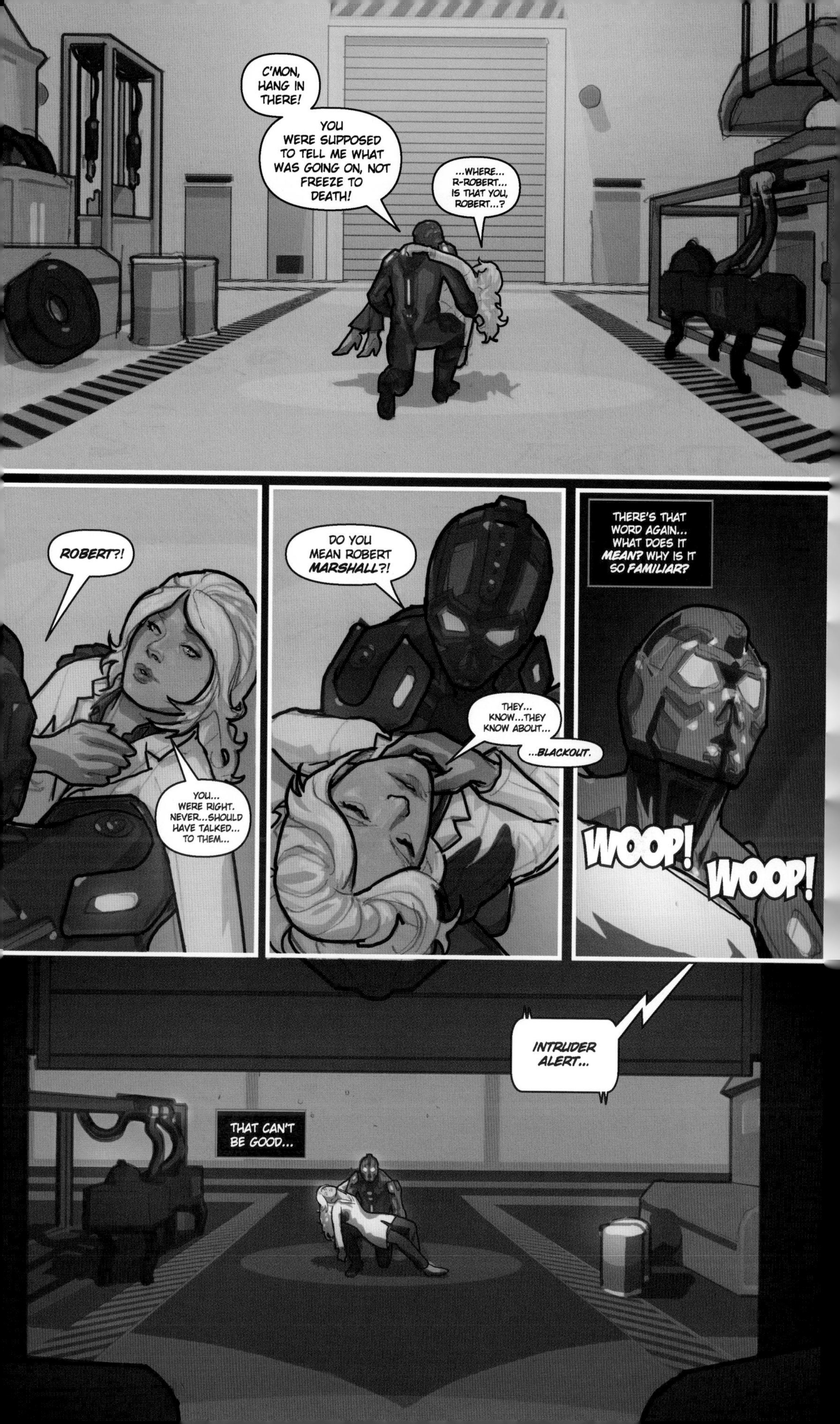
C'MON, HANG IN THERE!
YOU WERE SUPPOSED TO TELL ME WHAT WAS GOING ON, NOT FREEZE TO DEATH!
...WHERE... R-ROBERT... IS THAT YOU, ROBERT...?
ROBERT?!
YOU... WERE RIGHT. NEVER...SHOULD HAVE TALKED... TO THEM...
DO YOU MEAN ROBERT MARSHALL?!
THEY... KNOW...THEY KNOW ABOUT...
...BLACKOUT.
THERE'S THAT WORD AGAIN... WHAT DOES IT MEAN? WHY IS IT SO FAMILIAR?
WOOP! WOOP!
INTRUDER ALERT...
THAT CAN'T BE GOOD...

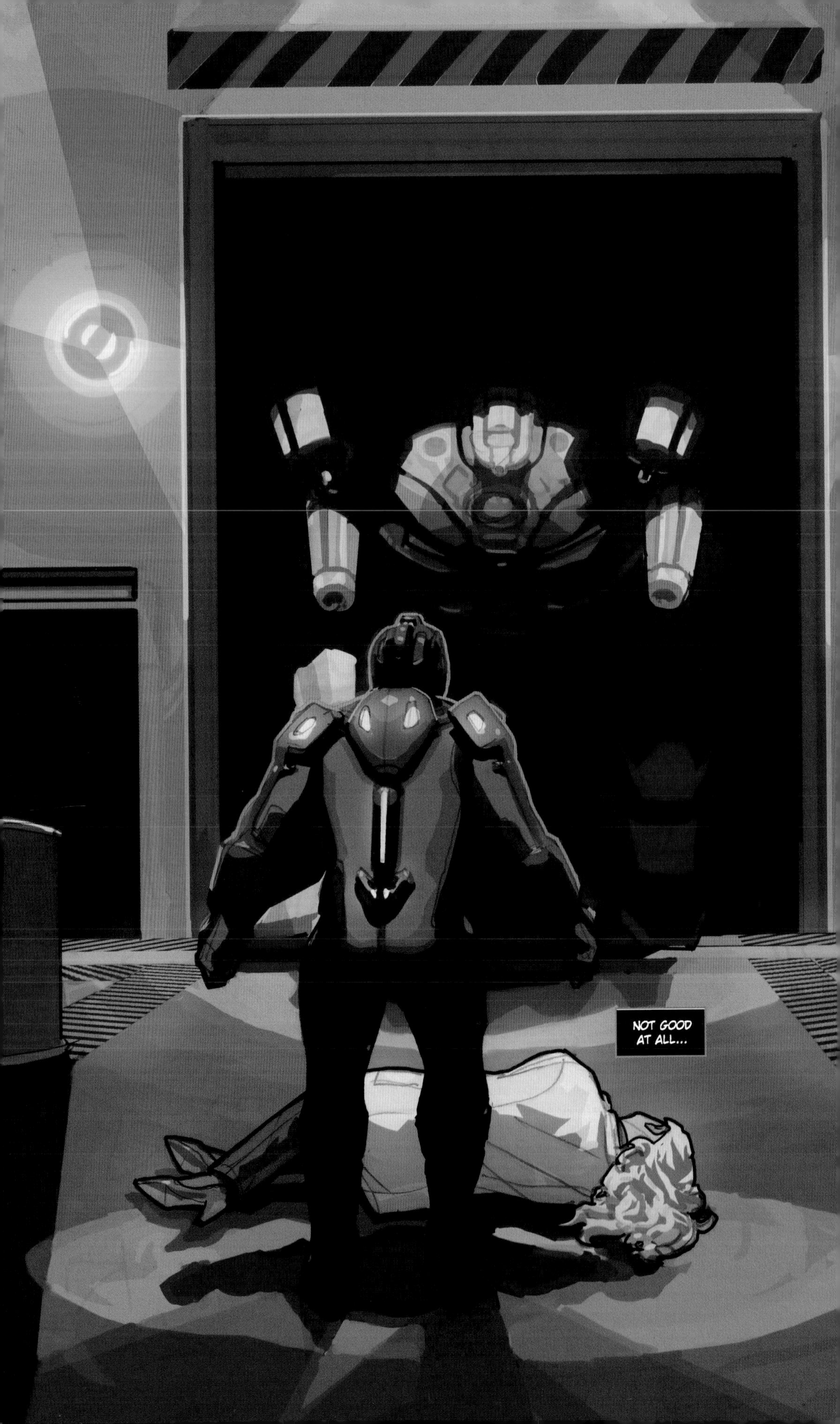
NOT GOOD
AT ALL...

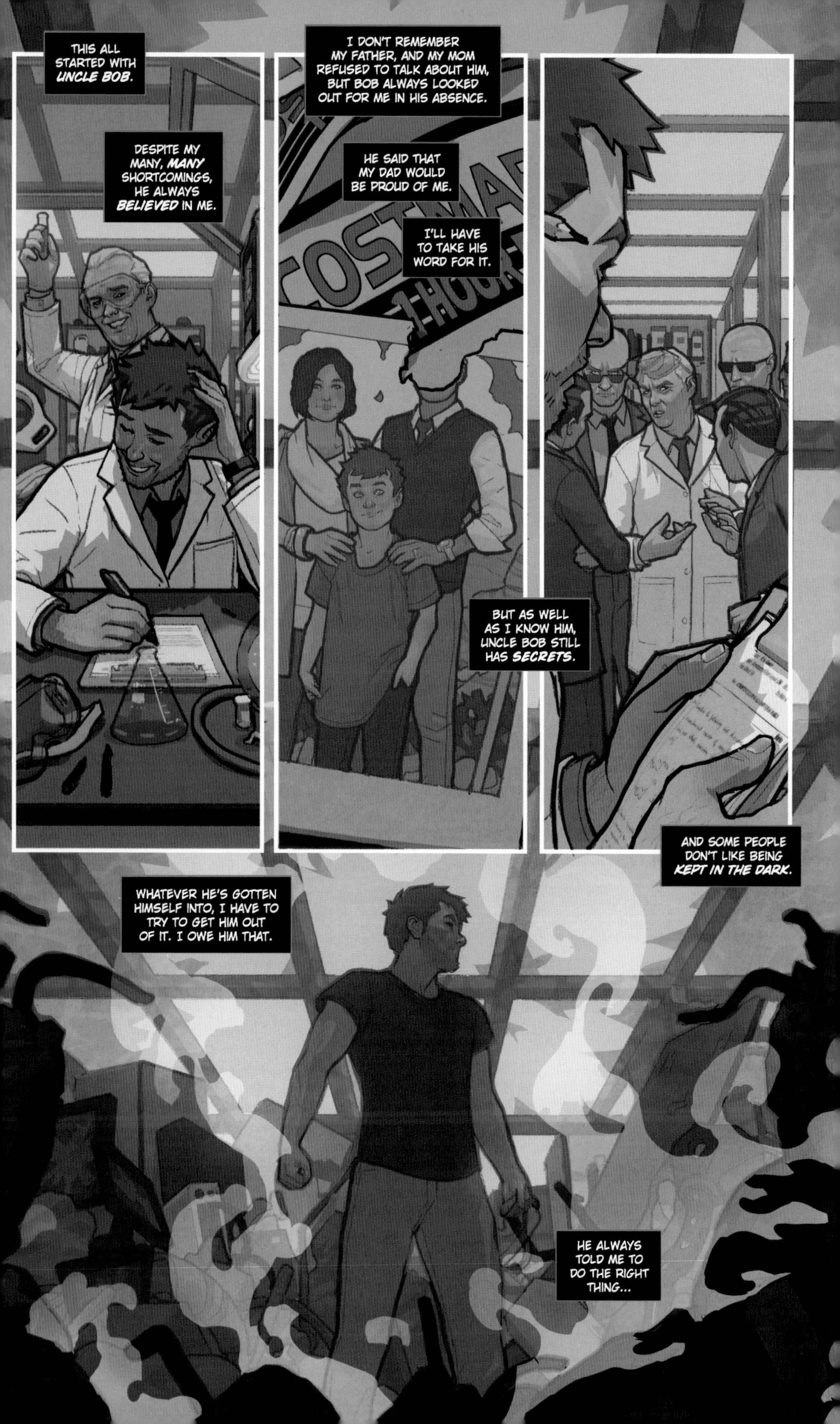

THIS ALL STARTED WITH *UNCLE BOB*.
DESPITE MY MANY, *MANY* SHORTCOMINGS, HE ALWAYS *BELIEVED* IN ME.
I DON'T REMEMBER MY FATHER, AND MY MOM REFUSED TO TALK ABOUT HIM, BUT BOB ALWAYS LOOKED OUT FOR ME IN HIS ABSENCE.
HE SAID THAT MY DAD WOULD BE PROUD OF ME.
I'LL HAVE TO TAKE HIS WORD FOR IT.
BUT AS WELL AS I KNOW HIM, UNCLE BOB STILL HAS *SECRETS*.
AND SOME PEOPLE DON'T LIKE BEING *KEPT IN THE DARK*.
WHATEVER HE'S GOTTEN HIMSELF INTO, I HAVE TO TRY TO GET HIM OUT OF IT. I OWE HIM THAT.
HE ALWAYS TOLD ME TO DO THE RIGHT THING...

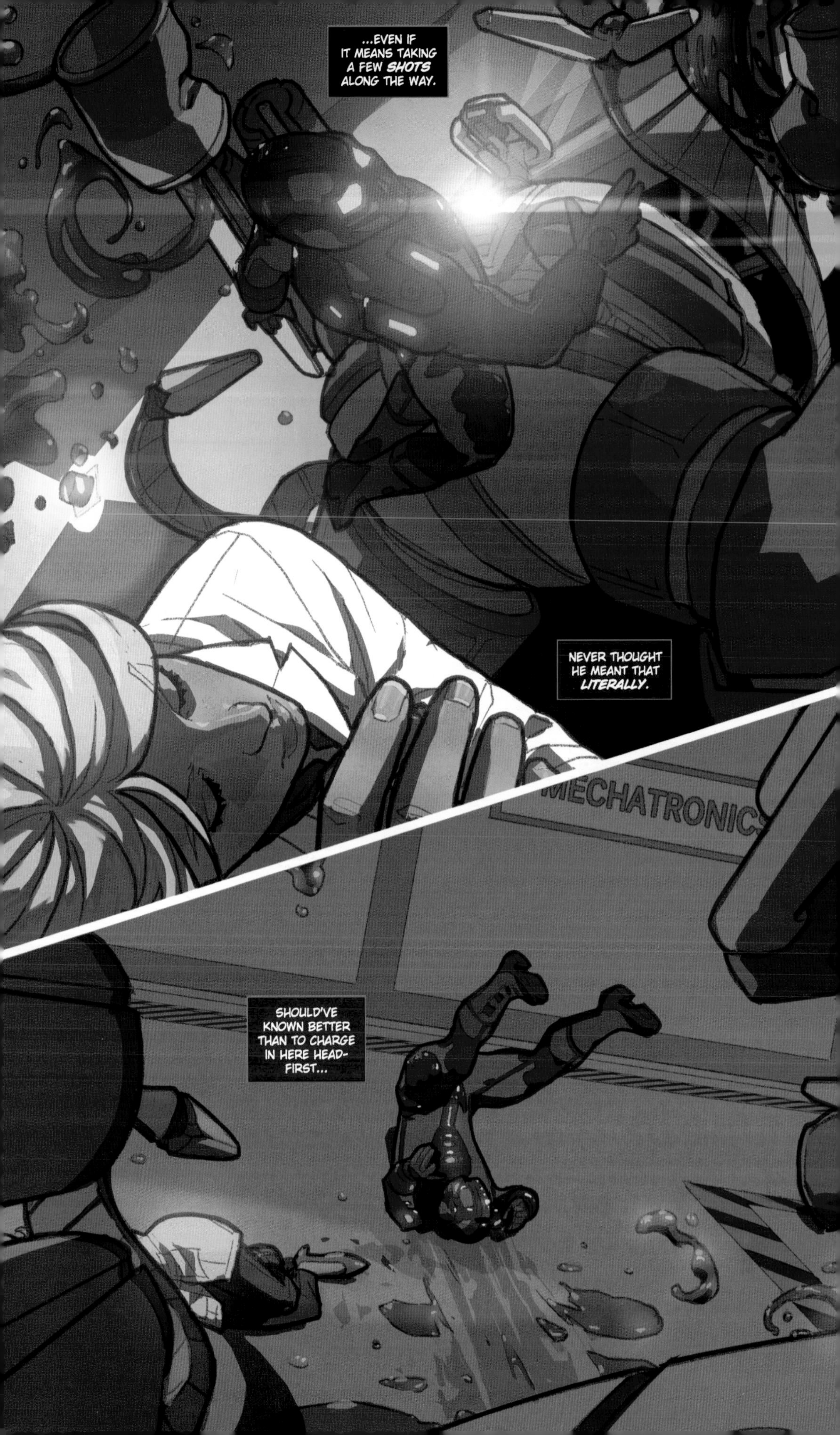
...EVEN IF IT MEANS TAKING A FEW *SHOTS* ALONG THE WAY.
NEVER THOUGHT HE MEANT THAT *LITERALLY*.
MECHATRONICS
SHOULD'VE KNOWN BETTER THAN TO CHARGE IN HERE HEAD-FIRST...

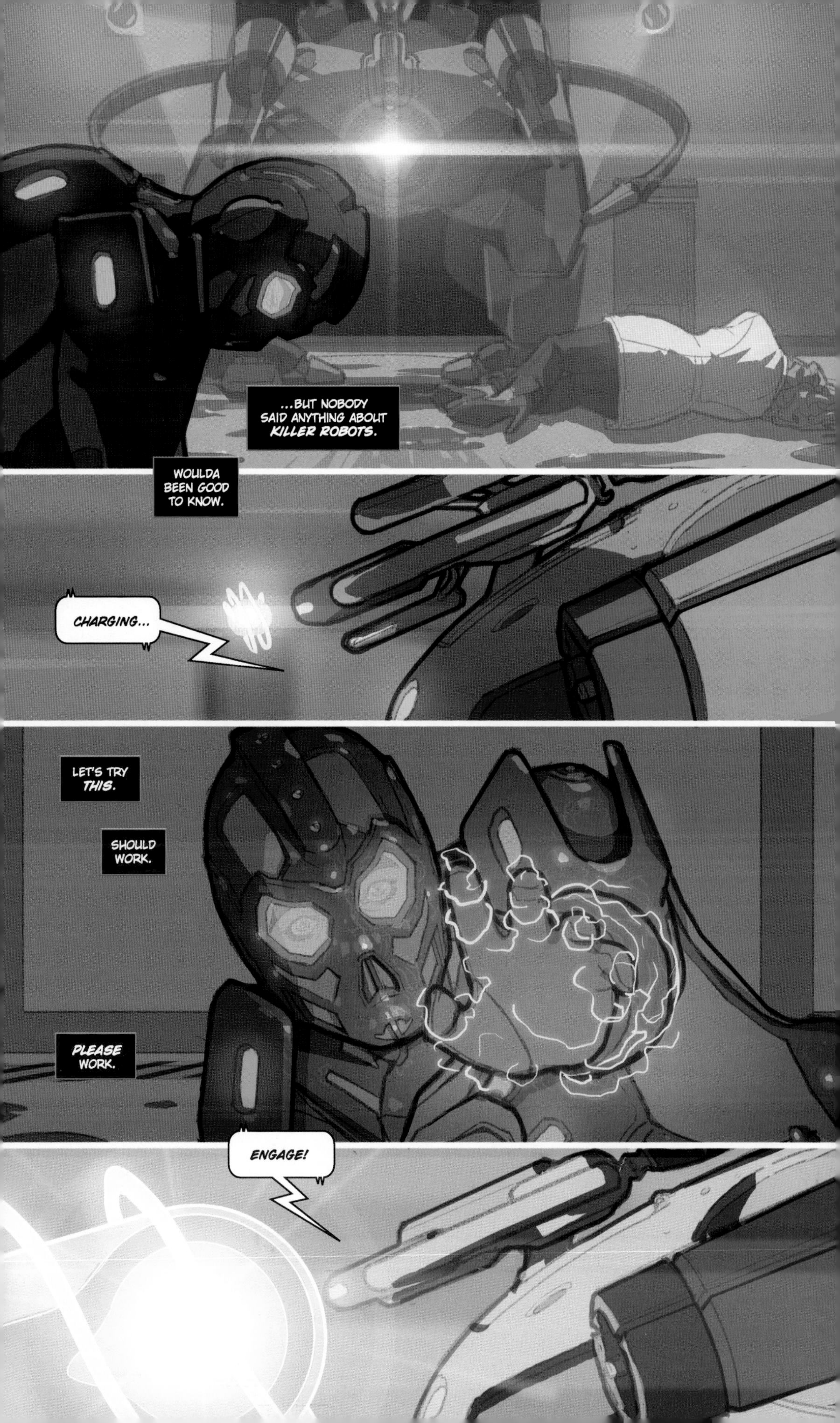

...BUT NOBODY SAID ANYTHING ABOUT *KILLER ROBOTS.*
WOULDA BEEN GOOD TO KNOW.
CHARGING...
LET'S TRY *THIS.*
SHOULD WORK.
PLEASE WORK.
ENGAGE!

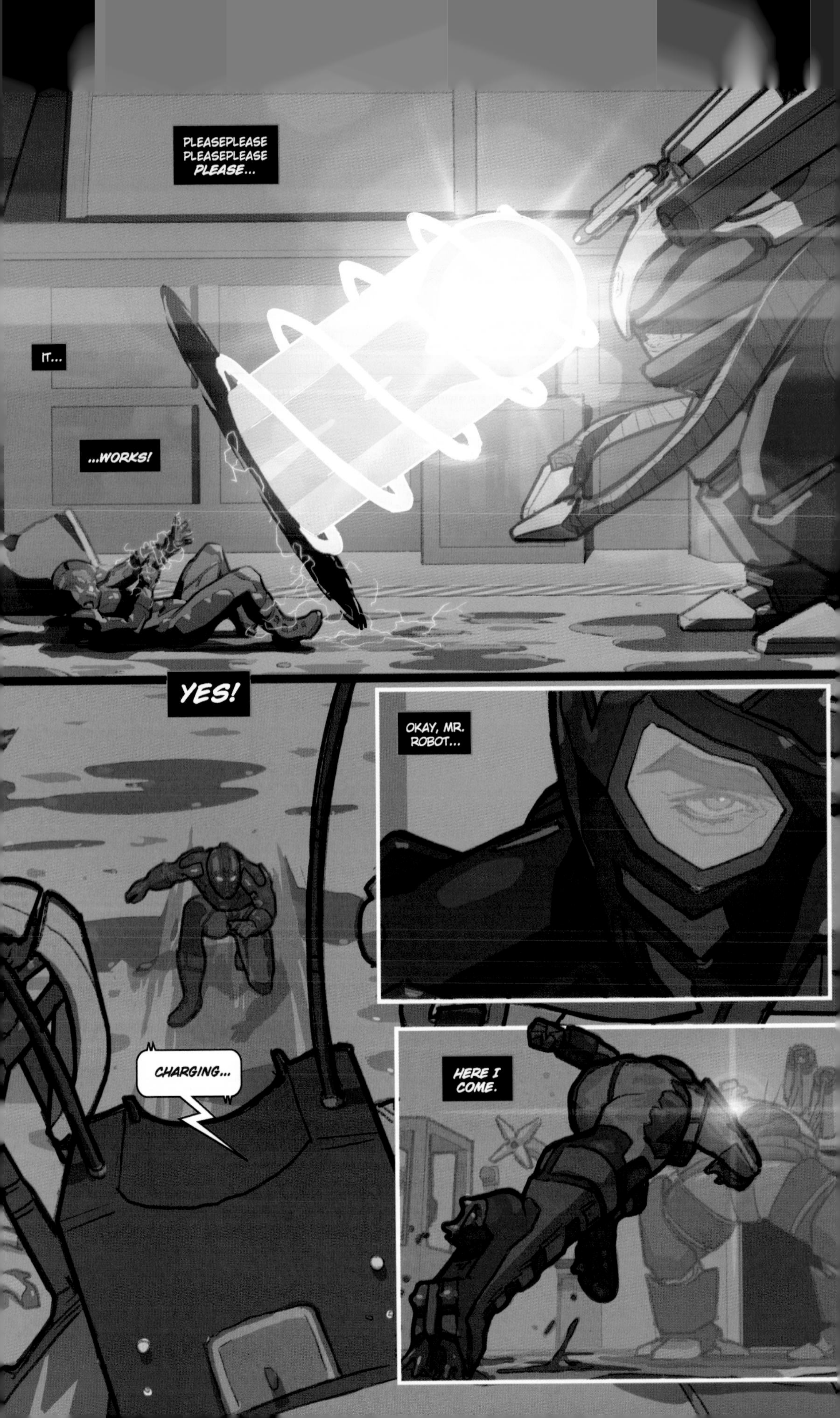
PLEASEPLEASE
PLEASEPLEASE
PLEASE...
IT...
...WORKS!
YES!
OKAY, MR. ROBOT...
CHARGING...
HERE I COME.

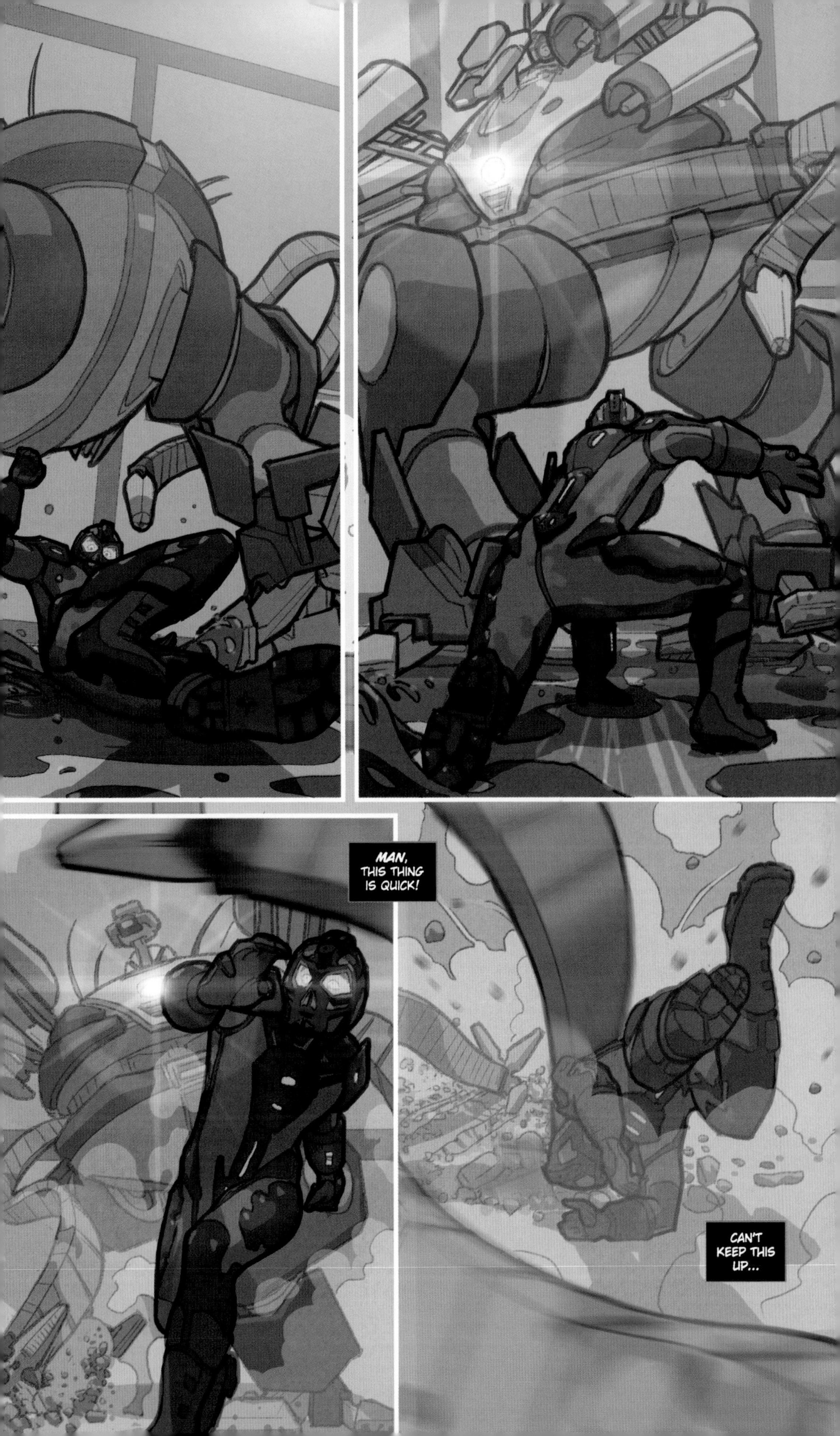
MAN, THIS THING IS QUICK!
CAN'T KEEP THIS UP...

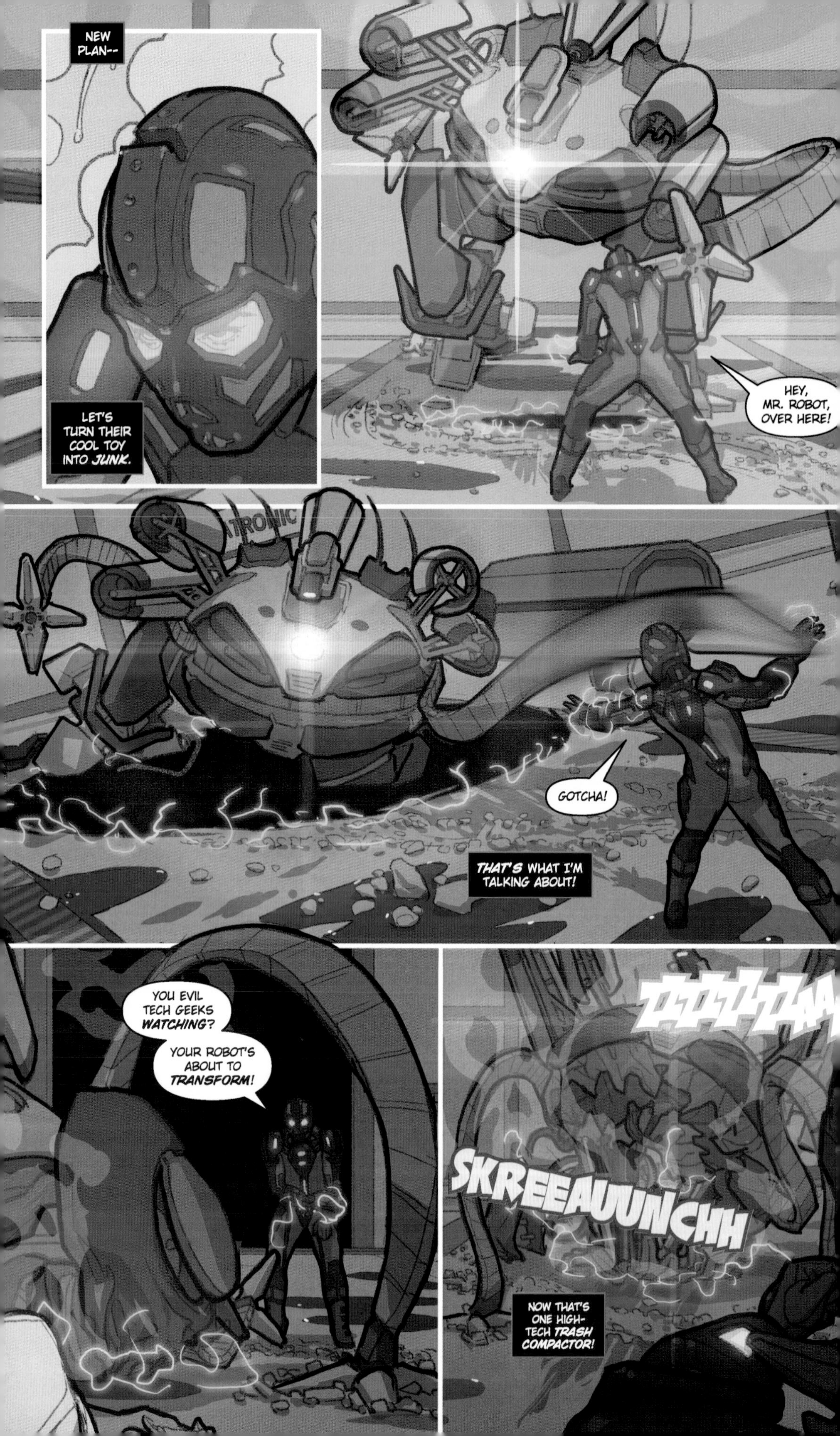

NEW PLAN--
LET'S TURN THEIR COOL TOY INTO JUNK.
HEY, MR. ROBOT, OVER HERE!
GOTCHA!
THAT'S WHAT I'M TALKING ABOUT!
YOU EVIL TECH GEEKS WATCHING?
YOUR ROBOT'S ABOUT TO TRANSFORM!
SKREEAUUNCHH
NOW THAT'S ONE HIGH-TECH TRASH COMPACTOR!

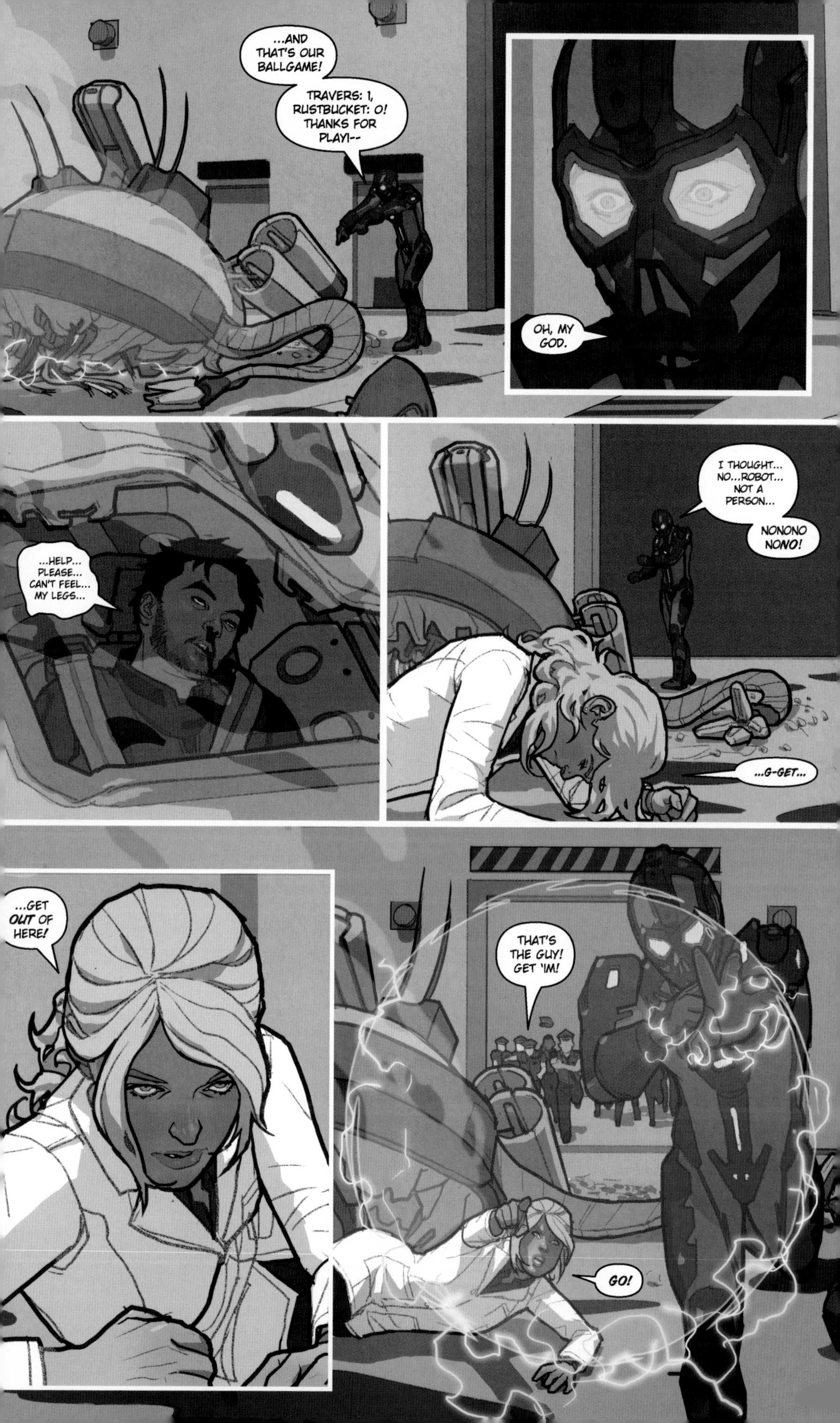
...AND THAT'S OUR BALLGAME!
TRAVERS: 1, RUSTBUCKET: 0! THANKS FOR PLAY!--
OH, MY GOD.
...HELP... PLEASE... CAN'T FEEL... MY LEGS...
I THOUGHT... NO...ROBOT... NOT A PERSON...
NONONO NONO!
...G-GET...
...GET OUT OF HERE!
THAT'S THE GUY! GET 'IM!
GO!

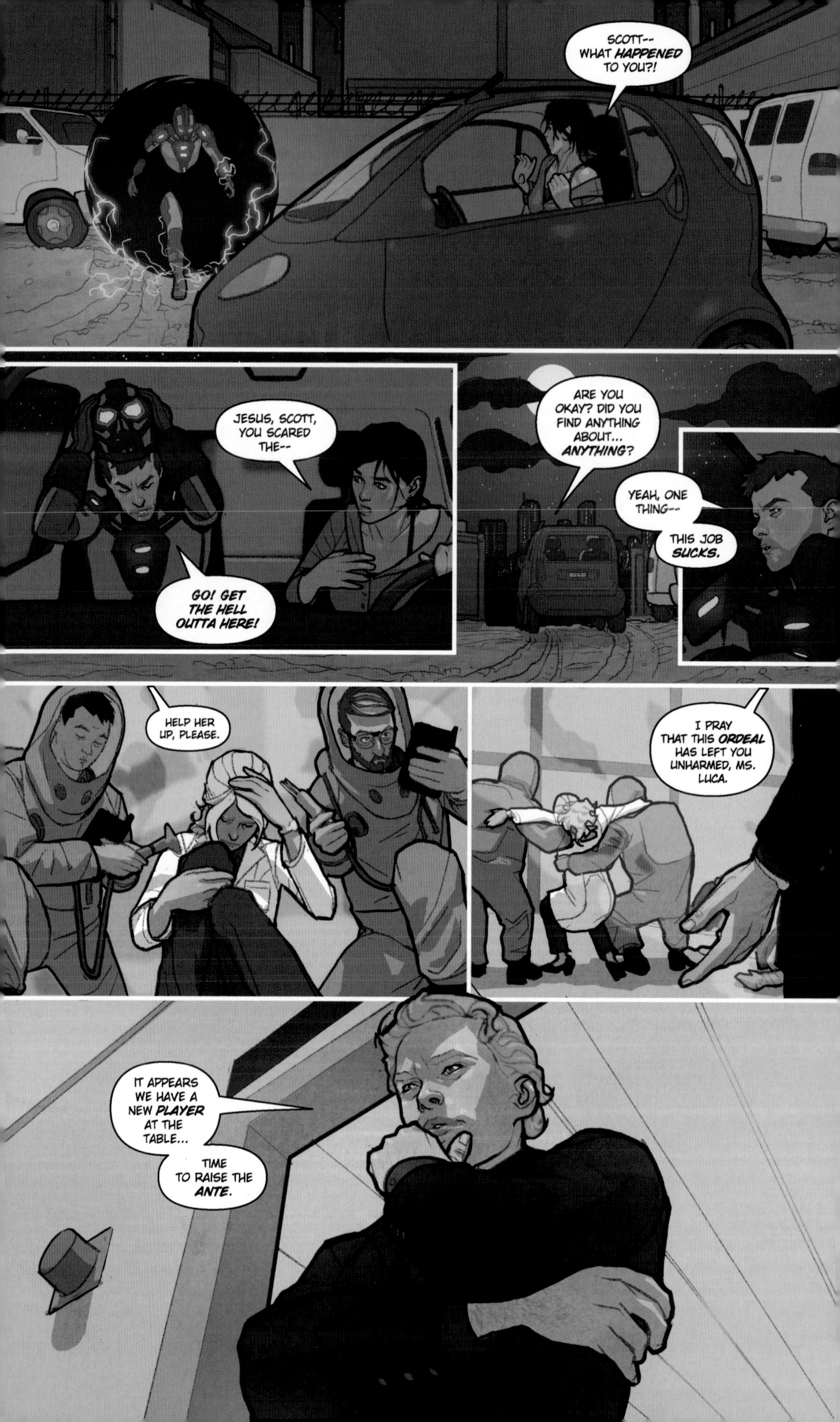
SCOTT--
WHAT HAPPENED
TO YOU?!
JESUS, SCOTT,
YOU SCARED
THE--
GO! GET
THE HELL
OUTTA HERE!
ARE YOU
OKAY? DID YOU
FIND ANYTHING
ABOUT...
ANYTHING?
YEAH, ONE
THING--
THIS JOB
SUCKS.
HELP HER
UP, PLEASE.
I PRAY
THAT THIS ORDEAL
HAS LEFT YOU
UNHARMED, MS.
LUCA.
IT APPEARS
WE HAVE A
NEW PLAYER
AT THE
TABLE...
TIME
TO RAISE THE
ANTE.

CHAPTER 1

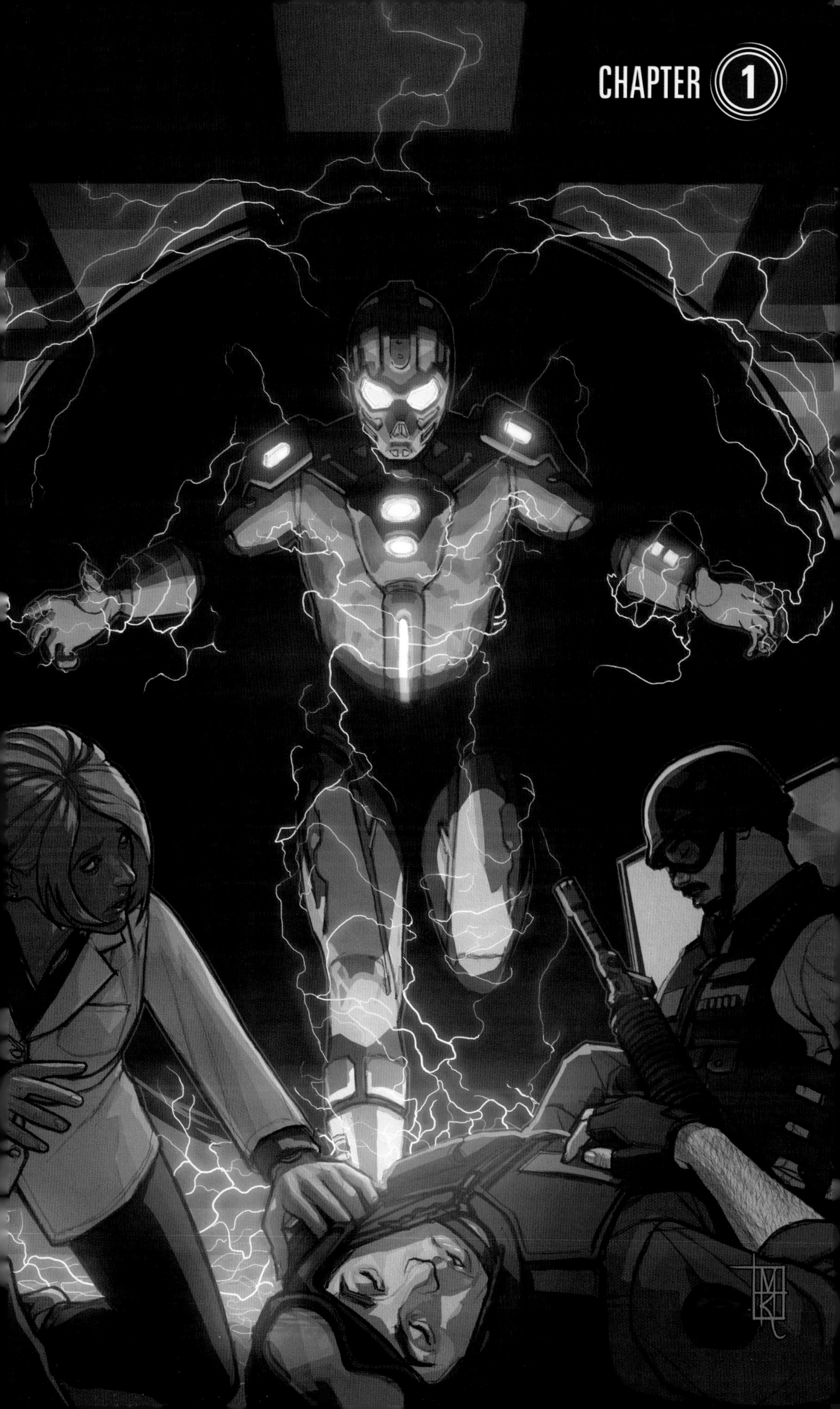

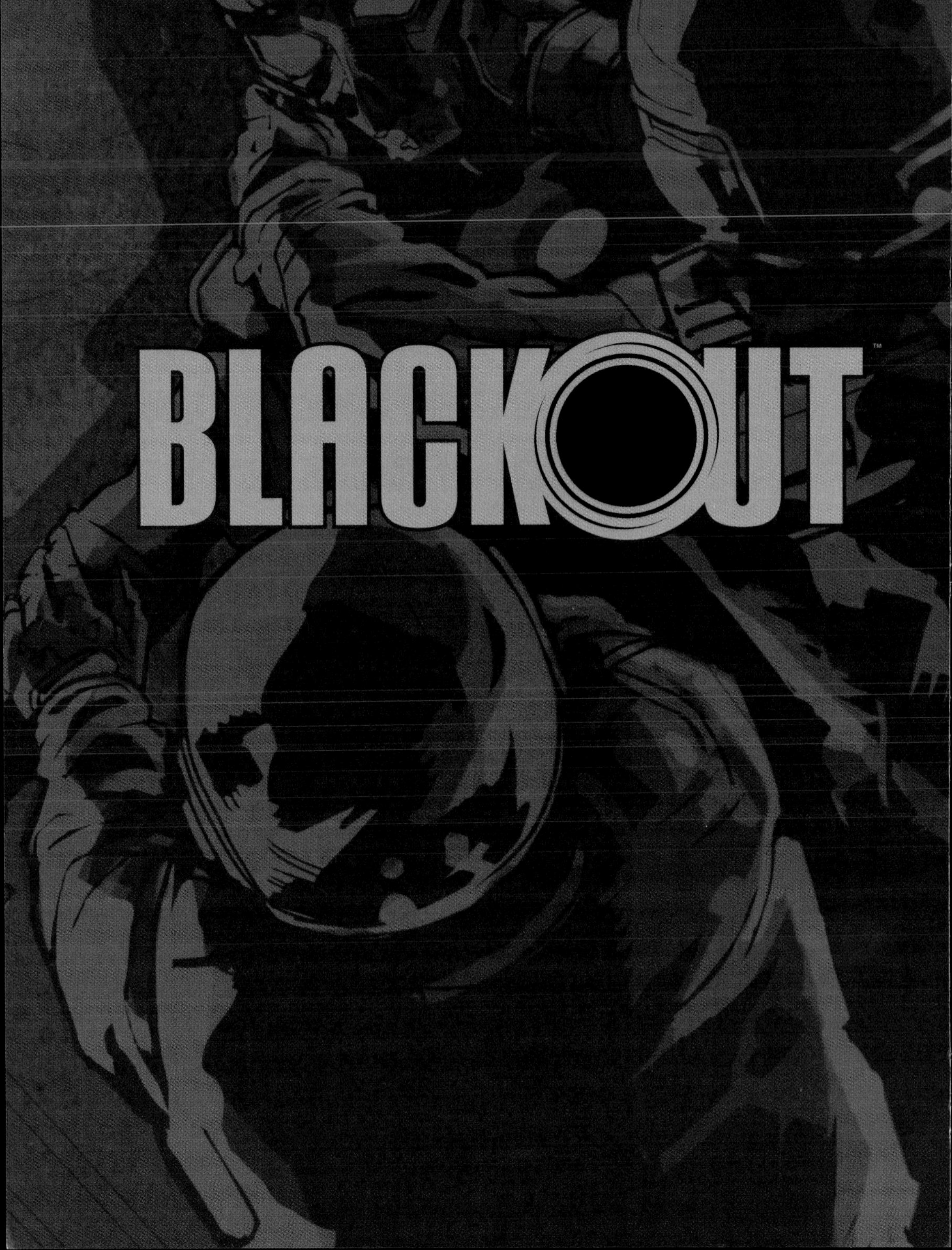
BLACKOUT™

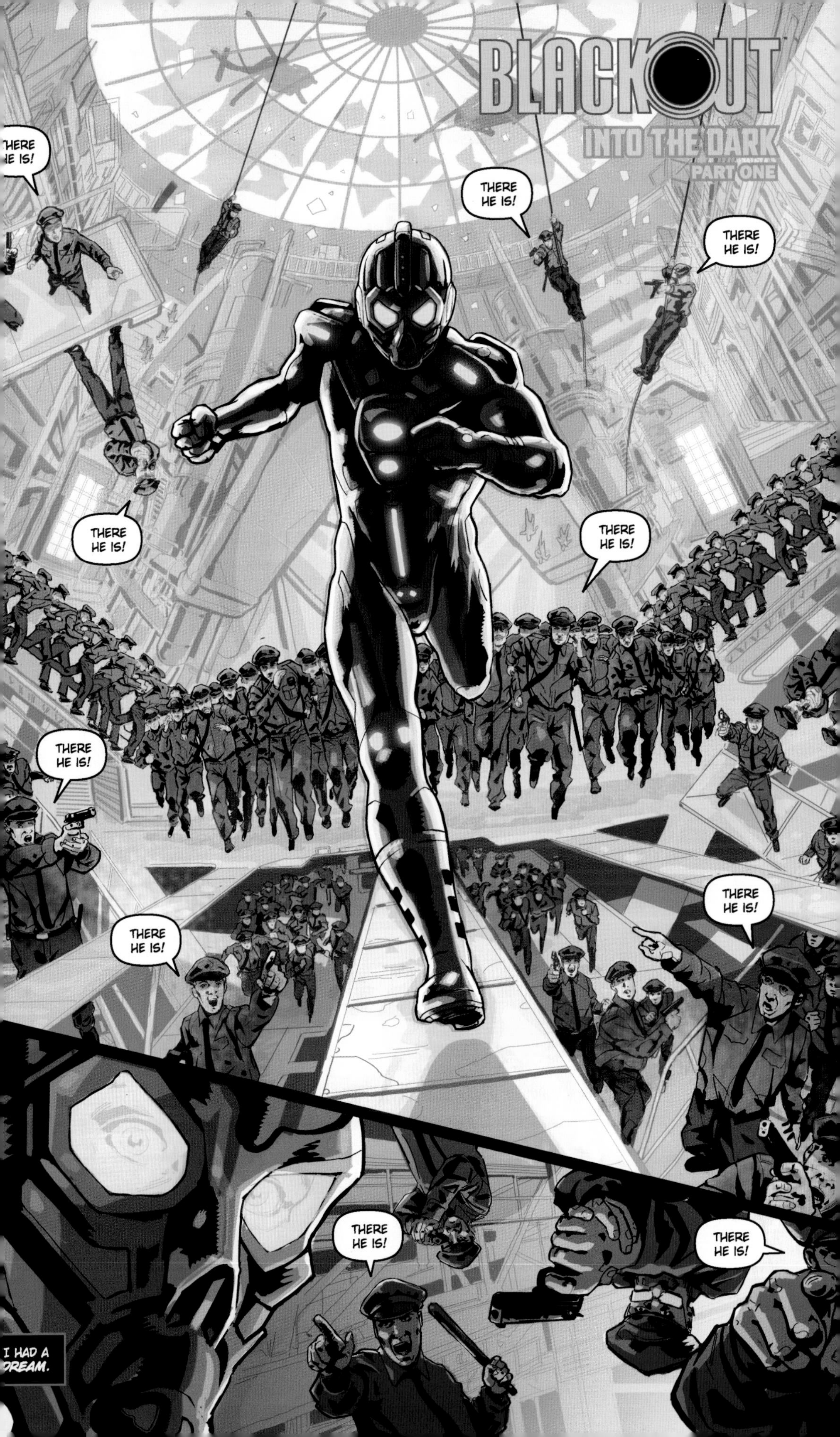
BLACKOUT
INTO THE DARK
PART ONE
HERE E IS!
THERE HE IS!
THERE HE IS!
THERE HE IS!
THERE HE IS!
THERE HE IS!
THERE HE IS!
THERE HE IS!
THERE HE IS!
THERE HE IS!
I HAD A DREAM.

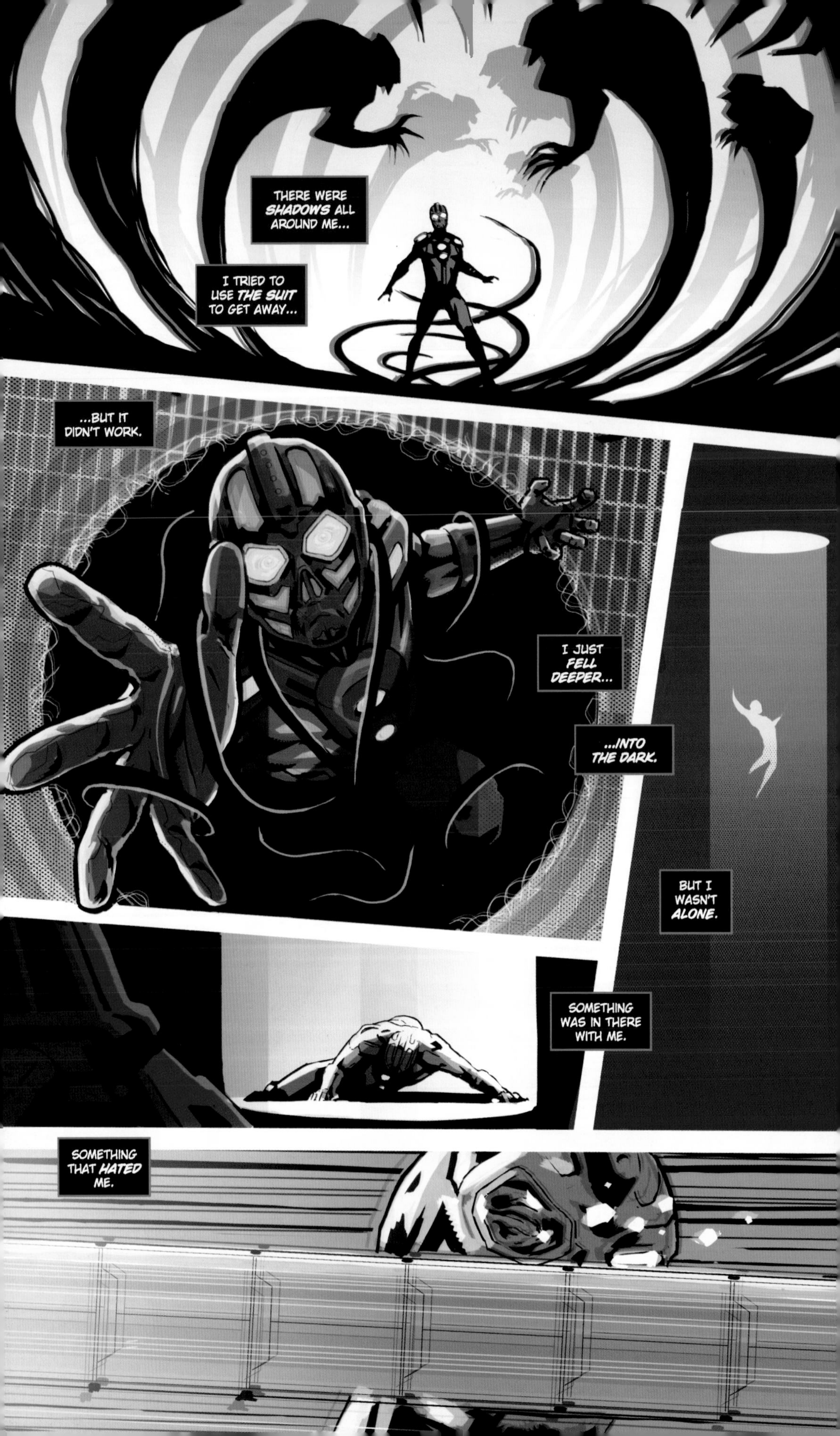
THERE WERE SHADOWS ALL AROUND ME...
I TRIED TO USE THE SUIT TO GET AWAY...
...BUT IT DIDN'T WORK.
I JUST FELL DEEPER...
...INTO THE DARK.
BUT I WASN'T ALONE.
SOMETHING WAS IN THERE WITH ME.
SOMETHING THAT HATED ME.

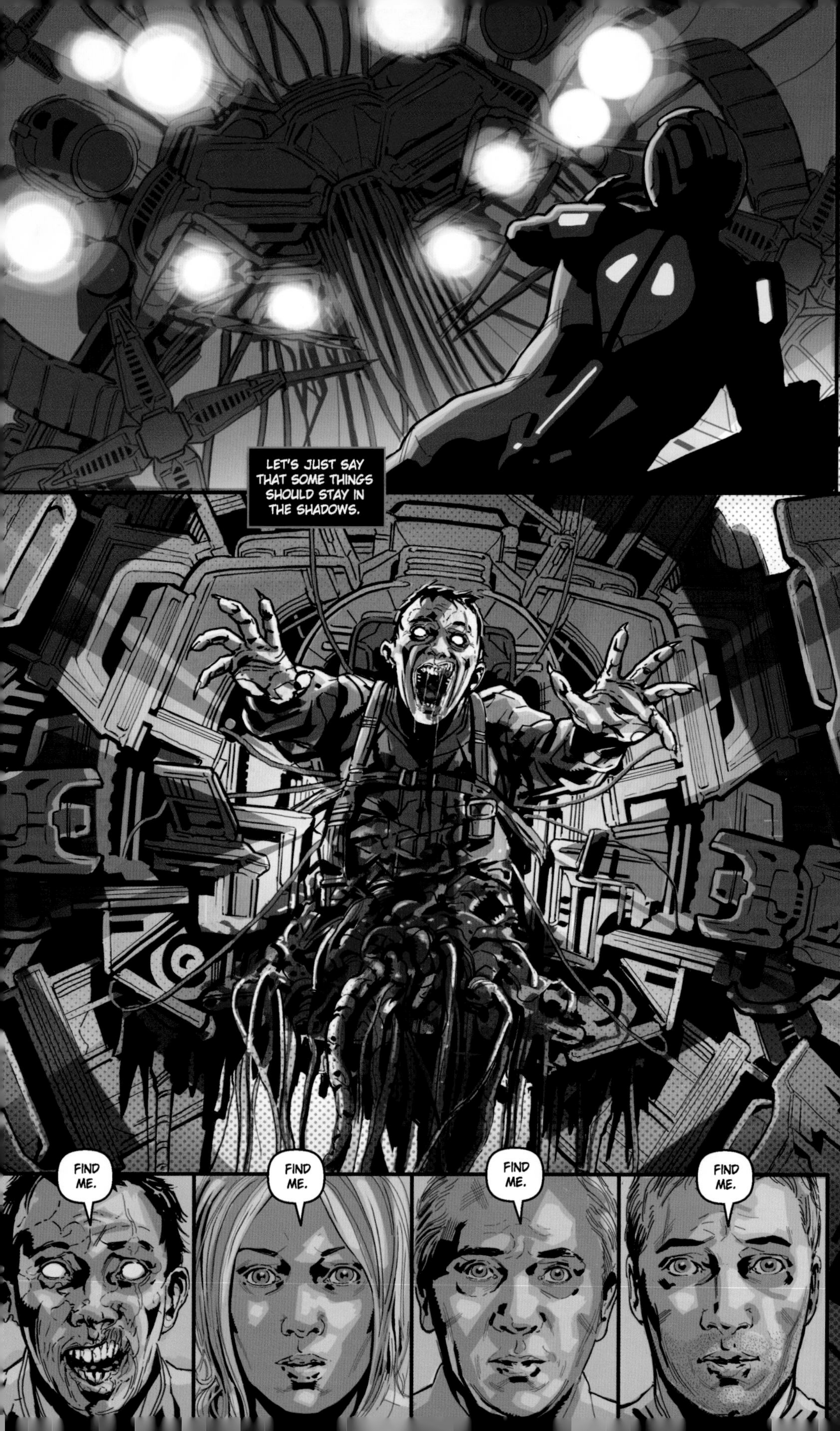
LET'S JUST SAY THAT SOME THINGS SHOULD STAY IN THE SHADOWS.
FIND ME.
FIND ME.
FIND ME.
FIND ME.

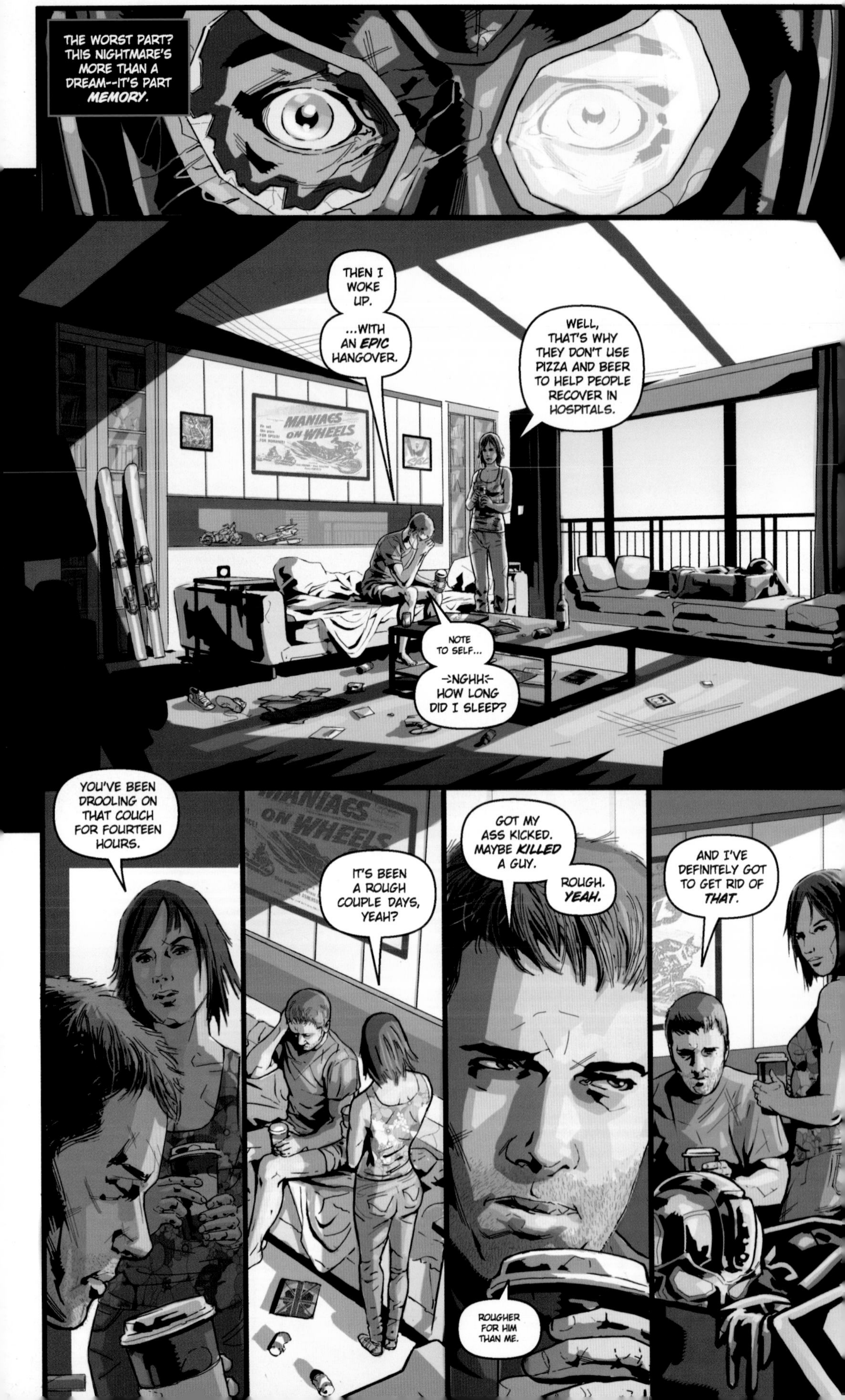

THE WORST PART? THIS NIGHTMARE'S MORE THAN A DREAM--IT'S PART *MEMORY*.
THEN I WOKE UP.
...WITH AN *EPIC* HANGOVER.
WELL, THAT'S WHY THEY DON'T USE PIZZA AND BEER TO HELP PEOPLE RECOVER IN HOSPITALS.
MANIACS ON WHEELS
NOTE TO SELF...
-NGHH- HOW LONG DID I SLEEP?
YOU'VE BEEN DROOLING ON THAT COUCH FOR FOURTEEN HOURS.
MANIACS ON WHEELS
IT'S BEEN A ROUGH COUPLE DAYS, YEAH?
GOT MY ASS KICKED. MAYBE *KILLED* A GUY.
ROUGH. ***YEAH.***
ROUGHER FOR HIM THAN ME.
AND I'VE DEFINITELY GOT TO GET RID OF *THAT*.

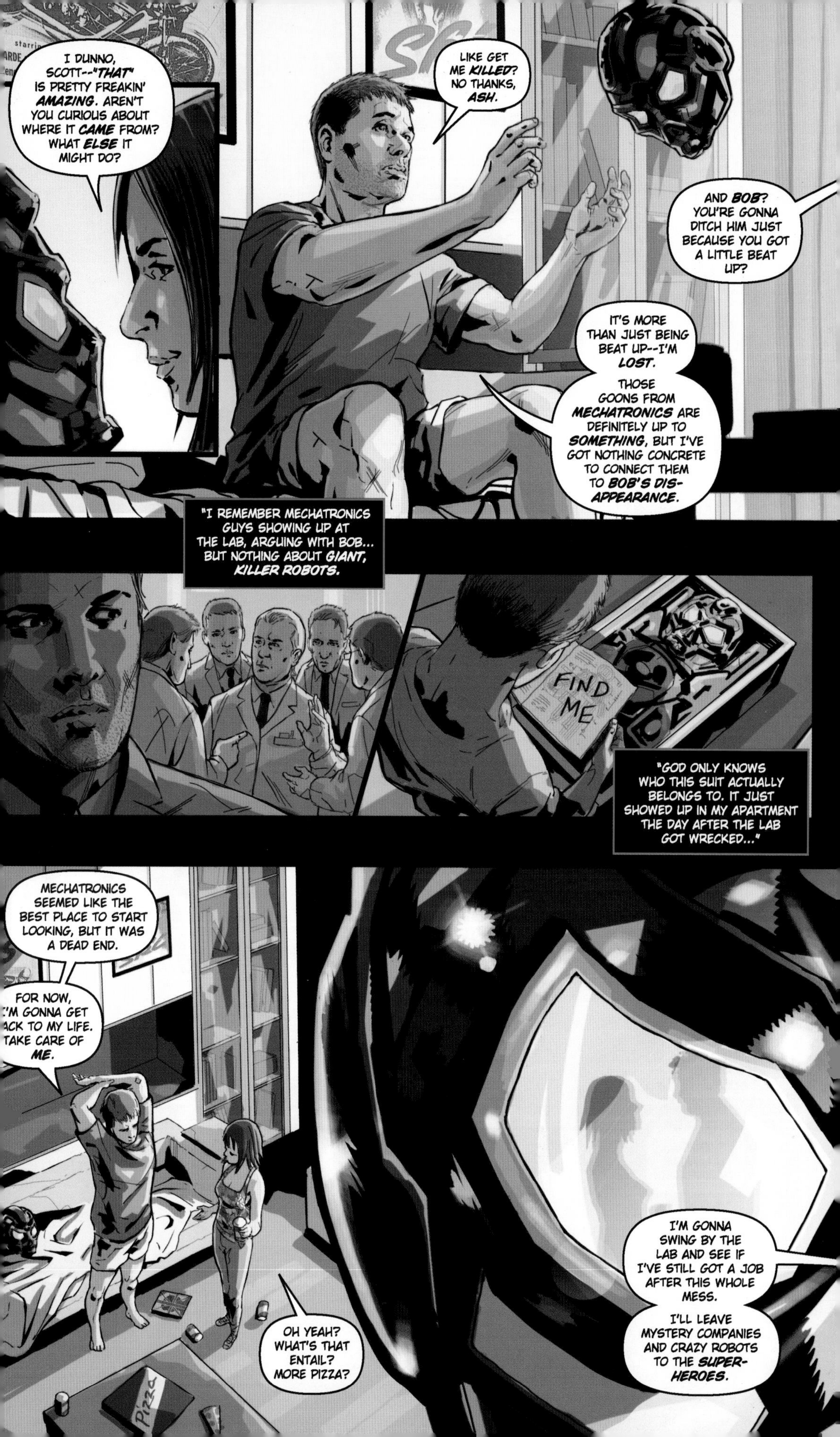

I DUNNO, SCOTT--"THAT" IS PRETTY FREAKIN' AMAZING. AREN'T YOU CURIOUS ABOUT WHERE IT CAME FROM? WHAT ELSE IT MIGHT DO?
LIKE GET ME KILLED? NO THANKS, ASH.
AND BOB? YOU'RE GONNA DITCH HIM JUST BECAUSE YOU GOT A LITTLE BEAT UP?
IT'S MORE THAN JUST BEING BEAT UP--I'M LOST.
THOSE GOONS FROM MECHATRONICS ARE DEFINITELY UP TO SOMETHING, BUT I'VE GOT NOTHING CONCRETE TO CONNECT THEM TO BOB'S DIS-APPEARANCE.
"I REMEMBER MECHATRONICS GUYS SHOWING UP AT THE LAB, ARGUING WITH BOB... BUT NOTHING ABOUT GIANT, KILLER ROBOTS.
FIND ME
"GOD ONLY KNOWS WHO THIS SUIT ACTUALLY BELONGS TO. IT JUST SHOWED UP IN MY APARTMENT THE DAY AFTER THE LAB GOT WRECKED..."
MECHATRONICS SEEMED LIKE THE BEST PLACE TO START LOOKING, BUT IT WAS A DEAD END.
FOR NOW, I'M GONNA GET BACK TO MY LIFE. TAKE CARE OF ME.
OH YEAH? WHAT'S THAT ENTAIL? MORE PIZZA?
I'M GONNA SWING BY THE LAB AND SEE IF I'VE STILL GOT A JOB AFTER THIS WHOLE MESS.
I'LL LEAVE MYSTERY COMPANIES AND CRAZY ROBOTS TO THE SUPER-HEROES.

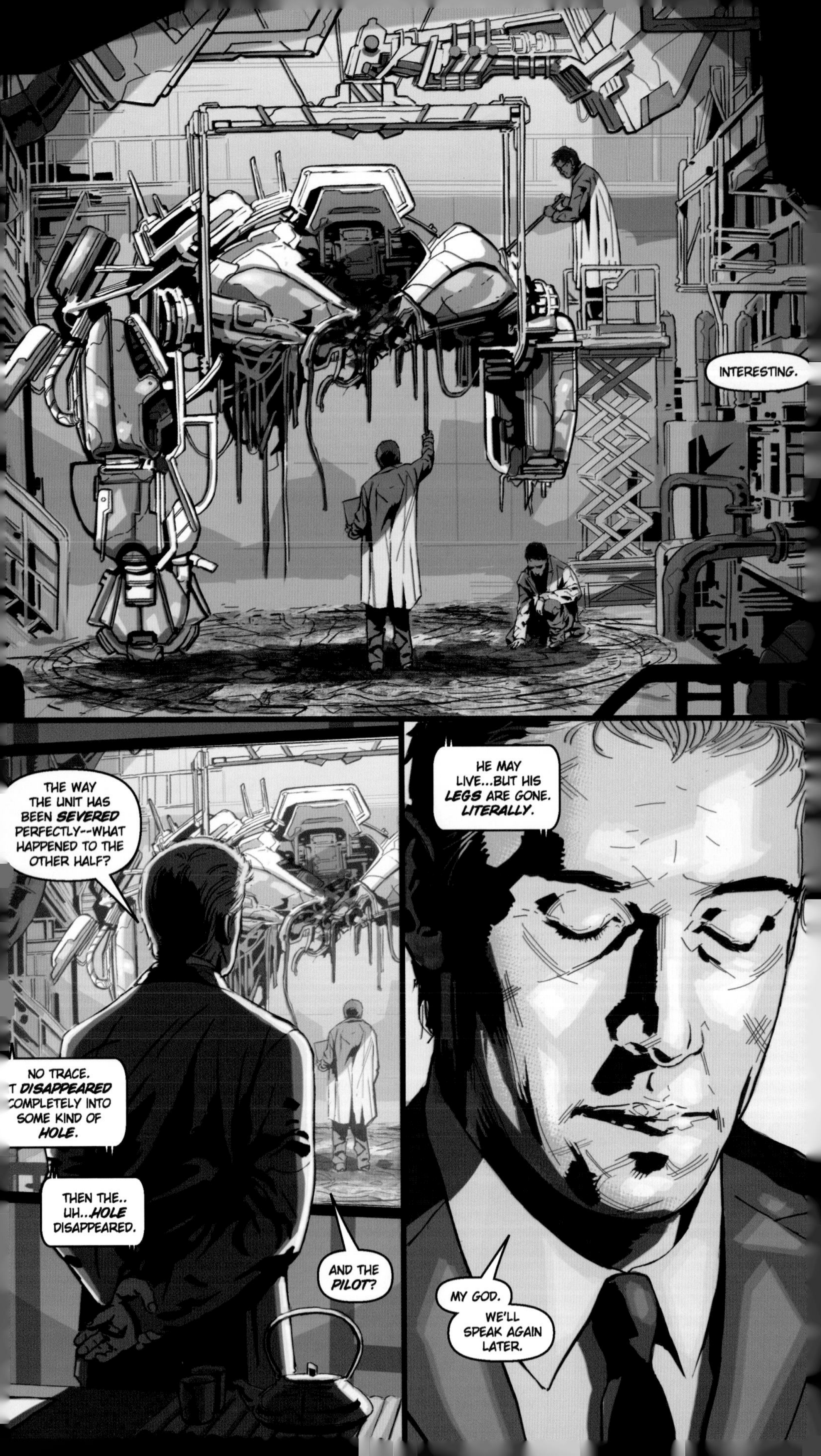
INTERESTING.
THE WAY THE UNIT HAS BEEN SEVERED PERFECTLY--WHAT HAPPENED TO THE OTHER HALF?
NO TRACE. IT DISAPPEARED COMPLETELY INTO SOME KIND OF HOLE.
THEN THE.. UH...HOLE DISAPPEARED.
AND THE PILOT?
HE MAY LIVE...BUT HIS LEGS ARE GONE. LITERALLY.
MY GOD.
WE'LL SPEAK AGAIN LATER.

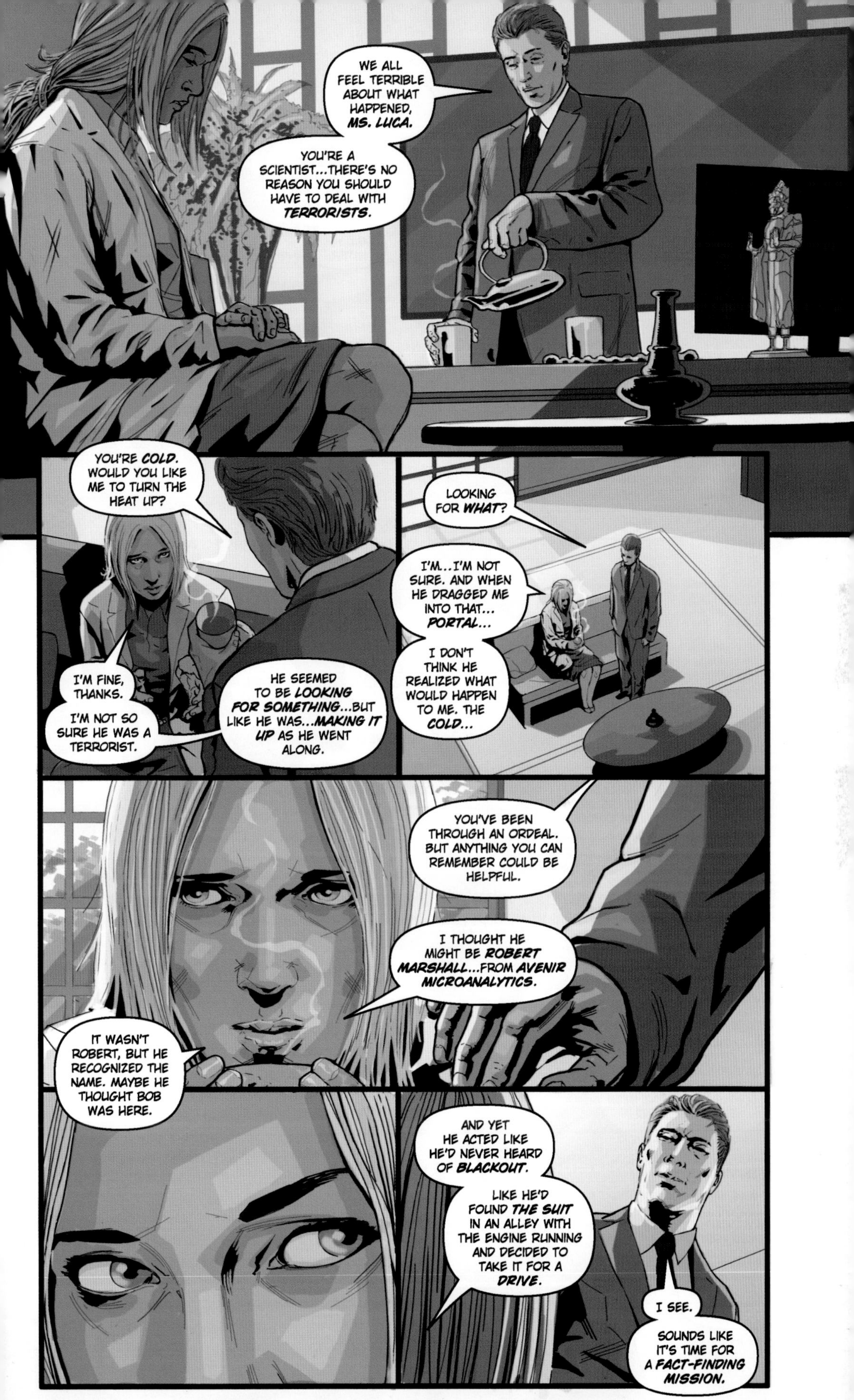
WE ALL FEEL TERRIBLE ABOUT WHAT HAPPENED, MS. LUCA.
YOU'RE A SCIENTIST...THERE'S NO REASON YOU SHOULD HAVE TO DEAL WITH TERRORISTS.
YOU'RE COLD. WOULD YOU LIKE ME TO TURN THE HEAT UP?
I'M FINE, THANKS.
I'M NOT SO SURE HE WAS A TERRORIST.
HE SEEMED TO BE LOOKING FOR SOMETHING...BUT LIKE HE WAS...MAKING IT UP AS HE WENT ALONG.
LOOKING FOR WHAT?
I'M...I'M NOT SURE. AND WHEN HE DRAGGED ME INTO THAT... PORTAL...
I DON'T THINK HE REALIZED WHAT WOULD HAPPEN TO ME. THE COLD...
YOU'VE BEEN THROUGH AN ORDEAL. BUT ANYTHING YOU CAN REMEMBER COULD BE HELPFUL.
I THOUGHT HE MIGHT BE ROBERT MARSHALL...FROM AVENIR MICROANALYTICS.
IT WASN'T ROBERT, BUT HE RECOGNIZED THE NAME. MAYBE HE THOUGHT BOB WAS HERE.
AND YET HE ACTED LIKE HE'D NEVER HEARD OF BLACKOUT.
LIKE HE'D FOUND THE SUIT IN AN ALLEY WITH THE ENGINE RUNNING AND DECIDED TO TAKE IT FOR A DRIVE.
I SEE.
SOUNDS LIKE IT'S TIME FOR A FACT-FINDING MISSION.

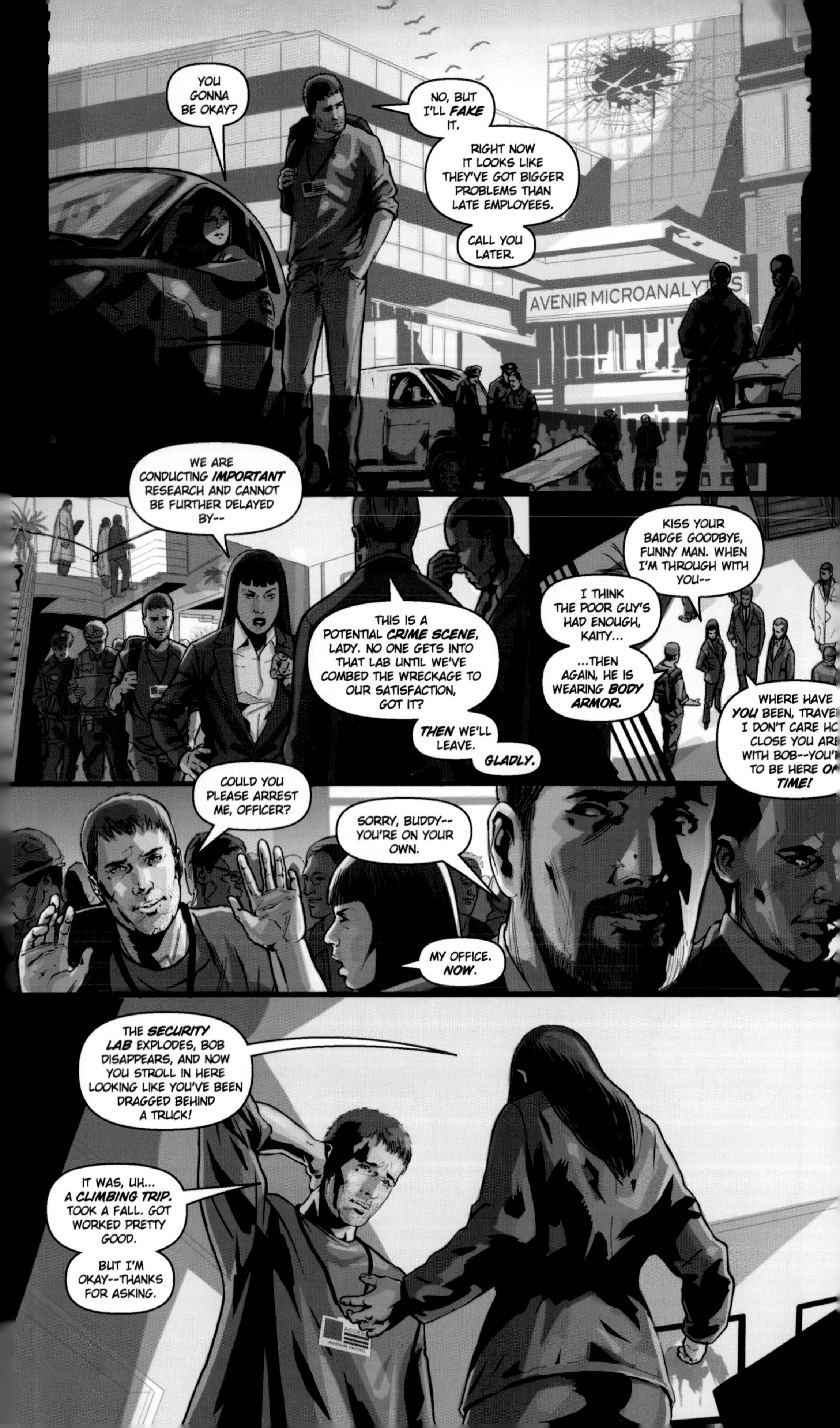
YOU GONNA BE OKAY?
NO, BUT I'LL FAKE IT.
RIGHT NOW IT LOOKS LIKE THEY'VE GOT BIGGER PROBLEMS THAN LATE EMPLOYEES.
CALL YOU LATER.
AVENIR MICROANALYT S
WE ARE CONDUCTING IMPORTANT RESEARCH AND CANNOT BE FURTHER DELAYED BY--
THIS IS A POTENTIAL CRIME SCENE, LADY. NO ONE GETS INTO THAT LAB UNTIL WE'VE COMBED THE WRECKAGE TO OUR SATISFACTION, GOT IT?
THEN WE'LL LEAVE.
GLADLY.
KISS YOUR BADGE GOODBYE, FUNNY MAN. WHEN I'M THROUGH WITH YOU--
I THINK THE POOR GUY'S HAD ENOUGH, KAITY...
...THEN AGAIN, HE IS WEARING BODY ARMOR.
WHERE HAVE YOU BEEN, TRAVE I DON'T CARE HO CLOSE YOU AR WITH BOB--YOU' TO BE HERE O TIME!
COULD YOU PLEASE ARREST ME, OFFICER?
SORRY, BUDDY-- YOU'RE ON YOUR OWN.
MY OFFICE. NOW.
THE SECURITY LAB EXPLODES, BOB DISAPPEARS, AND NOW YOU STROLL IN HERE LOOKING LIKE YOU'VE BEEN DRAGGED BEHIND A TRUCK!
IT WAS, UH... A CLIMBING TRIP. TOOK A FALL. GOT WORKED PRETTY GOOD.
BUT I'M OKAY--THANKS FOR ASKING.
ACCES AVENIR MICRO

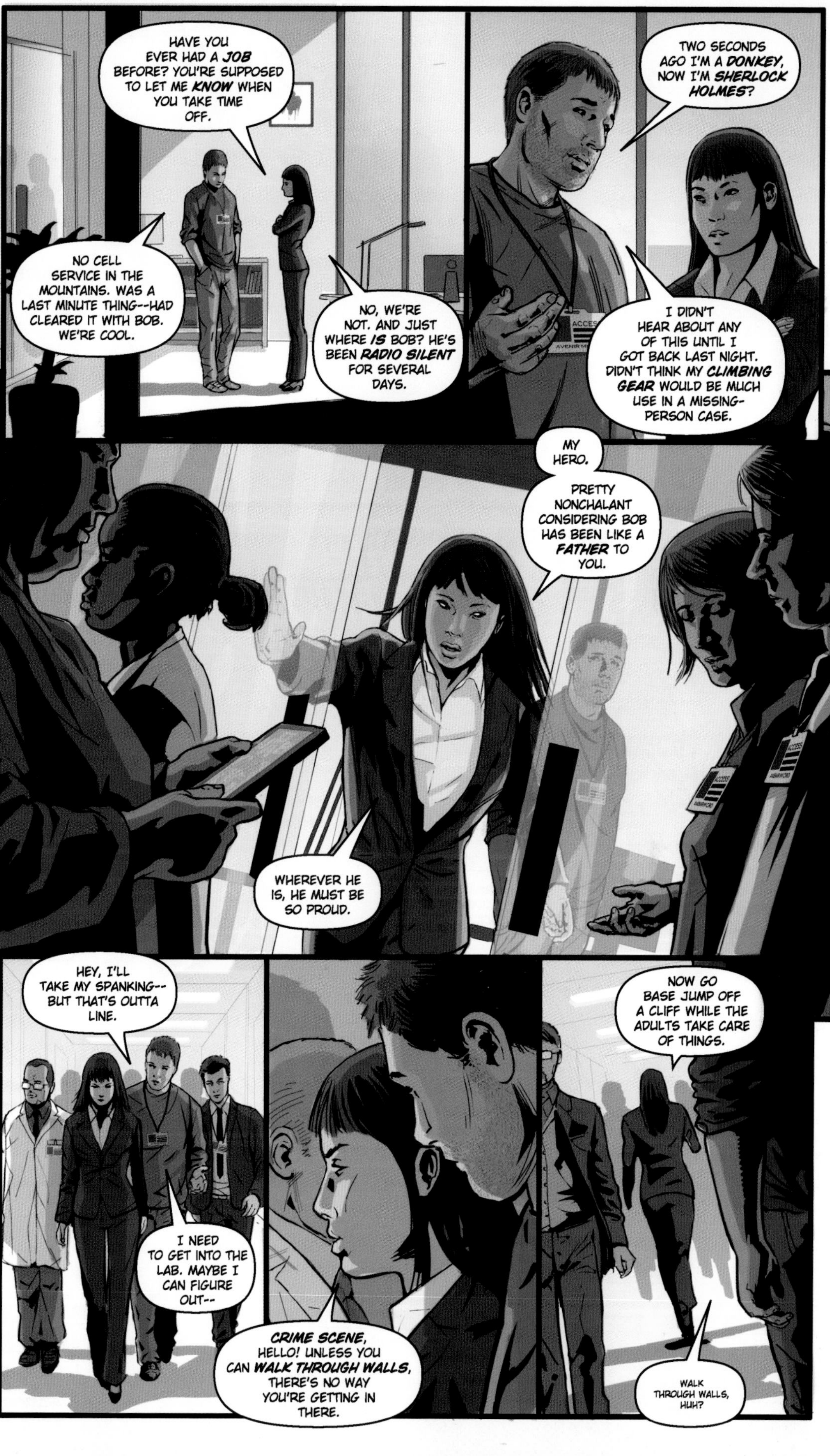
HAVE YOU EVER HAD A *JOB* BEFORE? YOU'RE SUPPOSED TO LET ME *KNOW* WHEN YOU TAKE TIME OFF.
NO CELL SERVICE IN THE MOUNTAINS. WAS A LAST MINUTE THING--HAD CLEARED IT WITH BOB. WE'RE COOL.
NO, WE'RE NOT. AND JUST WHERE *IS* BOB? HE'S BEEN *RADIO SILENT* FOR SEVERAL DAYS.
TWO SECONDS AGO I'M A *DONKEY*, NOW I'M *SHERLOCK HOLMES*?
I DIDN'T HEAR ABOUT ANY OF THIS UNTIL I GOT BACK LAST NIGHT. DIDN'T THINK MY *CLIMBING GEAR* WOULD BE MUCH USE IN A MISSING-PERSON CASE.
MY HERO.
PRETTY NONCHALANT CONSIDERING BOB HAS BEEN LIKE A *FATHER* TO YOU.
WHEREVER HE IS, HE MUST BE SO PROUD.
HEY, I'LL TAKE MY SPANKING--BUT THAT'S OUTTA LINE.
I NEED TO GET INTO THE LAB. MAYBE I CAN FIGURE OUT--
CRIME SCENE, HELLO! UNLESS YOU CAN *WALK THROUGH WALLS*, THERE'S NO WAY YOU'RE GETTING IN THERE.
NOW GO BASE JUMP OFF A CLIFF WHILE THE ADULTS TAKE CARE OF THINGS.
WALK THROUGH WALLS, HUH?

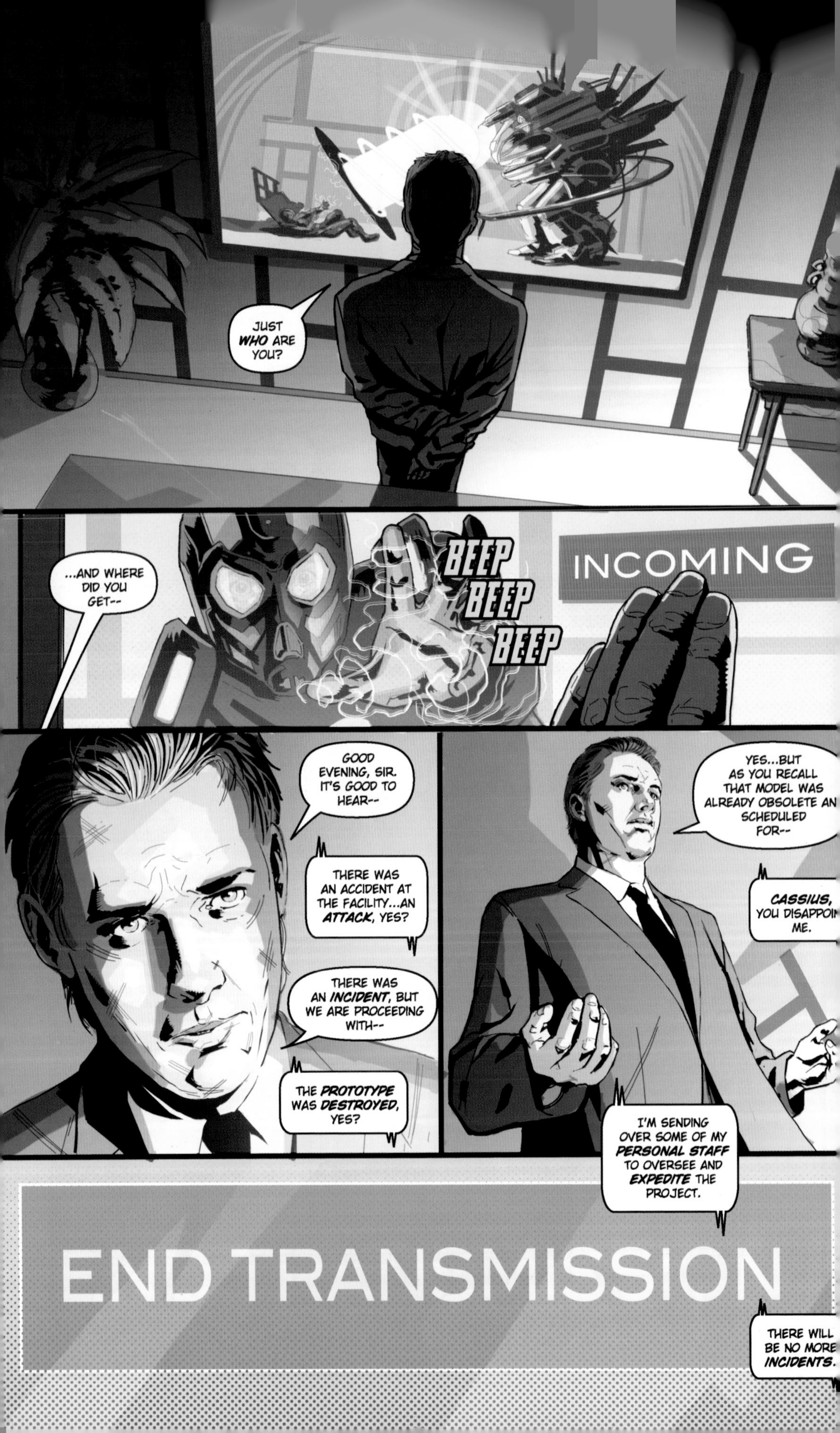
JUST WHO ARE YOU?
...AND WHERE DID YOU GET--
BEEP BEEP BEEP
INCOMING
GOOD EVENING, SIR. IT'S GOOD TO HEAR--
THERE WAS AN ACCIDENT AT THE FACILITY...AN ATTACK, YES?
THERE WAS AN INCIDENT, BUT WE ARE PROCEEDING WITH--
THE PROTOTYPE WAS DESTROYED, YES?
YES...BUT AS YOU RECALL THAT MODEL WAS ALREADY OBSOLETE AN SCHEDULED FOR--
CASSIUS, YOU DISAPPOI ME.
I'M SENDING OVER SOME OF MY PERSONAL STAFF TO OVERSEE AND EXPEDITE THE PROJECT.
END TRANSMISSION
THERE WILL BE NO MORE INCIDENTS.

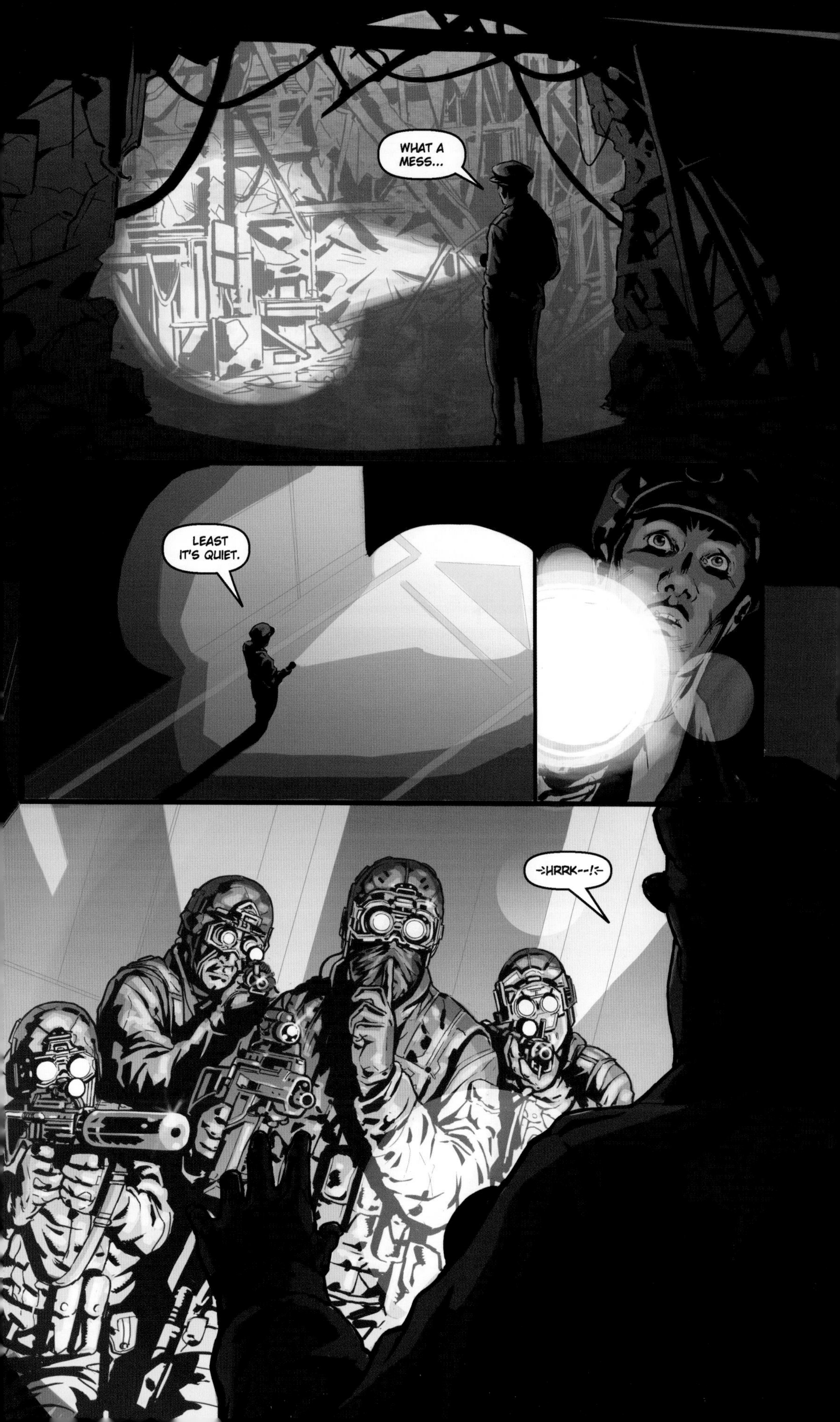
WHAT A MESS...
LEAST IT'S QUIET.
HRRK--!

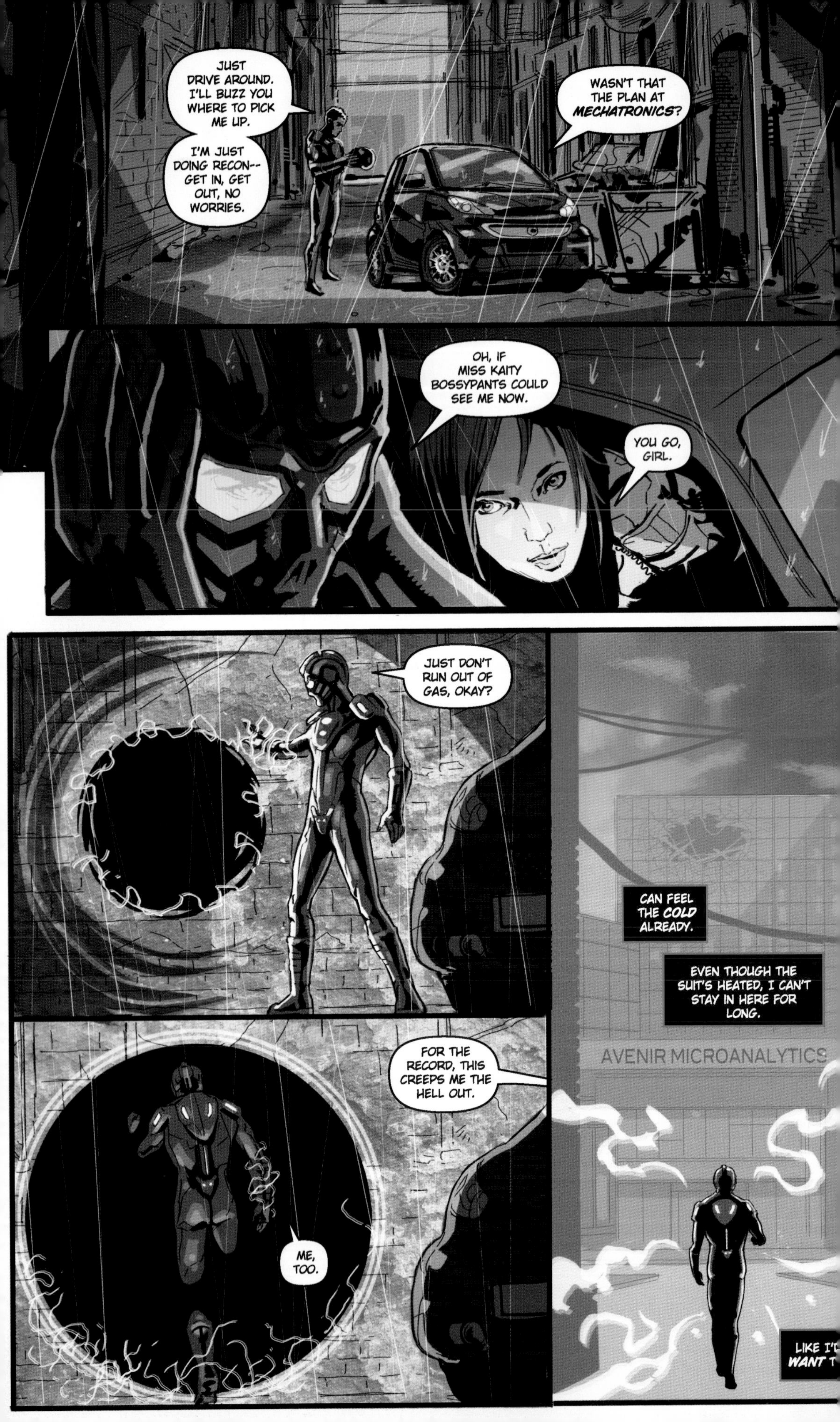
JUST DRIVE AROUND. I'LL BUZZ YOU WHERE TO PICK ME UP.
I'M JUST DOING RECON-- GET IN, GET OUT, NO WORRIES.
WASN'T THAT THE PLAN AT *MECHATRONICS*?
OH, IF MISS KAITY BOSSYPANTS COULD SEE ME NOW.
YOU GO, GIRL.
JUST DON'T RUN OUT OF GAS, OKAY?
FOR THE RECORD, THIS CREEPS ME THE HELL OUT.
ME, TOO.
CAN FEEL THE *COLD* ALREADY.
EVEN THOUGH THE SUIT'S HEATED, I CAN'T STAY IN HERE FOR LONG.
AVENIR MICROANALYTICS

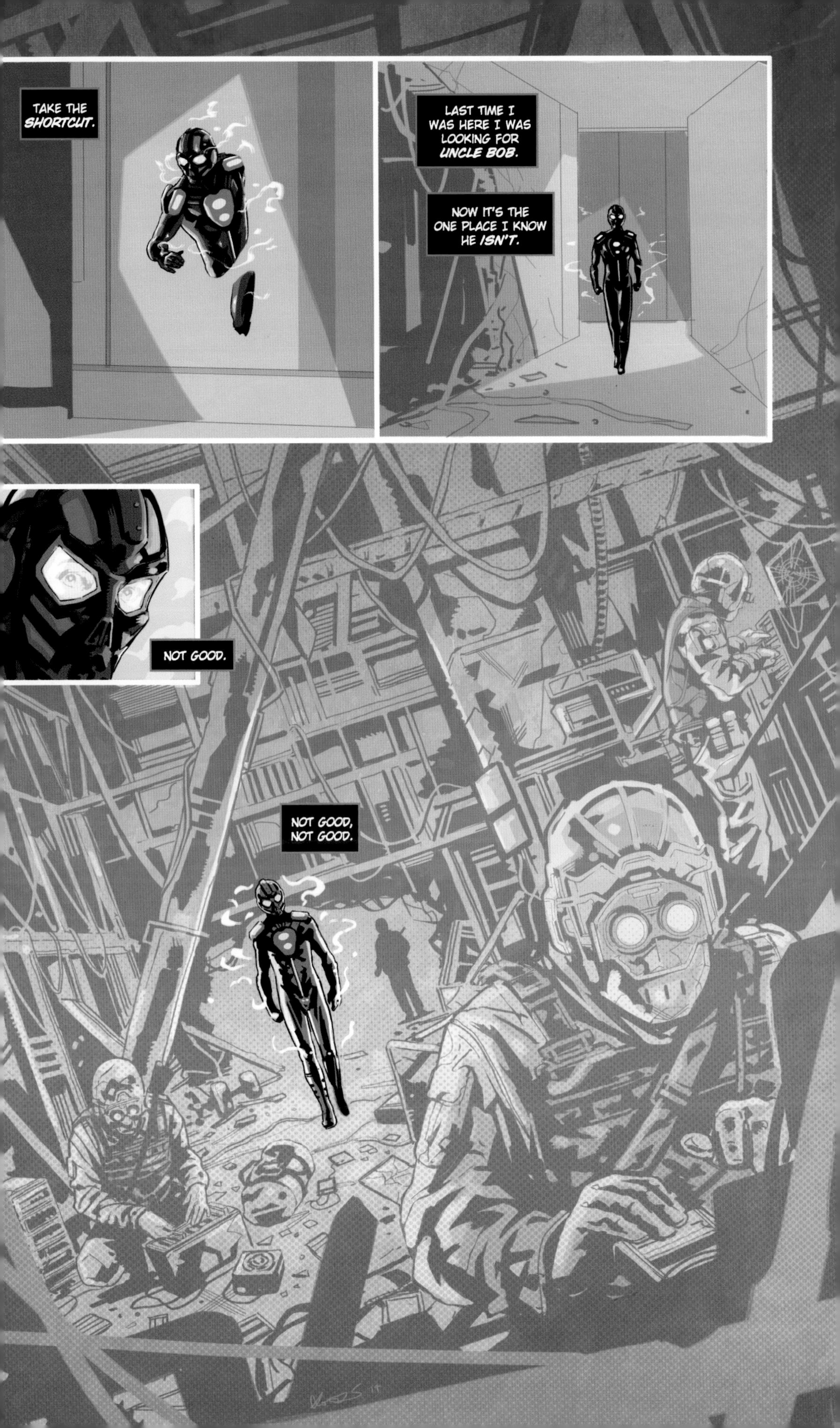
TAKE THE SHORTCUT.
LAST TIME I WAS HERE I WAS LOOKING FOR UNCLE BOB.
NOW IT'S THE ONE PLACE I KNOW HE ISN'T.
NOT GOOD.
NOT GOOD, NOT GOOD.

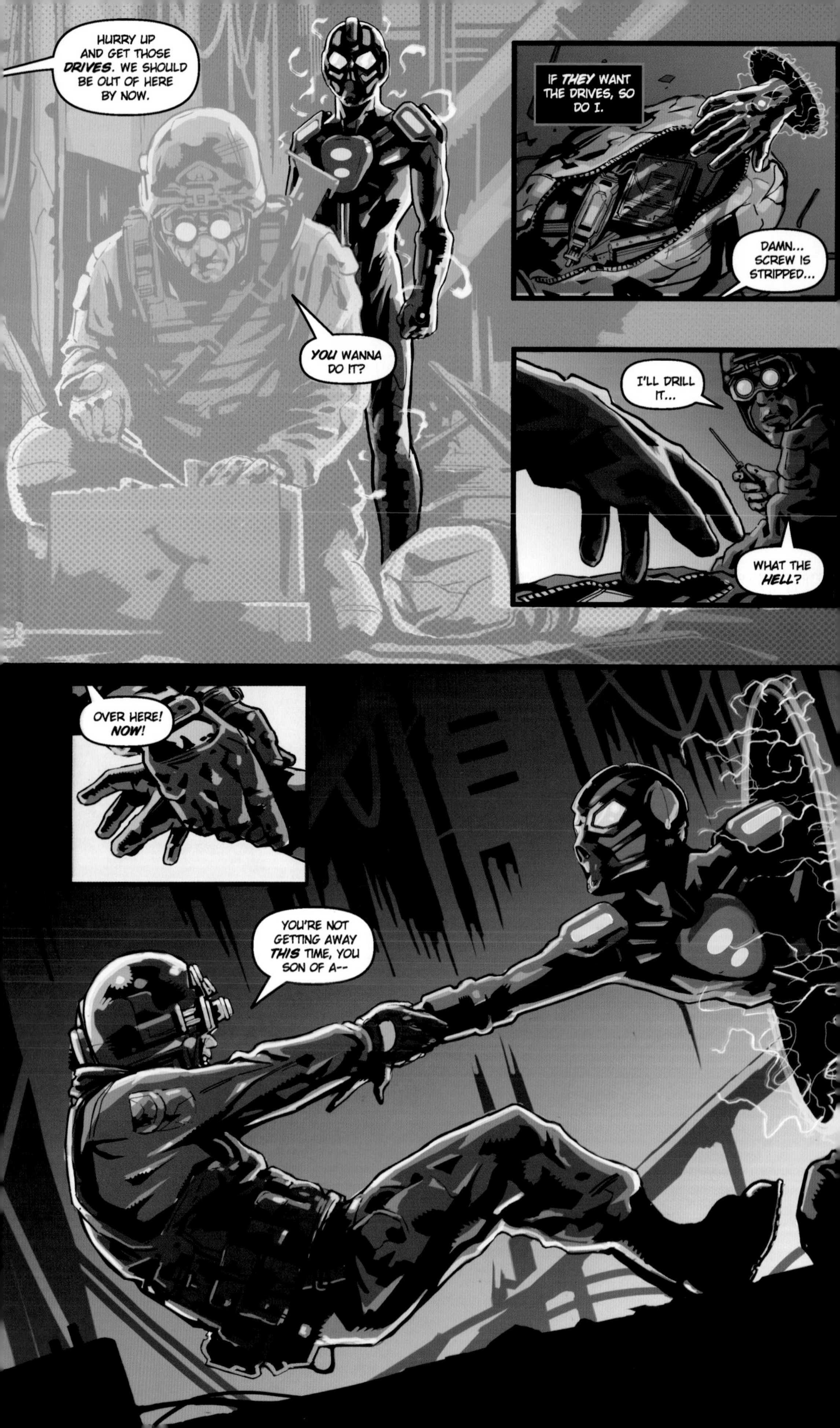
HURRY UP AND GET THOSE DRIVES. WE SHOULD BE OUT OF HERE BY NOW.
YOU WANNA DO IT?
IF THEY WANT THE DRIVES, SO DO I.
DAMN... SCREW IS STRIPPED...
I'LL DRILL IT...
WHAT THE HELL?
OVER HERE! NOW!
YOU'RE NOT GETTING AWAY THIS TIME, YOU SON OF A--

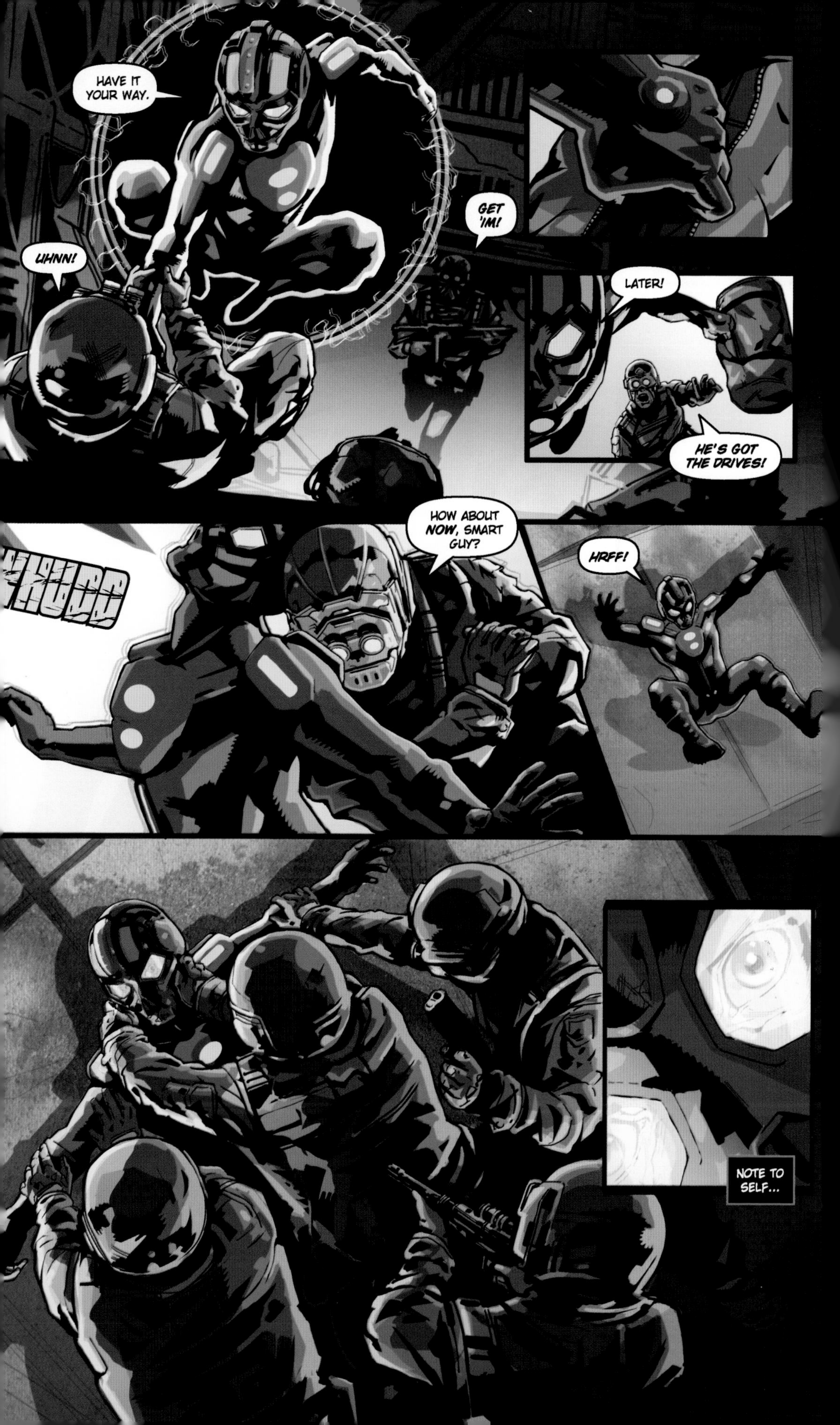
HAVE IT YOUR WAY.
UHNN!
GET 'IM!
LATER!
HE'S GOT THE DRIVES!
HOW ABOUT NOW, SMART GUY?
HRFF!
NOTE TO SELF...

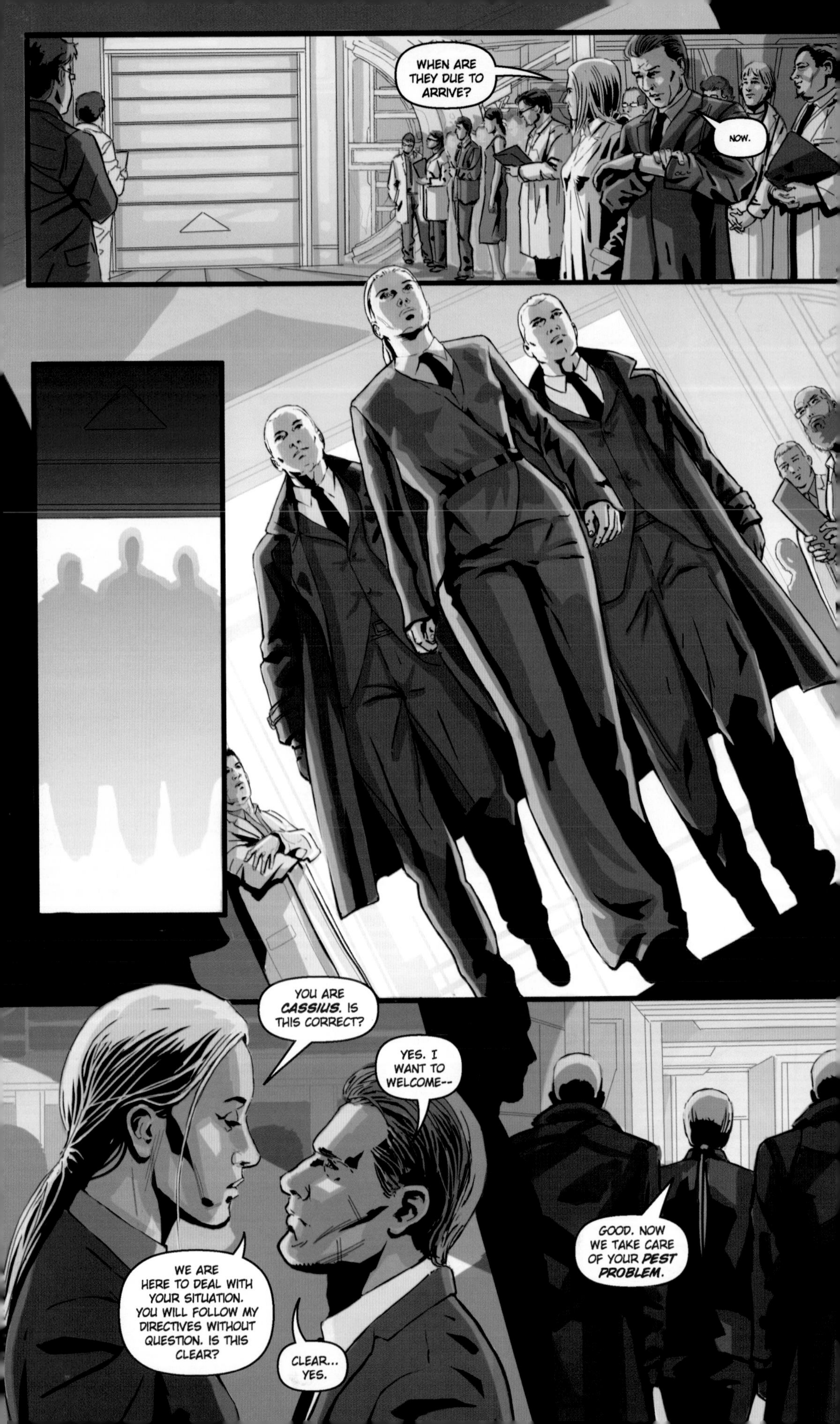
WHEN ARE THEY DUE TO ARRIVE?
NOW.
YOU ARE *CASSIUS*. IS THIS CORRECT?
YES. I WANT TO WELCOME--
WE ARE HERE TO DEAL WITH YOUR SITUATION. YOU WILL FOLLOW MY DIRECTIVES WITHOUT QUESTION. IS THIS CLEAR?
CLEAR... YES.
GOOD. NOW WE TAKE CARE OF YOUR *PEST PROBLEM*.

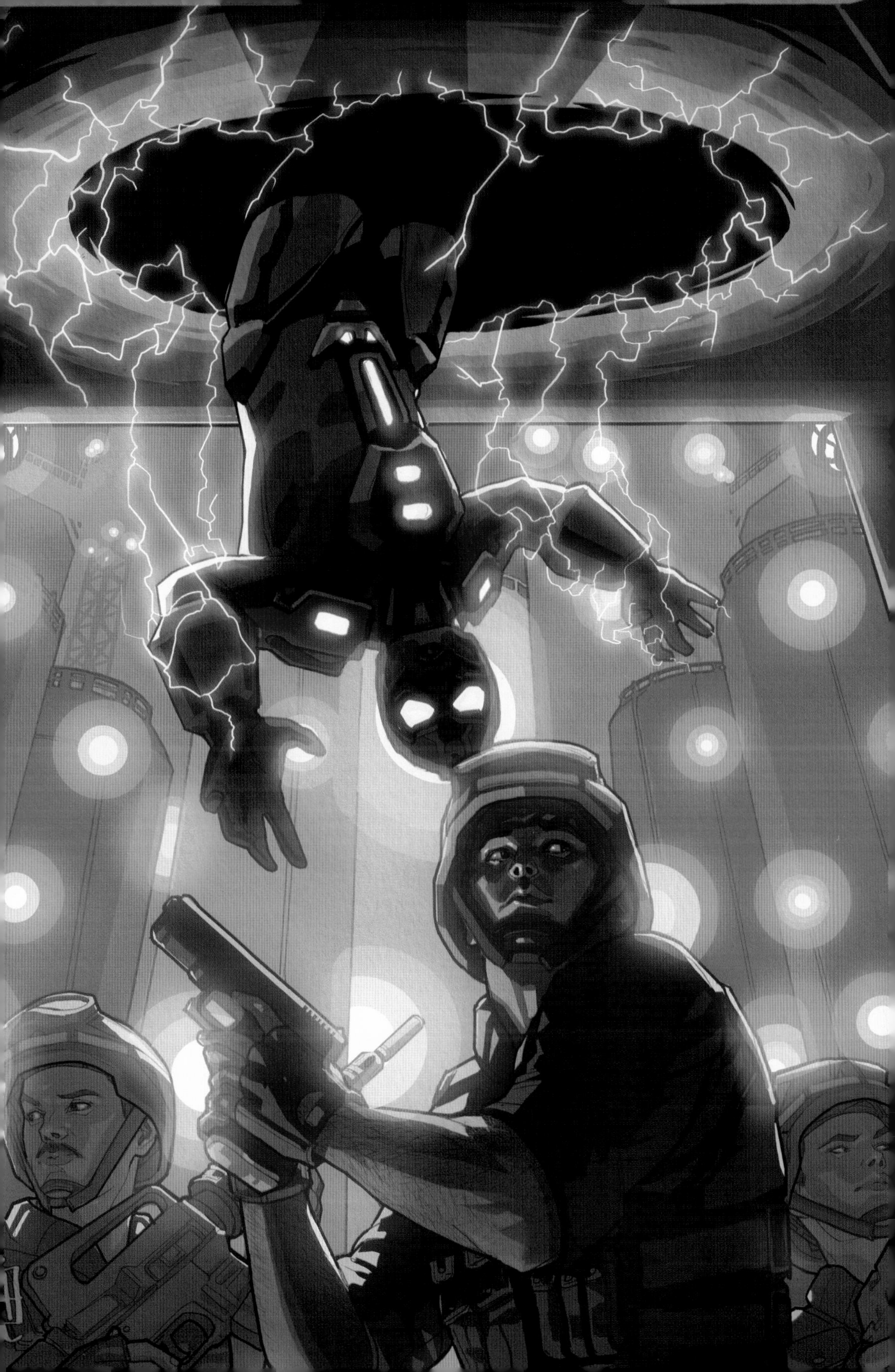

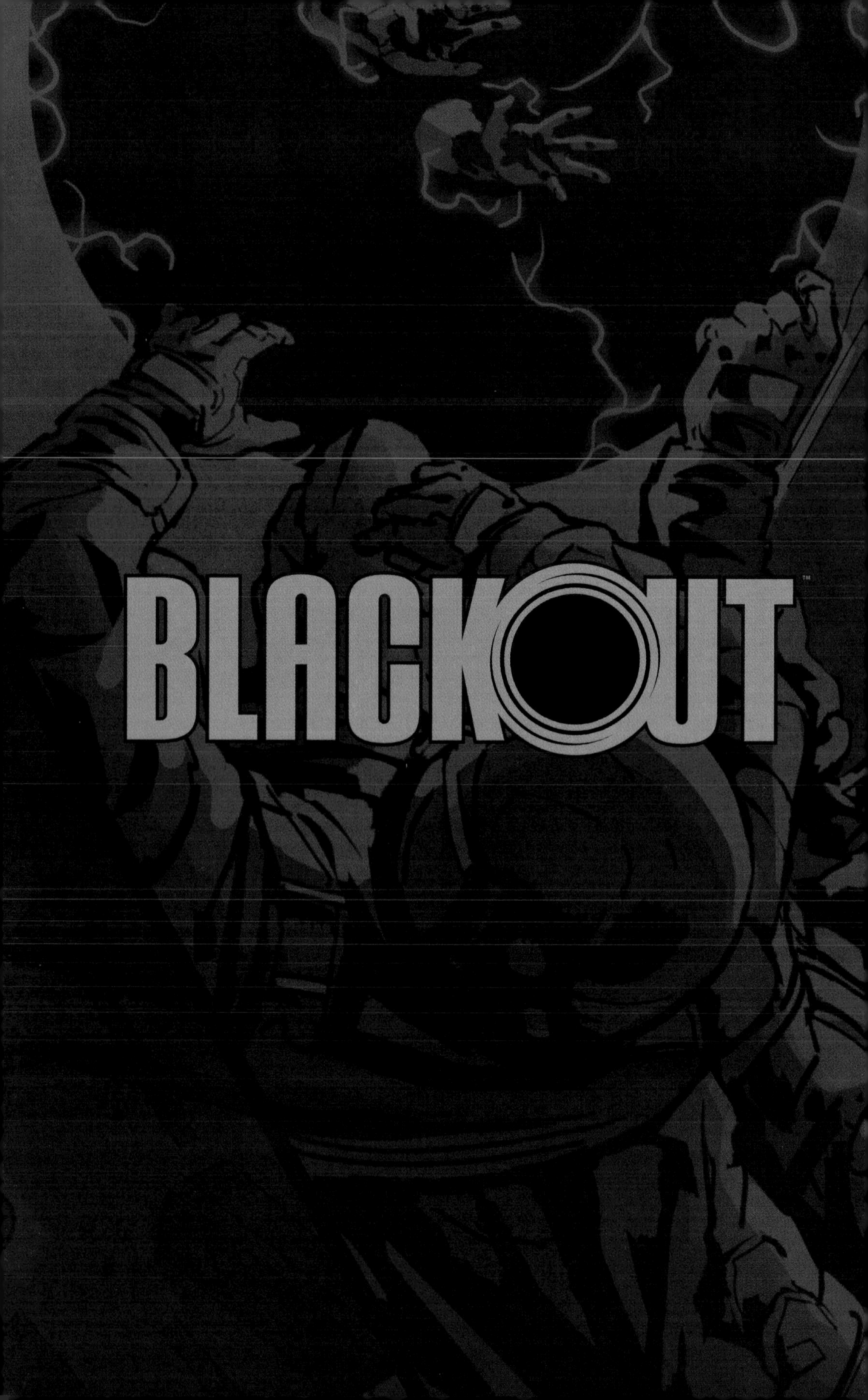
BLACKOUT™

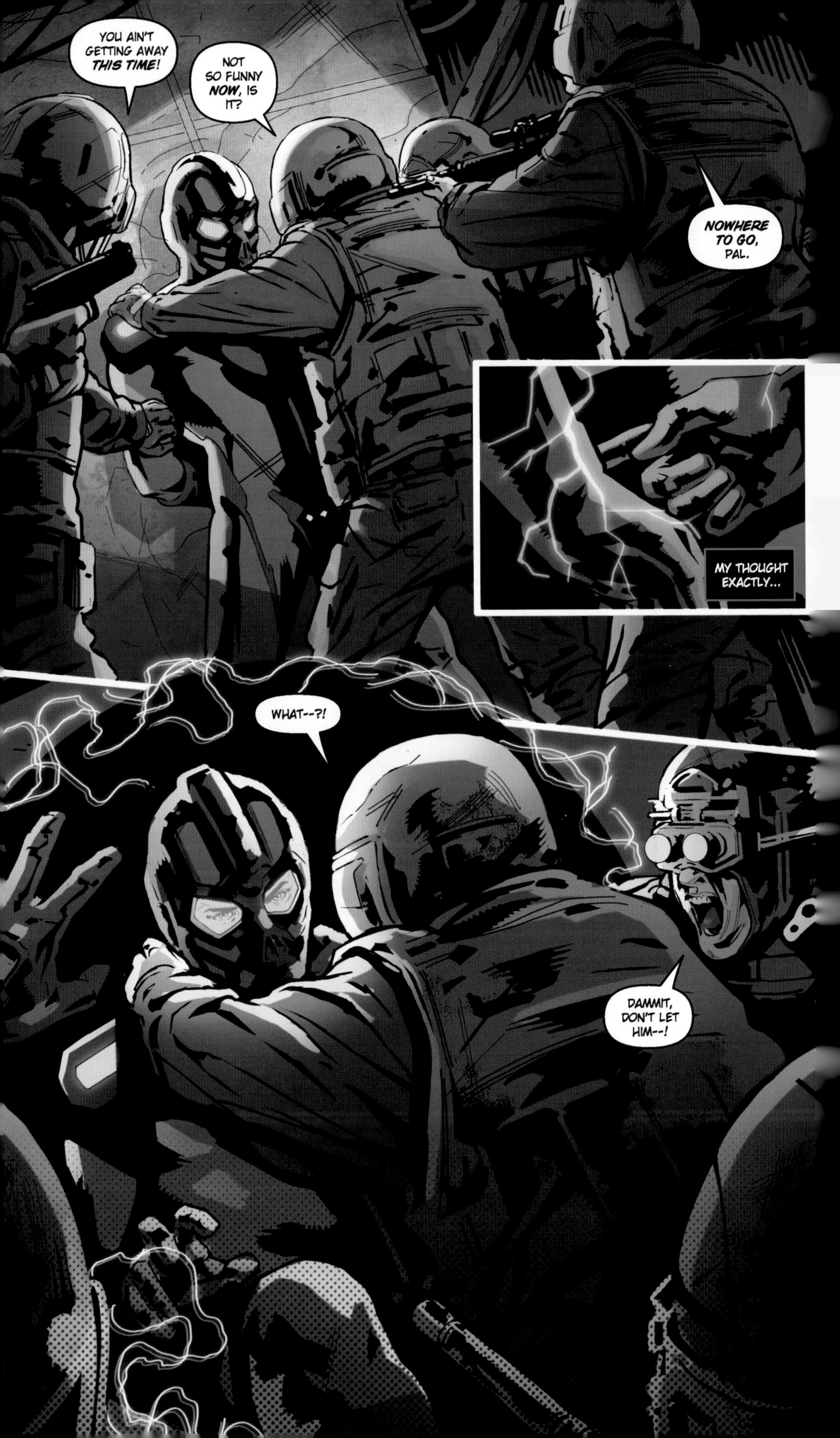
YOU AIN'T GETTING AWAY THIS TIME!
NOT SO FUNNY NOW, IS IT?
NOWHERE TO GO, PAL.
MY THOUGHT EXACTLY...
WHAT--?!
DAMMIT, DON'T LET HIM--!

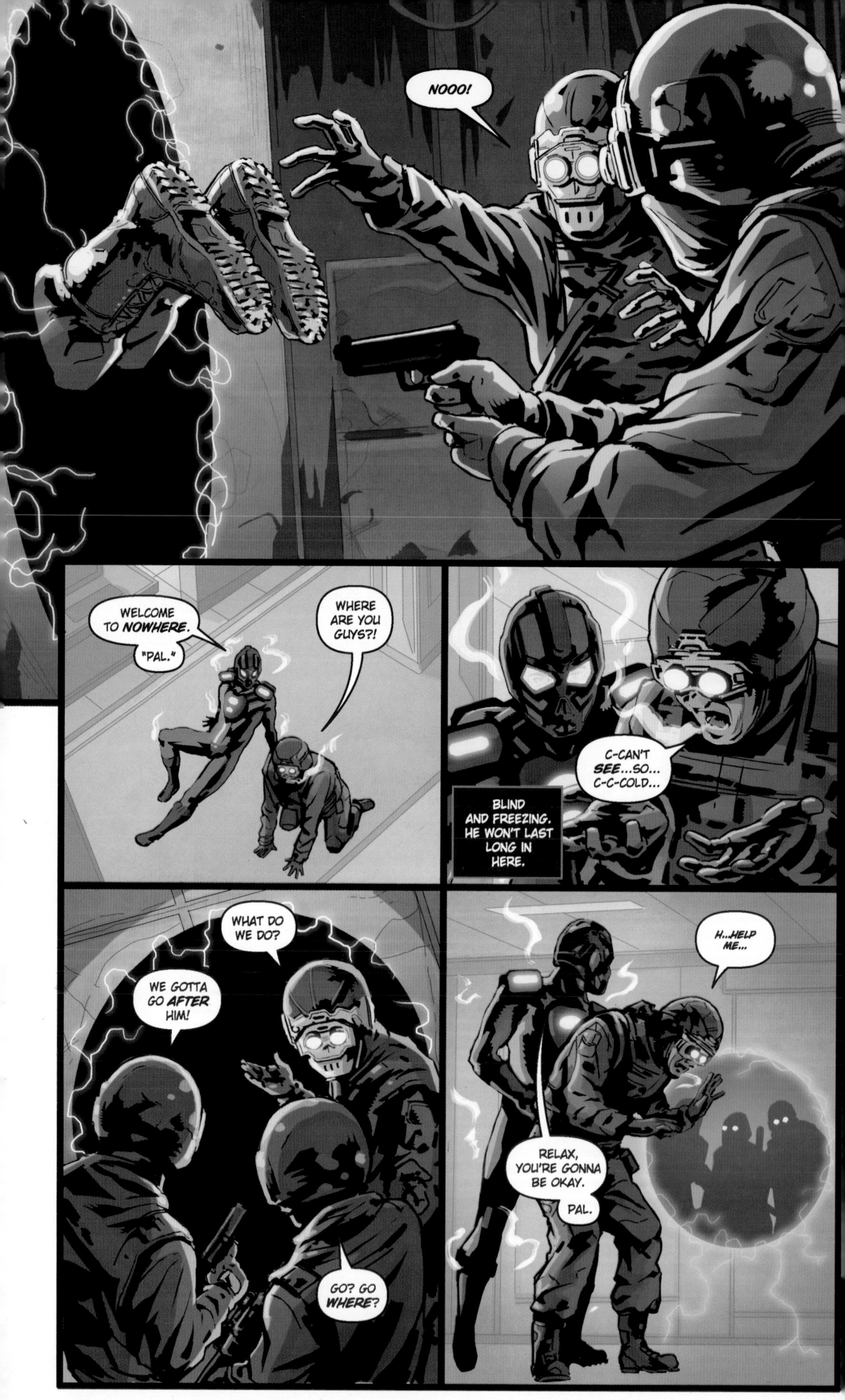
NOOO!
WELCOME TO NOWHERE.
"PAL."
WHERE ARE YOU GUYS?!
C-CAN'T SEE...SO... C-C-COLD...
BLIND AND FREEZING. HE WON'T LAST LONG IN HERE.
WHAT DO WE DO?
WE GOTTA GO AFTER HIM!
GO? GO WHERE?
H...HELP ME...
RELAX, YOU'RE GONNA BE OKAY.
PAL.

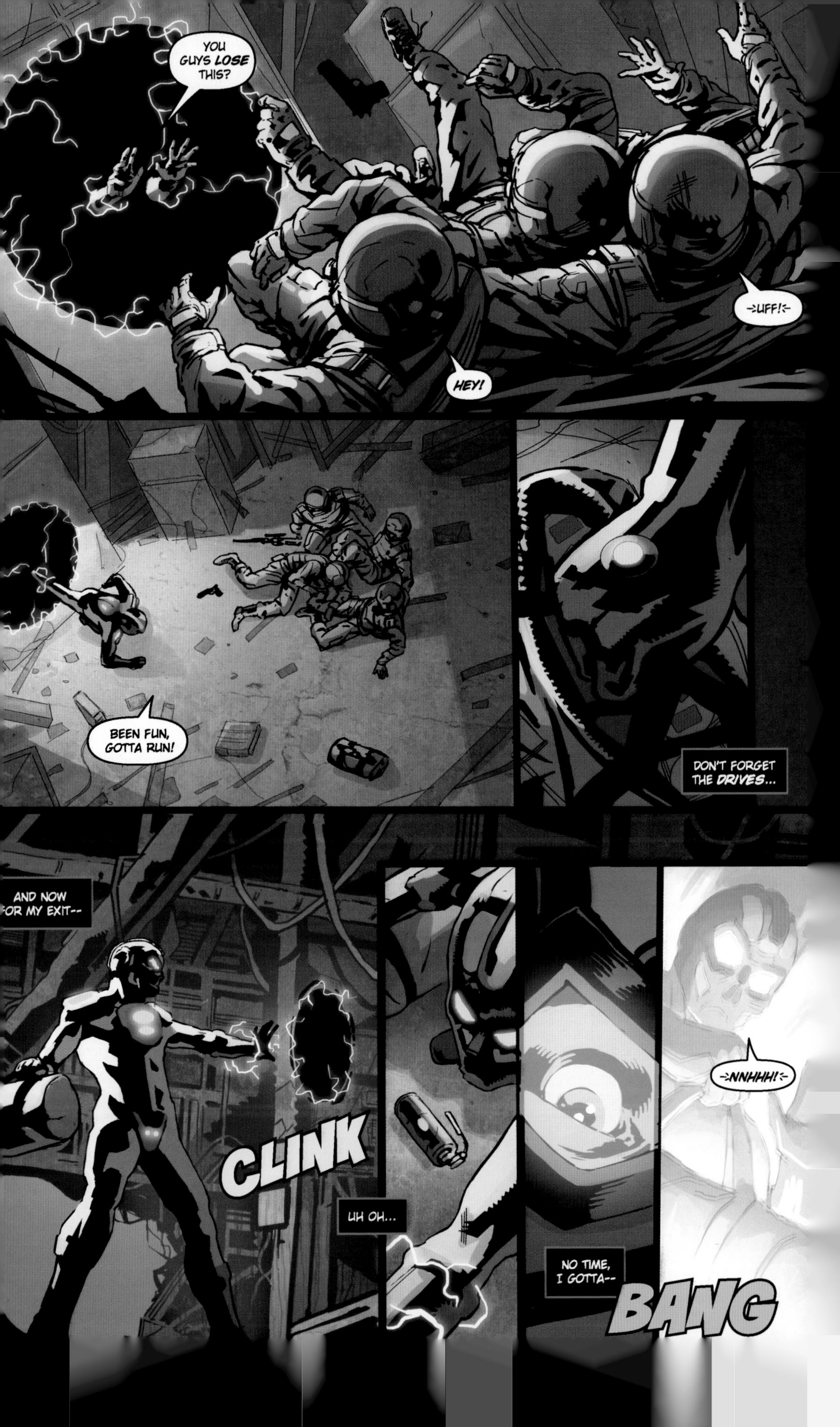
YOU GUYS LOSE THIS?
-UFF!-
HEY!
BEEN FUN, GOTTA RUN!
DON'T FORGET THE DRIVES...
AND NOW FOR MY EXIT--
CLINK
UH OH...
-NNHHH!-
NO TIME, I GOTTA--
BANG

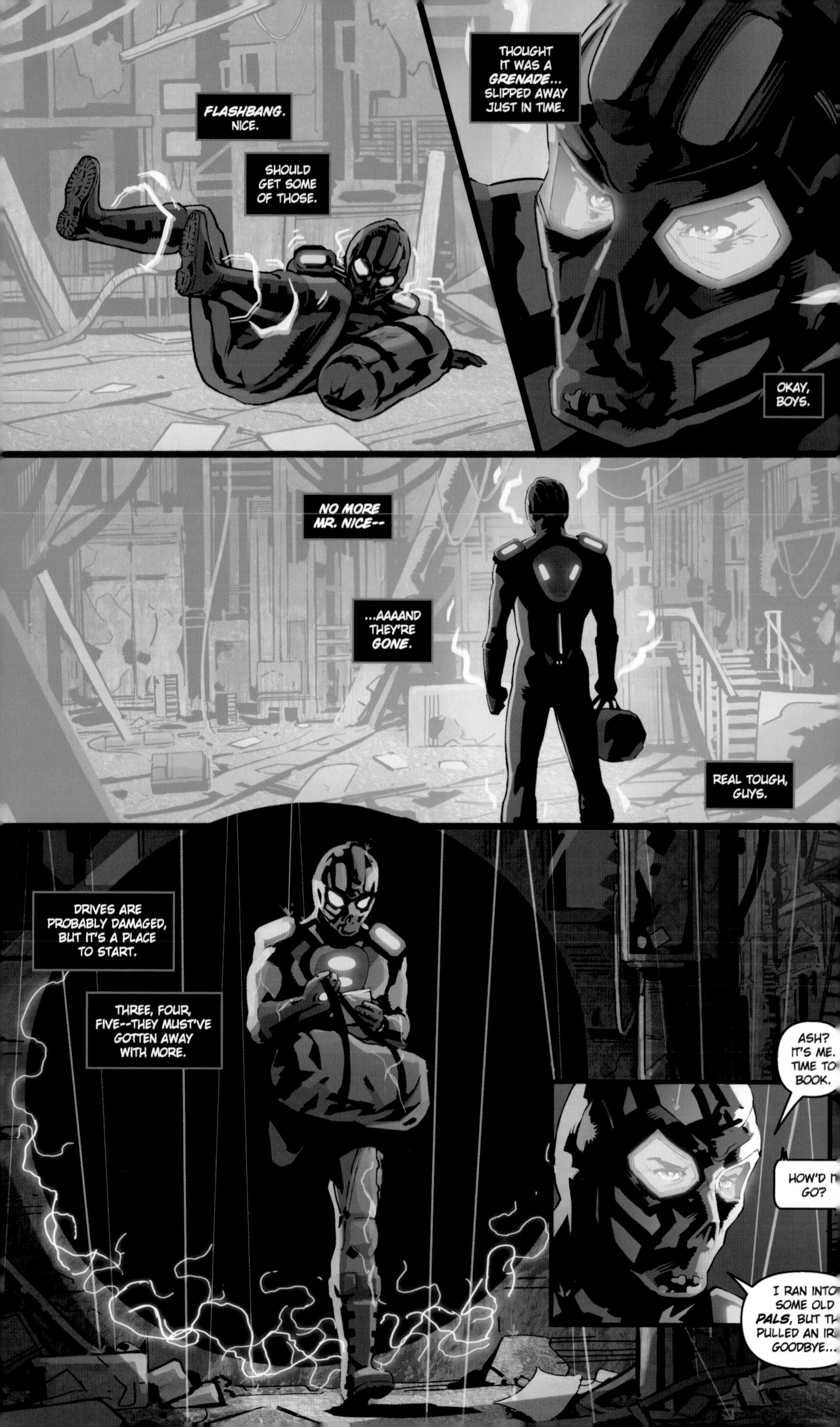

FLASHBANG. NICE.
SHOULD GET SOME OF THOSE.
THOUGHT IT WAS A GRENADE... SLIPPED AWAY JUST IN TIME.
OKAY, BOYS.
NO MORE MR. NICE--
...AAAAND THEY'RE GONE.
REAL TOUGH, GUYS.
DRIVES ARE PROBABLY DAMAGED, BUT IT'S A PLACE TO START.
THREE, FOUR, FIVE--THEY MUST'VE GOTTEN AWAY WITH MORE.
ASH? IT'S ME. TIME TO BOOK.
HOW'D GO?
I RAN INTO SOME OLD PALS, BUT PULLED AN GOODBYE...

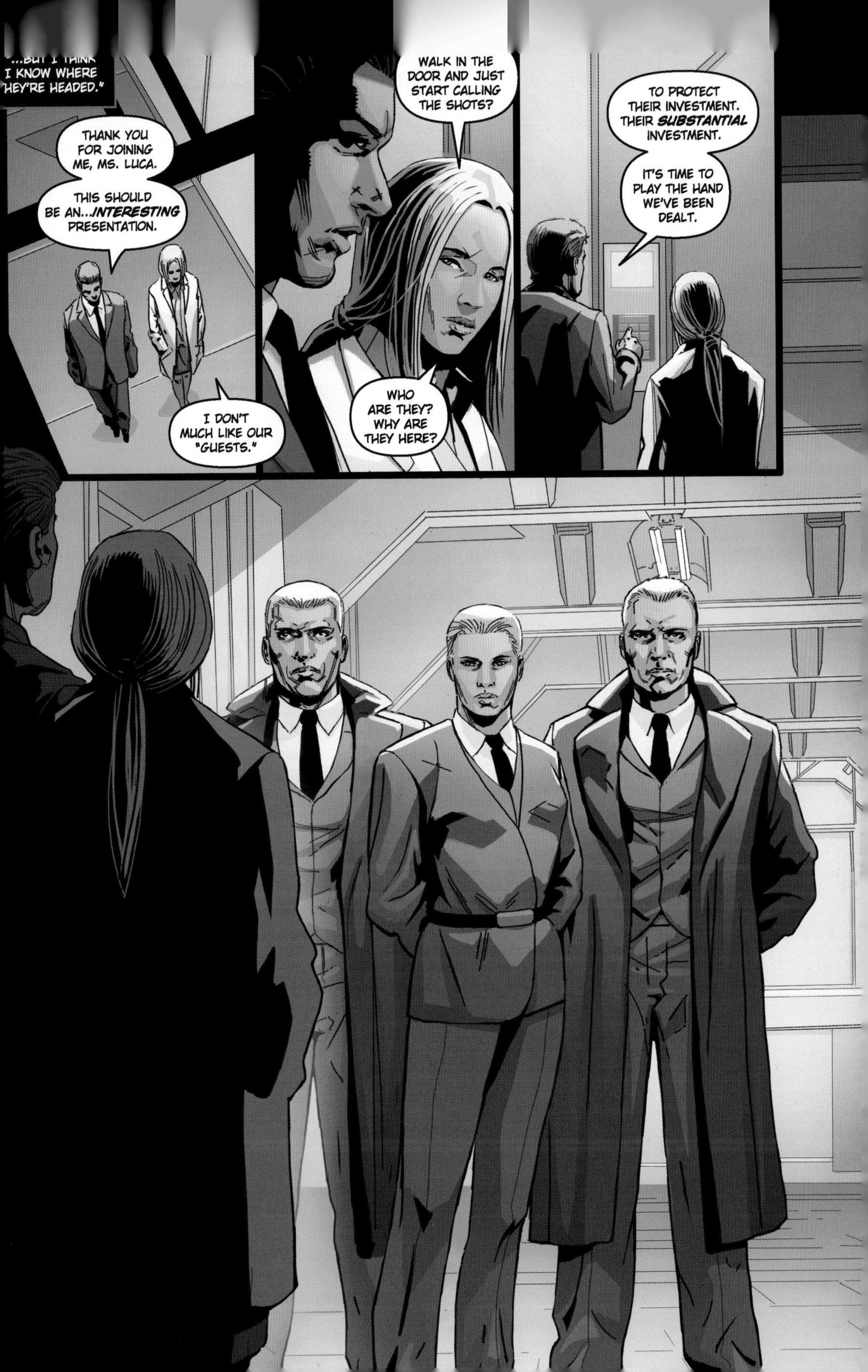

...BUT I THINK I KNOW WHERE HEY'RE HEADED."
THANK YOU FOR JOINING ME, MS. LUCA.
THIS SHOULD BE AN...*INTERESTING* PRESENTATION.
I DON'T MUCH LIKE OUR "GUESTS."
WHO ARE THEY? WHY ARE THEY HERE?
WALK IN THE DOOR AND JUST START CALLING THE SHOTS?
TO PROTECT THEIR INVESTMENT. THEIR *SUBSTANTIAL* INVESTMENT.
IT'S TIME TO PLAY THE HAND WE'VE BEEN DEALT.

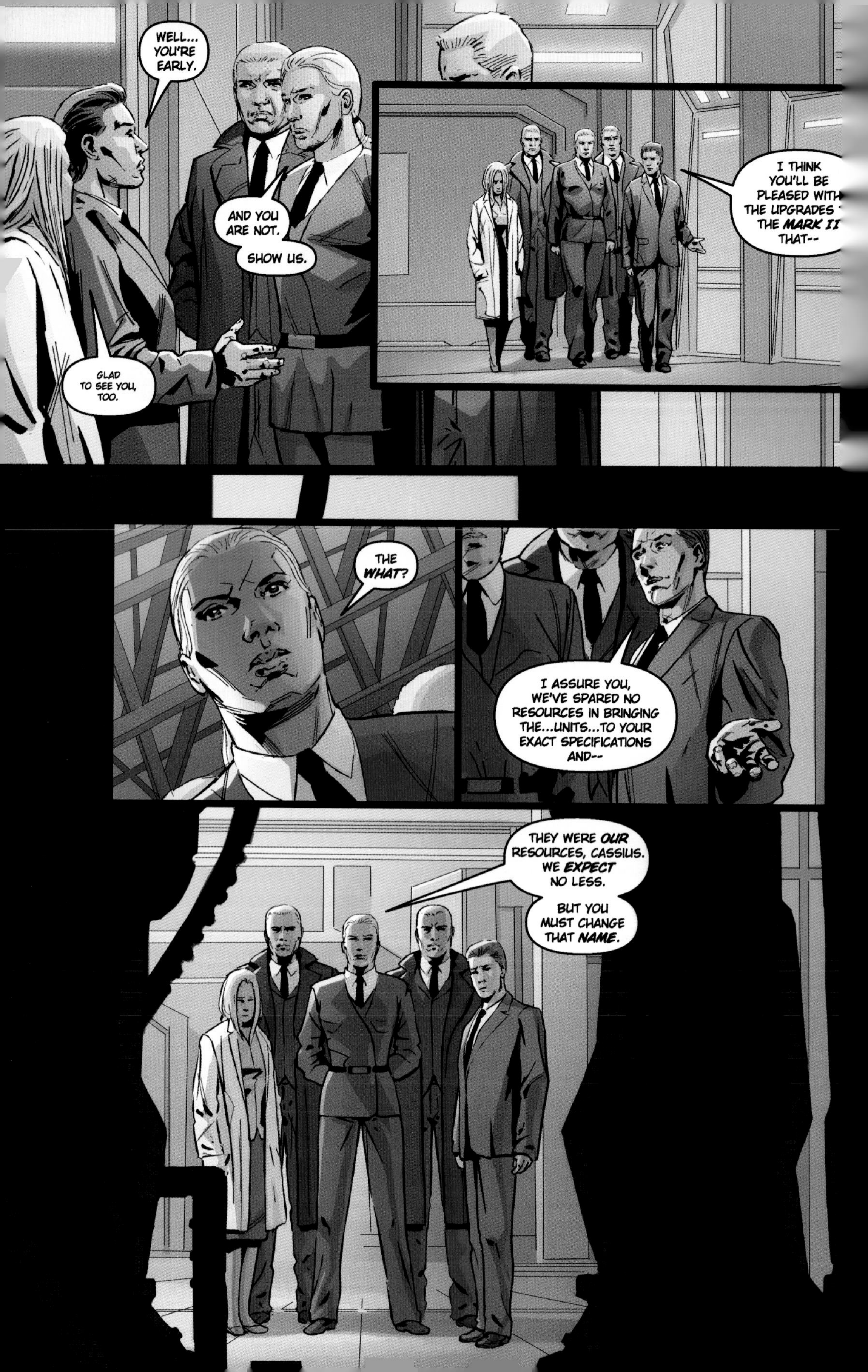
WELL... YOU'RE EARLY.
AND YOU ARE NOT.
SHOW US.
GLAD TO SEE YOU, TOO.
I THINK YOU'LL BE PLEASED WITH THE UPGRADES THE MARK II THAT--
THE WHAT?
I ASSURE YOU, WE'VE SPARED NO RESOURCES IN BRINGING THE...UNITS...TO YOUR EXACT SPECIFICATIONS AND--
THEY WERE OUR RESOURCES, CASSIUS. WE EXPECT NO LESS.
BUT YOU MUST CHANGE THAT NAME.

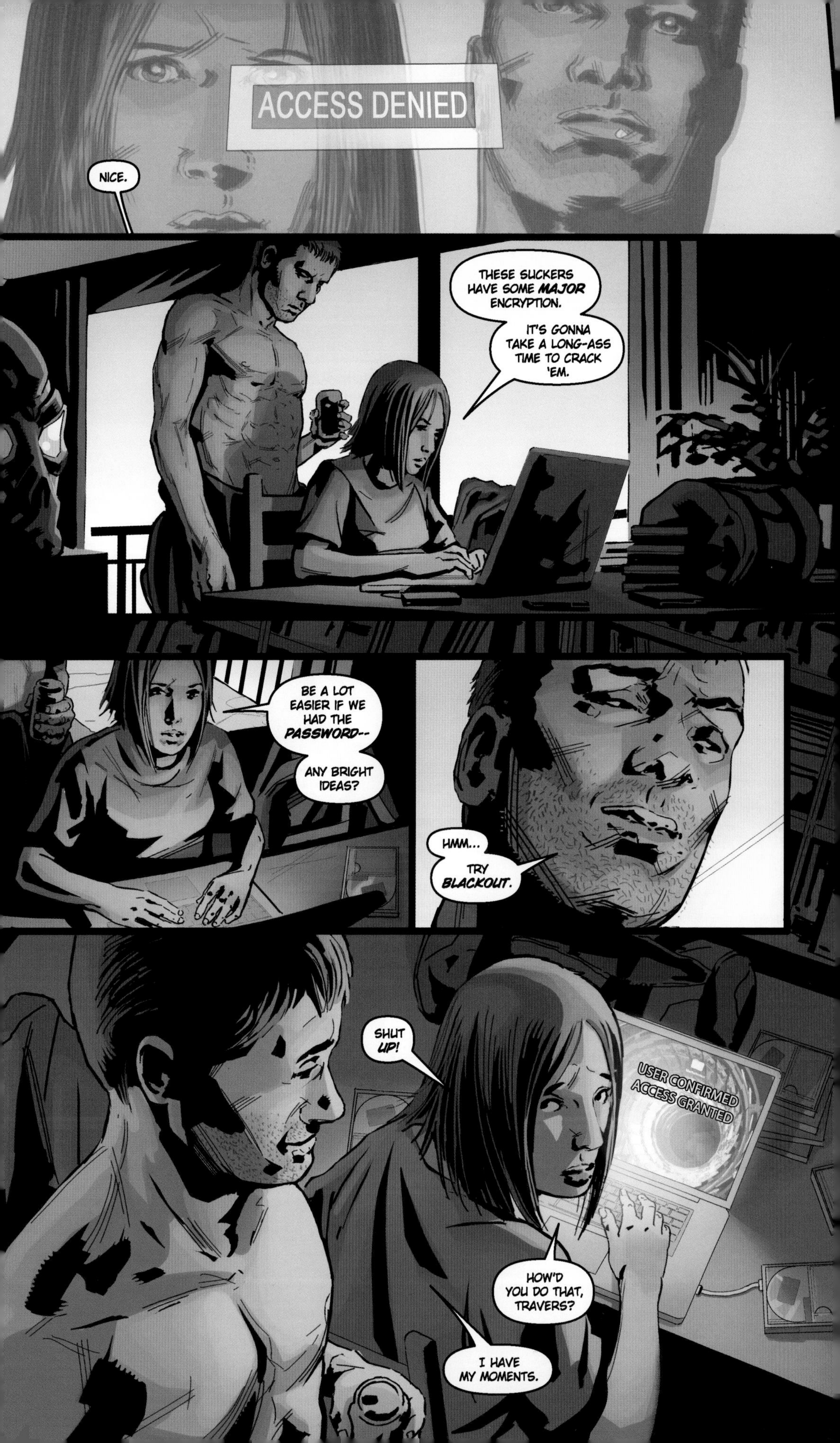
ACCESS DENIED
NICE.
THESE SUCKERS HAVE SOME MAJOR ENCRYPTION.
IT'S GONNA TAKE A LONG-ASS TIME TO CRACK 'EM.
BE A LOT EASIER IF WE HAD THE PASSWORD--
ANY BRIGHT IDEAS?
HMM...
TRY BLACKOUT.
USER CONFIRMED ACCESS GRANTED
SHUT UP!
HOW'D YOU DO THAT, TRAVERS?
I HAVE MY MOMENTS.

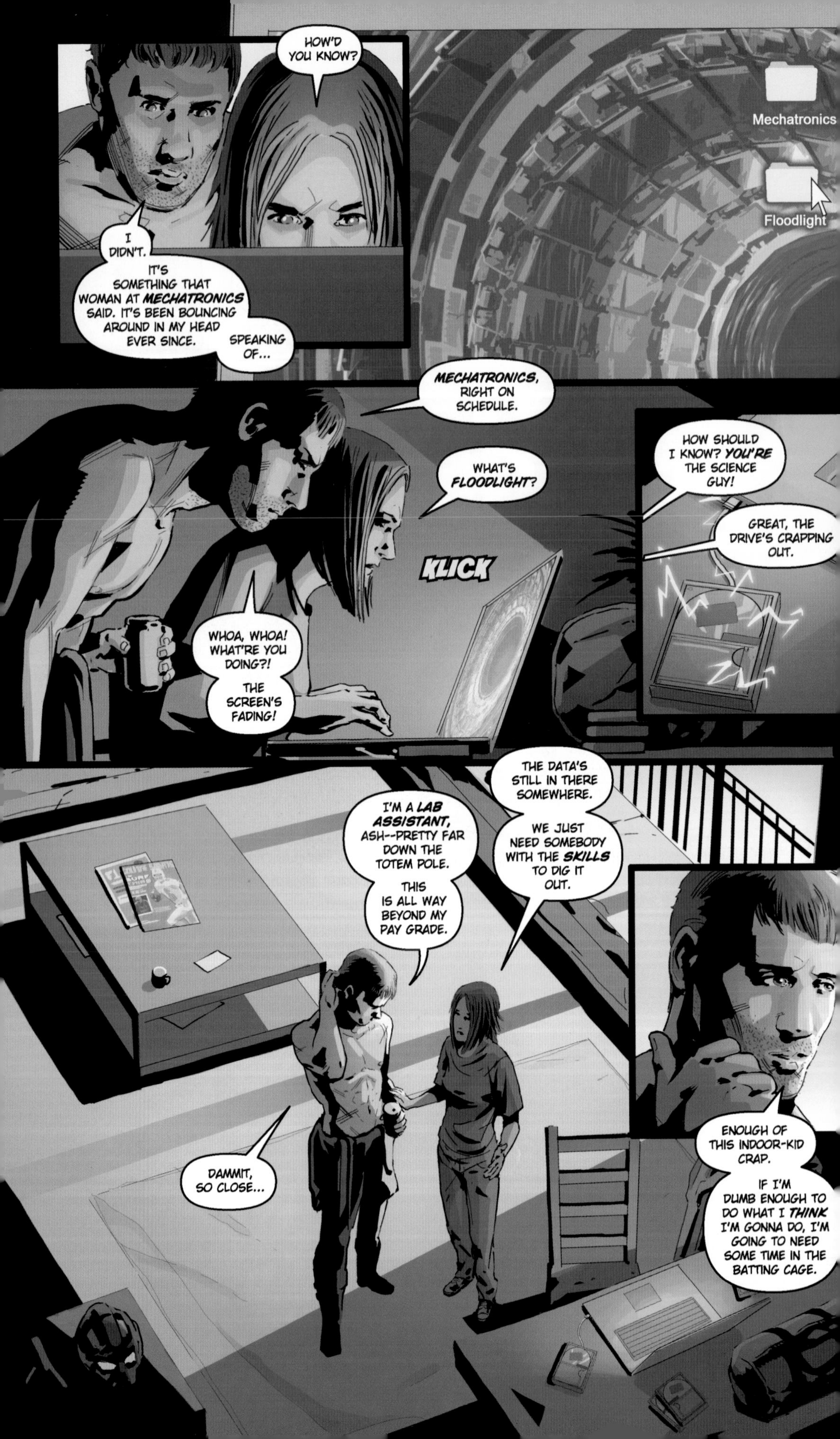
HOW'D YOU KNOW?
I DIDN'T.
IT'S SOMETHING THAT WOMAN AT MECHATRONICS SAID. IT'S BEEN BOUNCING AROUND IN MY HEAD EVER SINCE.
SPEAKING OF...
Mechatronics
Floodlight
MECHATRONICS, RIGHT ON SCHEDULE.
WHAT'S FLOODLIGHT?
KLICK
WHOA, WHOA! WHAT'RE YOU DOING?!
THE SCREEN'S FADING!
HOW SHOULD I KNOW? YOU'RE THE SCIENCE GUY!
GREAT, THE DRIVE'S CRAPPING OUT.
I'M A LAB ASSISTANT, ASH--PRETTY FAR DOWN THE TOTEM POLE.
THIS IS ALL WAY BEYOND MY PAY GRADE.
THE DATA'S STILL IN THERE SOMEWHERE.
WE JUST NEED SOMEBODY WITH THE SKILLS TO DIG IT OUT.
DAMMIT, SO CLOSE...
ENOUGH OF THIS INDOOR-KID CRAP.
IF I'M DUMB ENOUGH TO DO WHAT I THINK I'M GONNA DO, I'M GOING TO NEED SOME TIME IN THE BATTING CAGE.

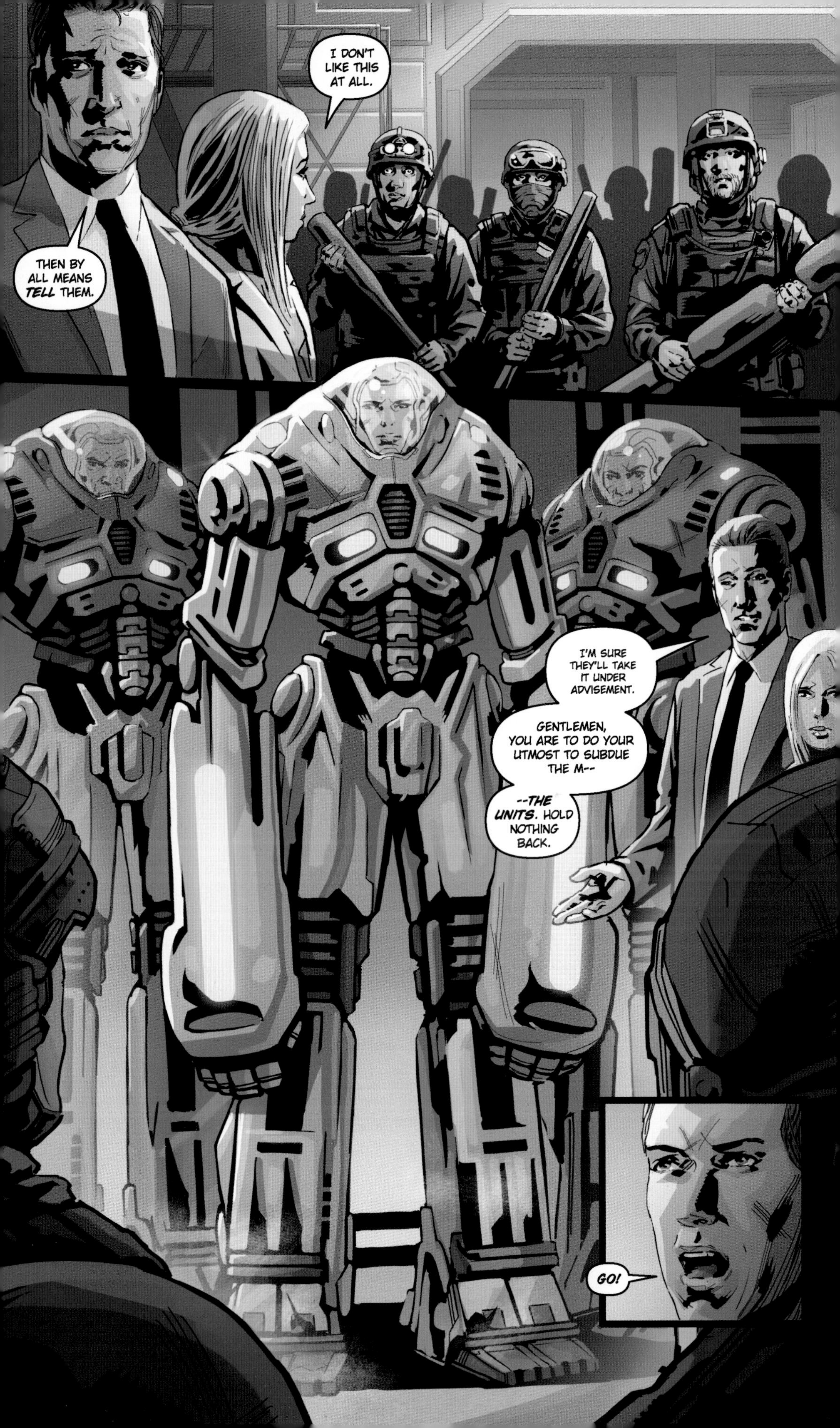
I DON'T LIKE THIS AT ALL.
THEN BY ALL MEANS TELL THEM.
I'M SURE THEY'LL TAKE IT UNDER ADVISEMENT.
GENTLEMEN, YOU ARE TO DO YOUR UTMOST TO SUBDUE THE M--
--THE UNITS. HOLD NOTHING BACK.
GO!

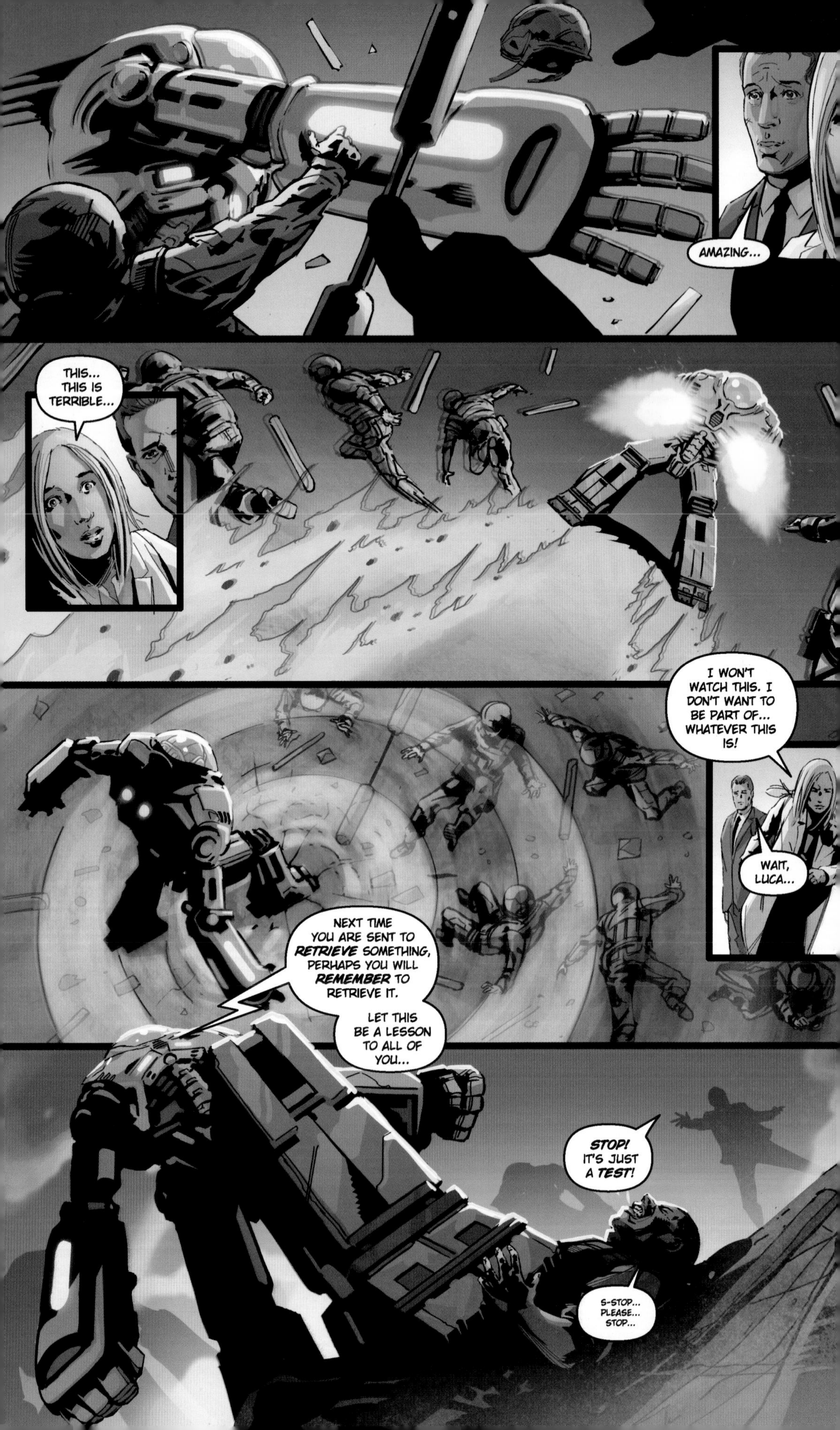
AMAZING...
THIS... THIS IS TERRIBLE...
I WON'T WATCH THIS. I DON'T WANT TO BE PART OF... WHATEVER THIS IS!
WAIT, LUCA...
NEXT TIME YOU ARE SENT TO RETRIEVE SOMETHING, PERHAPS YOU WILL REMEMBER TO RETRIEVE IT.
LET THIS BE A LESSON TO ALL OF YOU...
STOP! IT'S JUST A TEST!
S-STOP... PLEASE... STOP...

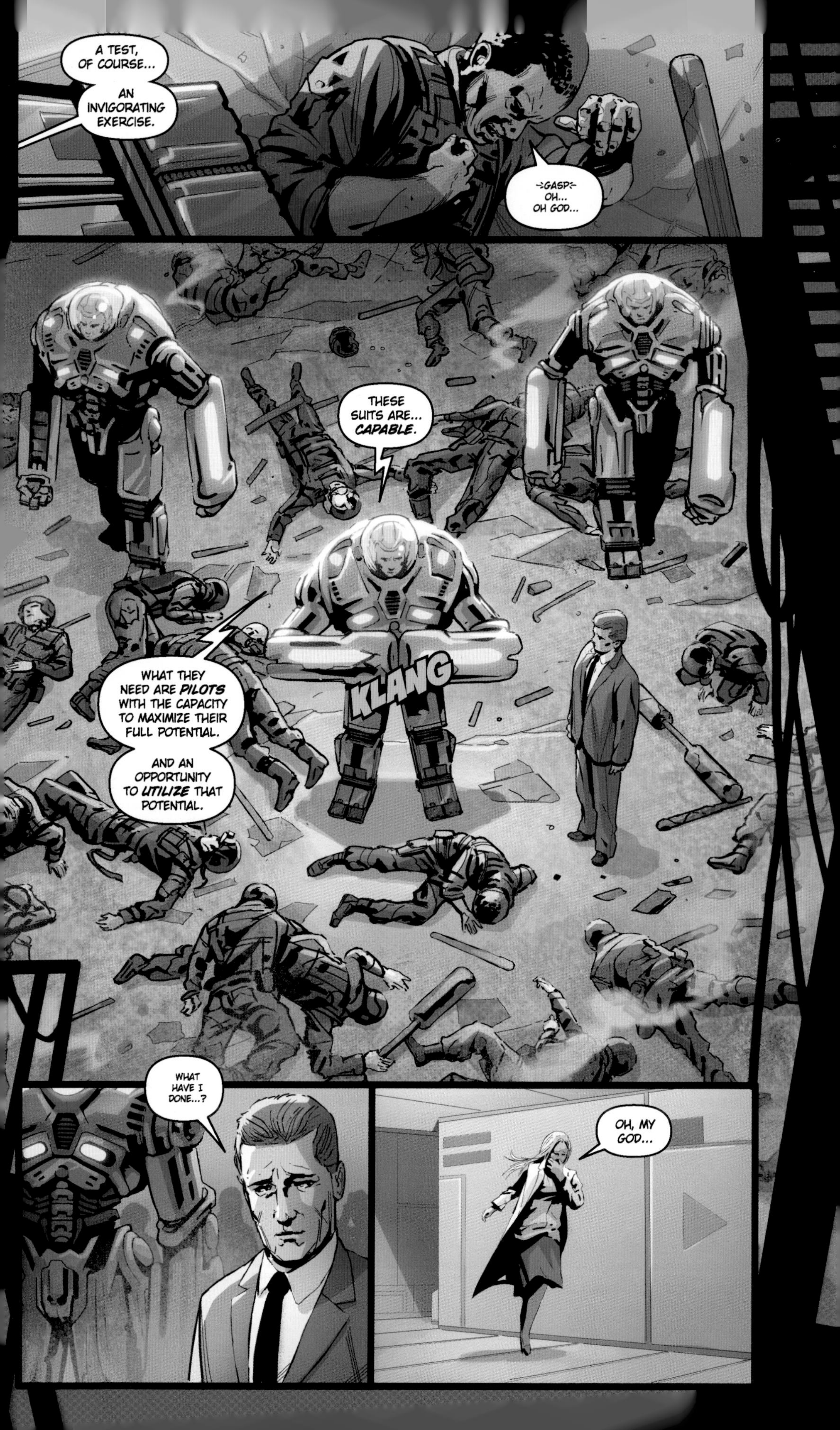
A TEST, OF COURSE...
AN INVIGORATING EXERCISE.
-GASP- OH... OH GOD...
THESE SUITS ARE... CAPABLE.
KLANG
WHAT THEY NEED ARE PILOTS WITH THE CAPACITY TO MAXIMIZE THEIR FULL POTENTIAL.
AND AN OPPORTUNITY TO UTILIZE THAT POTENTIAL.
WHAT HAVE I DONE...?
OH, MY GOD...

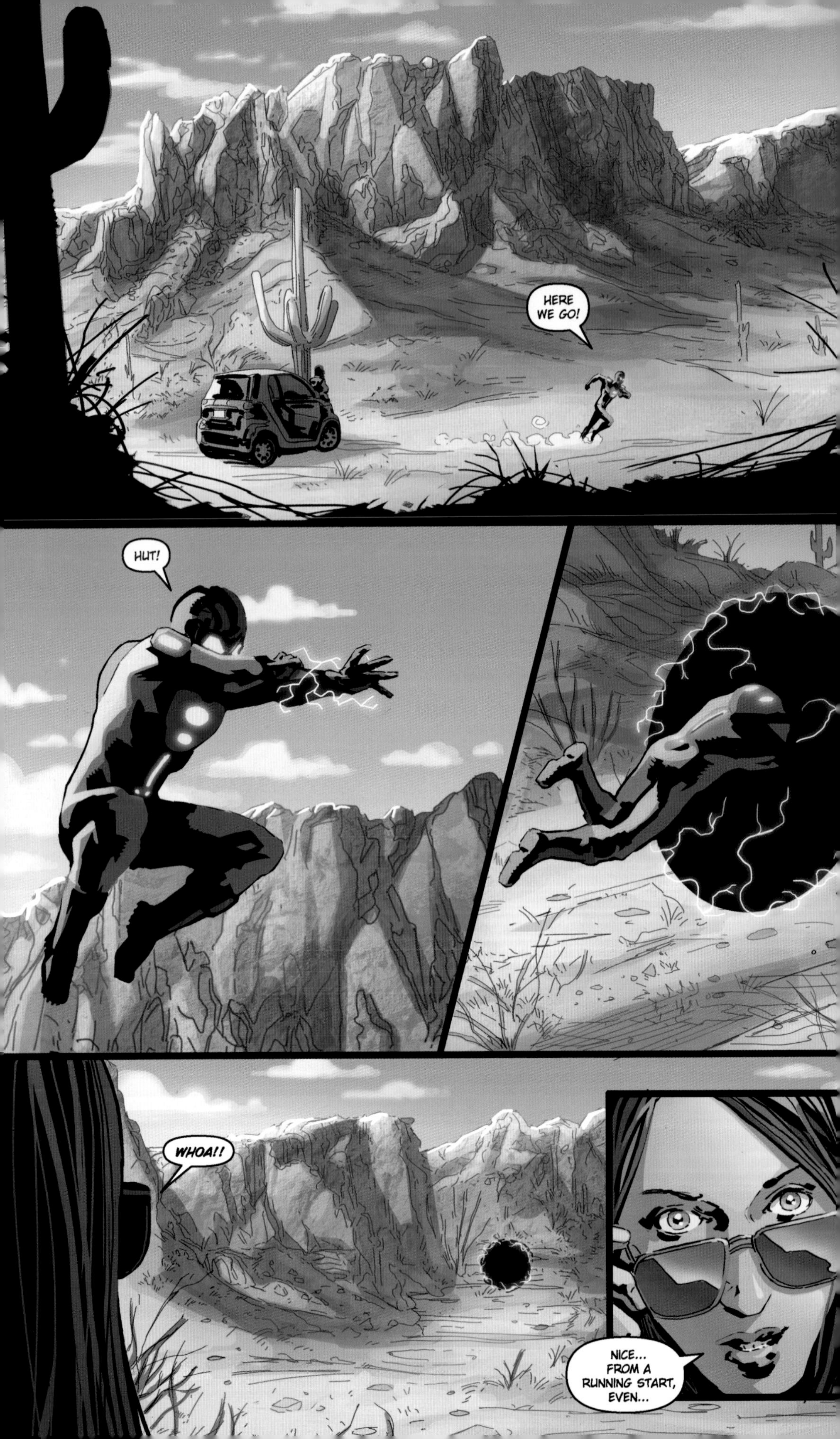
HERE WE GO!
HUT!
WHOA!!
NICE... FROM A RUNNING START, EVEN...

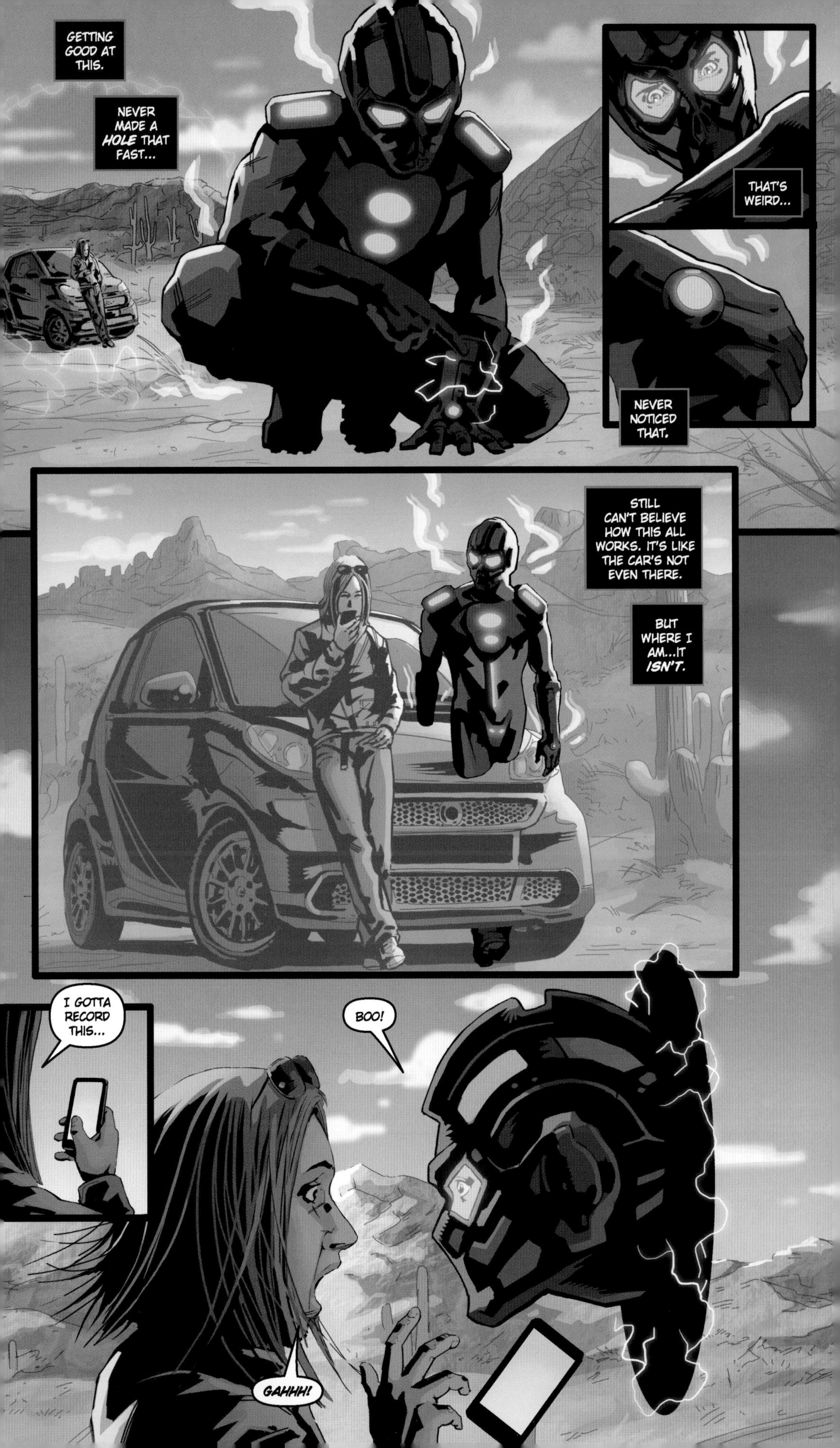
GETTING GOOD AT THIS.
NEVER MADE A *HOLE* THAT FAST...
THAT'S WEIRD...
NEVER NOTICED THAT.
STILL CAN'T BELIEVE HOW THIS ALL WORKS. IT'S LIKE THE CAR'S NOT EVEN THERE.
BUT WHERE I AM...IT *ISN'T*.
I GOTTA RECORD THIS...
BOO!
GAHHH!

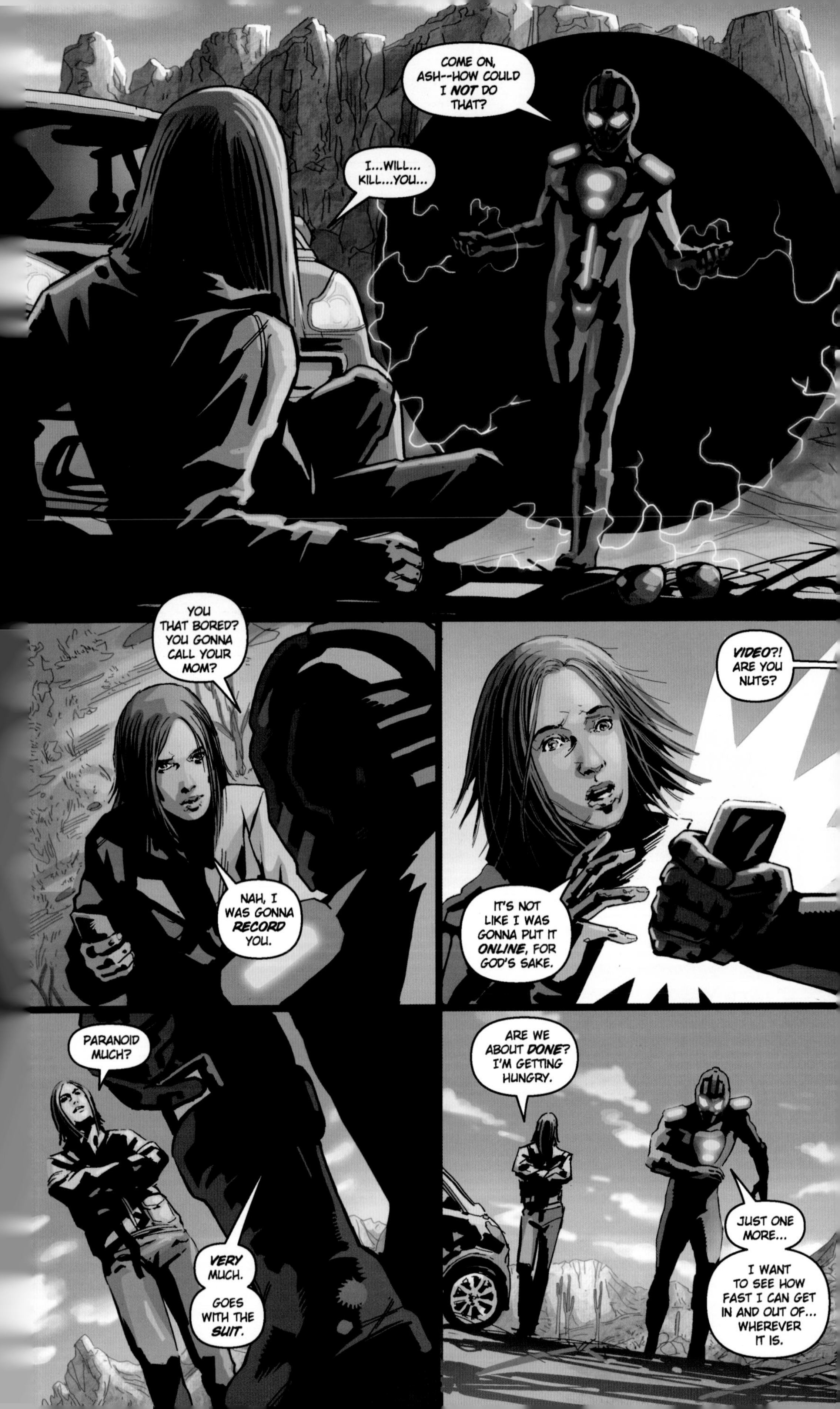
COME ON, ASH--HOW COULD I *NOT* DO THAT?
I...WILL... KILL...YOU...
YOU THAT BORED? YOU GONNA CALL YOUR MOM?
NAH, I WAS GONNA *RECORD* YOU.
VIDEO?! ARE YOU NUTS?
IT'S NOT LIKE I WAS GONNA PUT IT *ONLINE*, FOR GOD'S SAKE.
PARANOID MUCH?
VERY MUCH.
GOES WITH THE *SUIT*.
ARE WE ABOUT *DONE*? I'M GETTING HUNGRY.
JUST ONE MORE...
I WANT TO SEE HOW FAST I CAN GET IN AND OUT OF... WHEREVER IT IS.

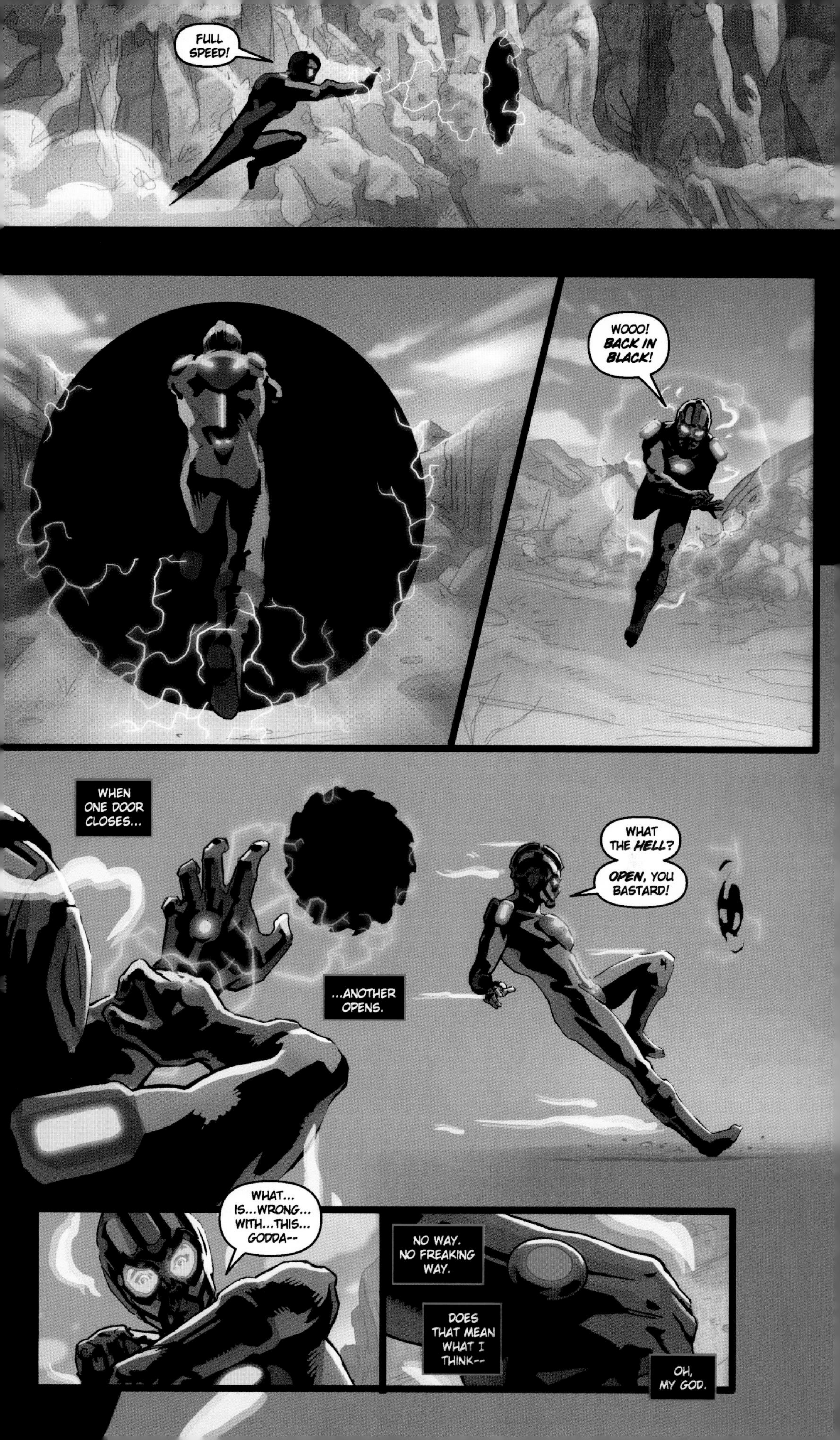
FULL SPEED!
WOOO! BACK IN BLACK!
WHEN ONE DOOR CLOSES...
...ANOTHER OPENS.
WHAT THE HELL?
OPEN, YOU BASTARD!
WHAT... IS...WRONG... WITH...THIS... GODDA--
NO WAY. NO FREAKING WAY.
DOES THAT MEAN WHAT I THINK--
OH, MY GOD.

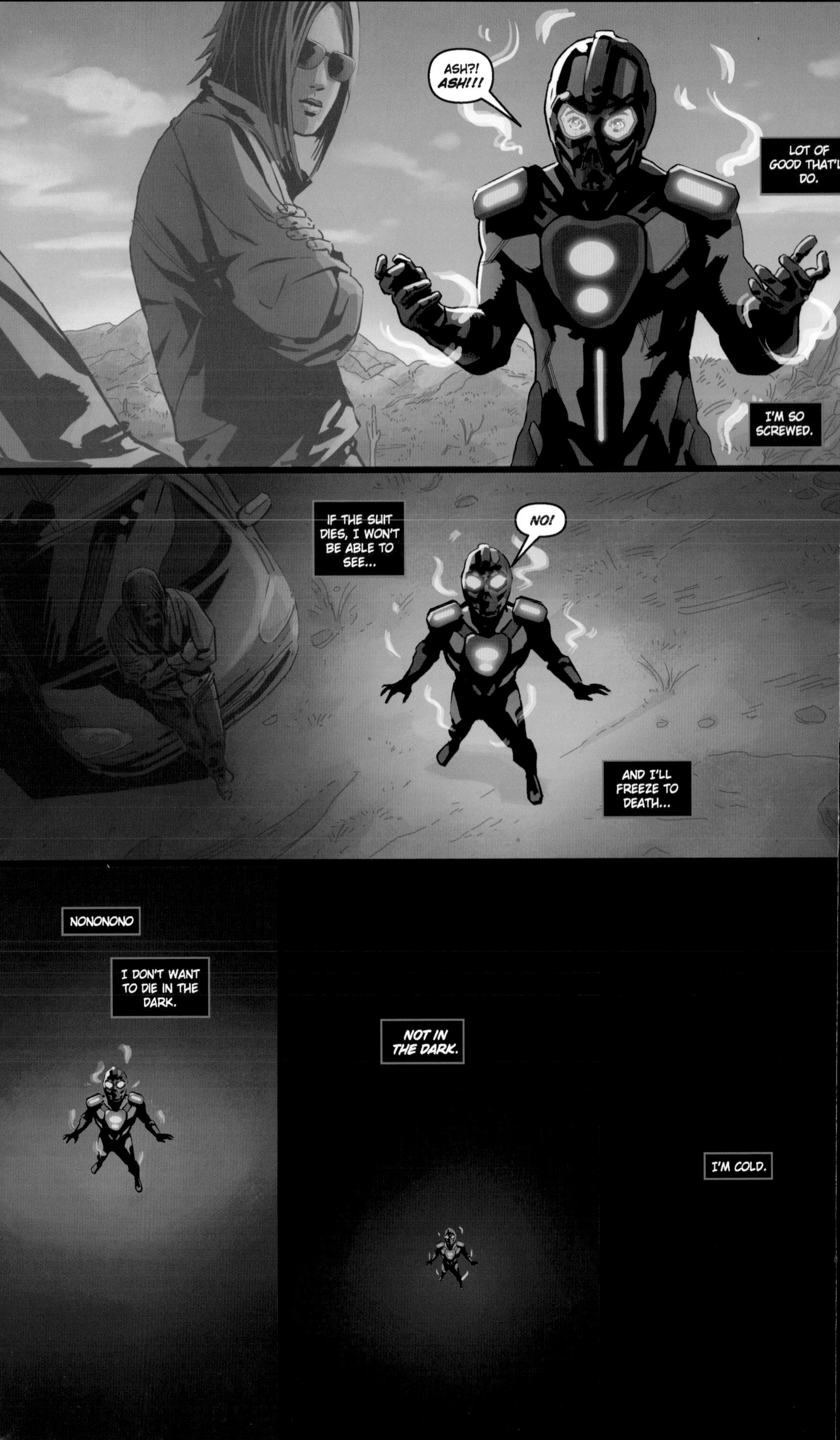
ASH?!
ASH!!!
LOT OF GOOD THAT'LL DO.
I'M SO SCREWED.
IF THE SUIT DIES, I WON'T BE ABLE TO SEE...
NO!
AND I'LL FREEZE TO DEATH...
NONONONO
I DON'T WANT TO DIE IN THE DARK.
NOT IN THE DARK.
I'M COLD.

CHAPTER 3

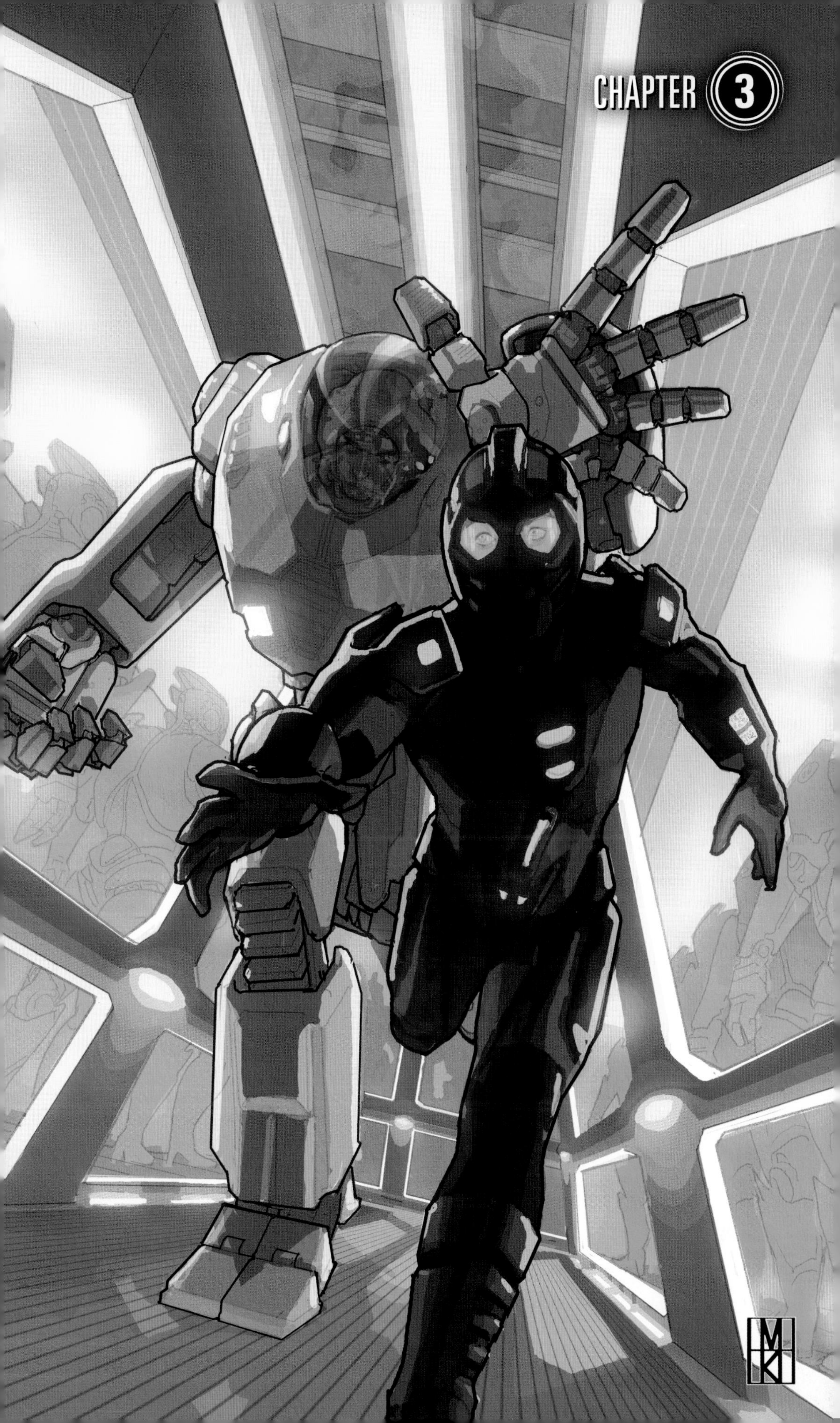

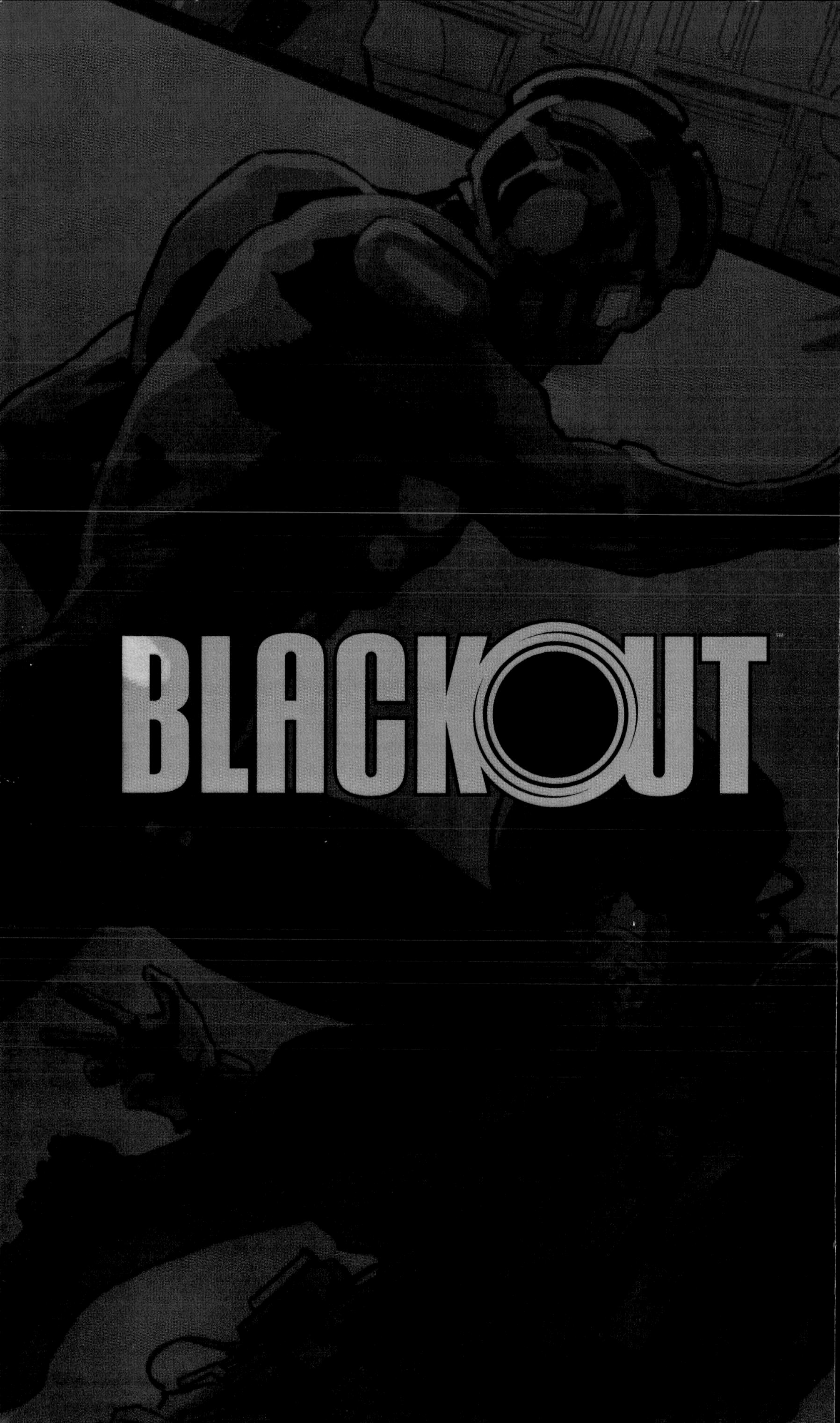
BLACKOUT™

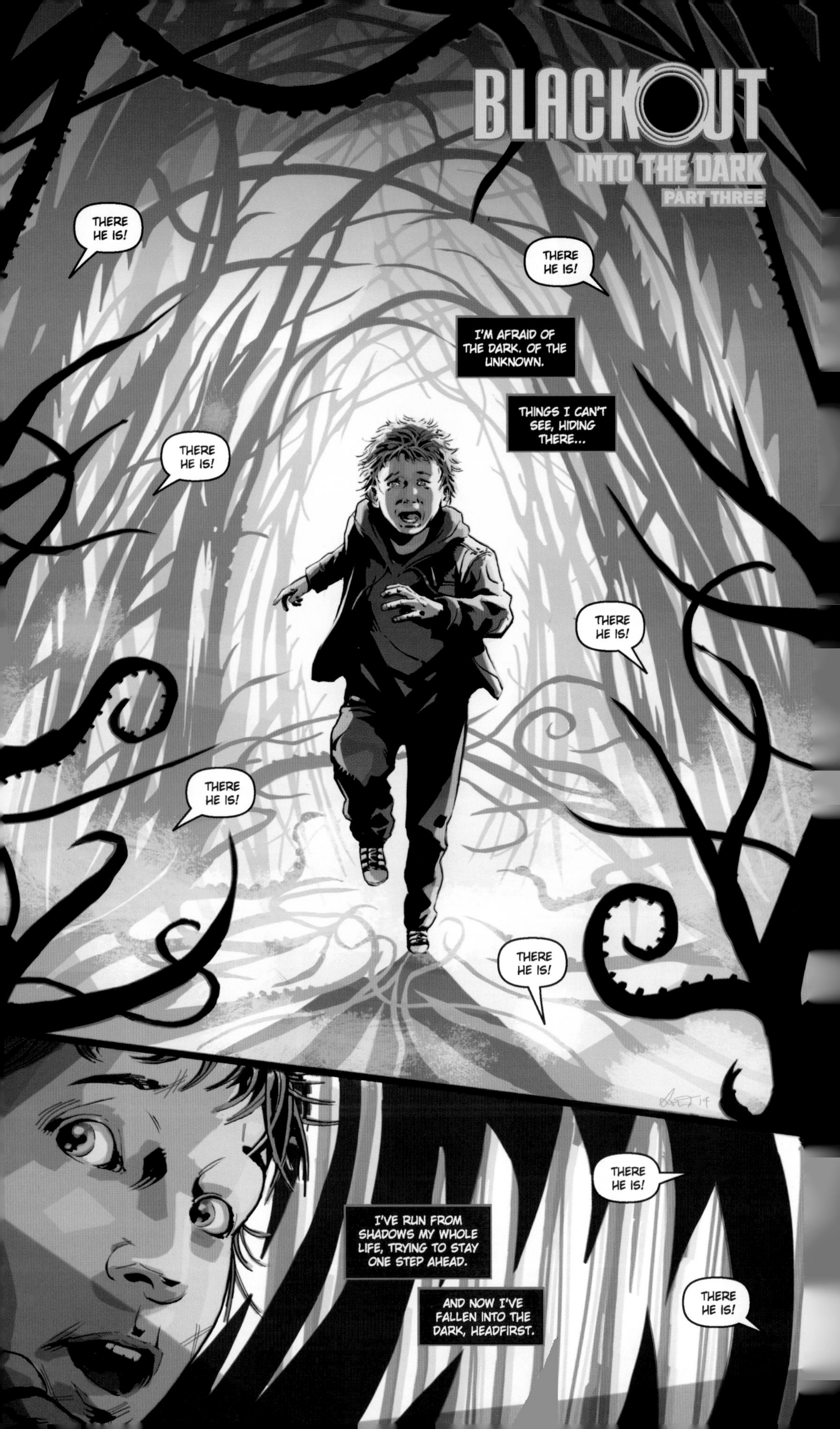

BLACKOUT
INTO THE DARK
PART THREE
THERE HE IS!
THERE HE IS!
I'M AFRAID OF THE DARK. OF THE UNKNOWN.
THINGS I CAN'T SEE, HIDING THERE...
THERE HE IS!
THERE HE IS!
THERE HE IS!
THERE HE IS!
THERE HE IS!
I'VE RUN FROM SHADOWS MY WHOLE LIFE, TRYING TO STAY ONE STEP AHEAD.
AND NOW I'VE FALLEN INTO THE DARK, HEADFIRST.
THERE HE IS!

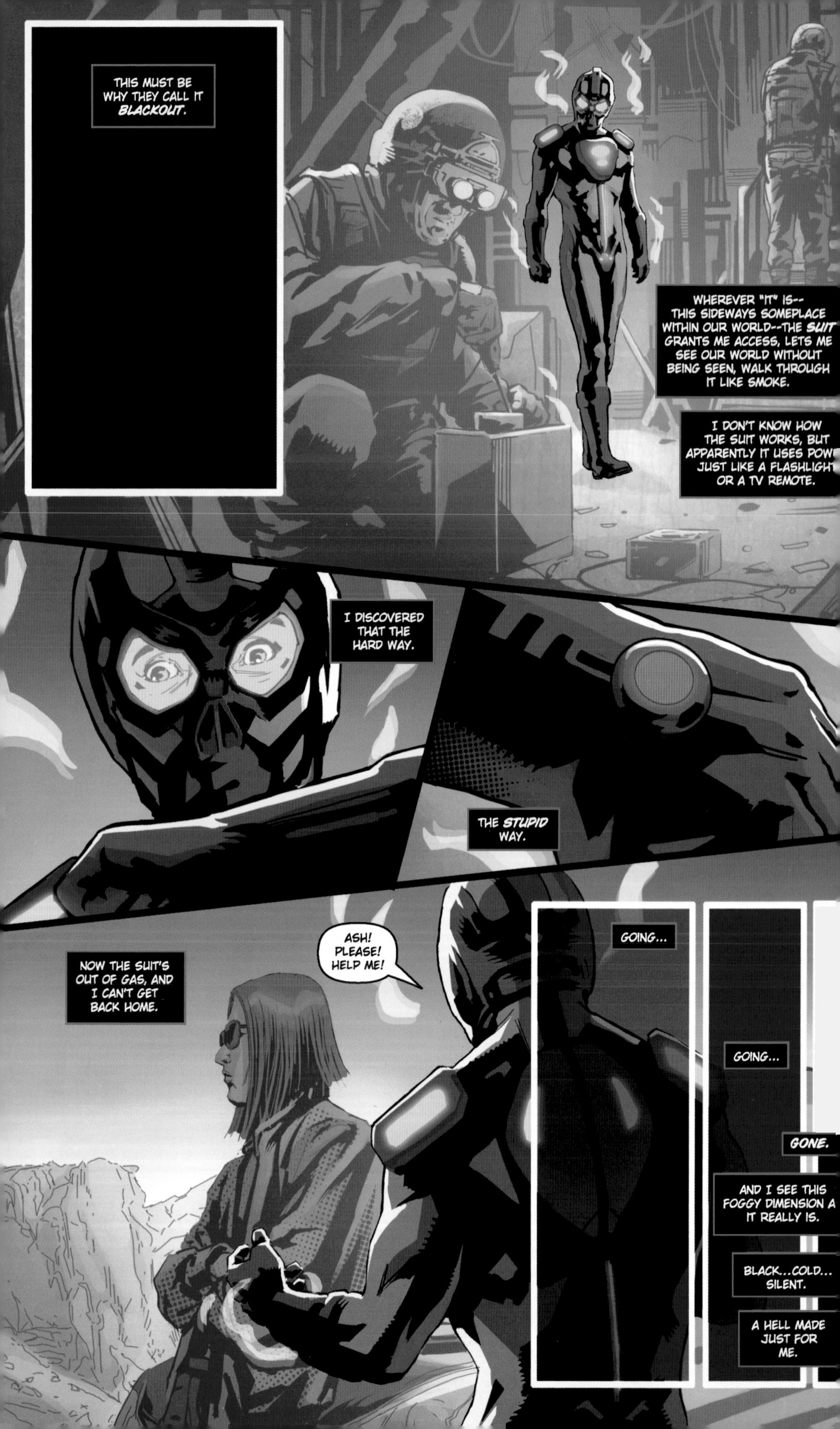
THIS MUST BE WHY THEY CALL IT *BLACKOUT*.
WHEREVER "IT" IS-- THIS SIDEWAYS SOMEPLACE WITHIN OUR WORLD--THE *SUIT* GRANTS ME ACCESS, LETS ME SEE OUR WORLD WITHOUT BEING SEEN, WALK THROUGH IT LIKE SMOKE.
I DON'T KNOW HOW THE SUIT WORKS, BUT APPARENTLY IT USES POW JUST LIKE A FLASHLIGH OR A TV REMOTE.
I DISCOVERED THAT THE HARD WAY.
THE *STUPID* WAY.
NOW THE SUIT'S OUT OF GAS, AND I CAN'T GET BACK HOME.
ASH! PLEASE! HELP ME!
GOING...
GOING...
GONE.
AND I SEE THIS FOGGY DIMENSION A IT REALLY IS.
BLACK...COLD... SILENT.
A HELL MADE JUST FOR ME.

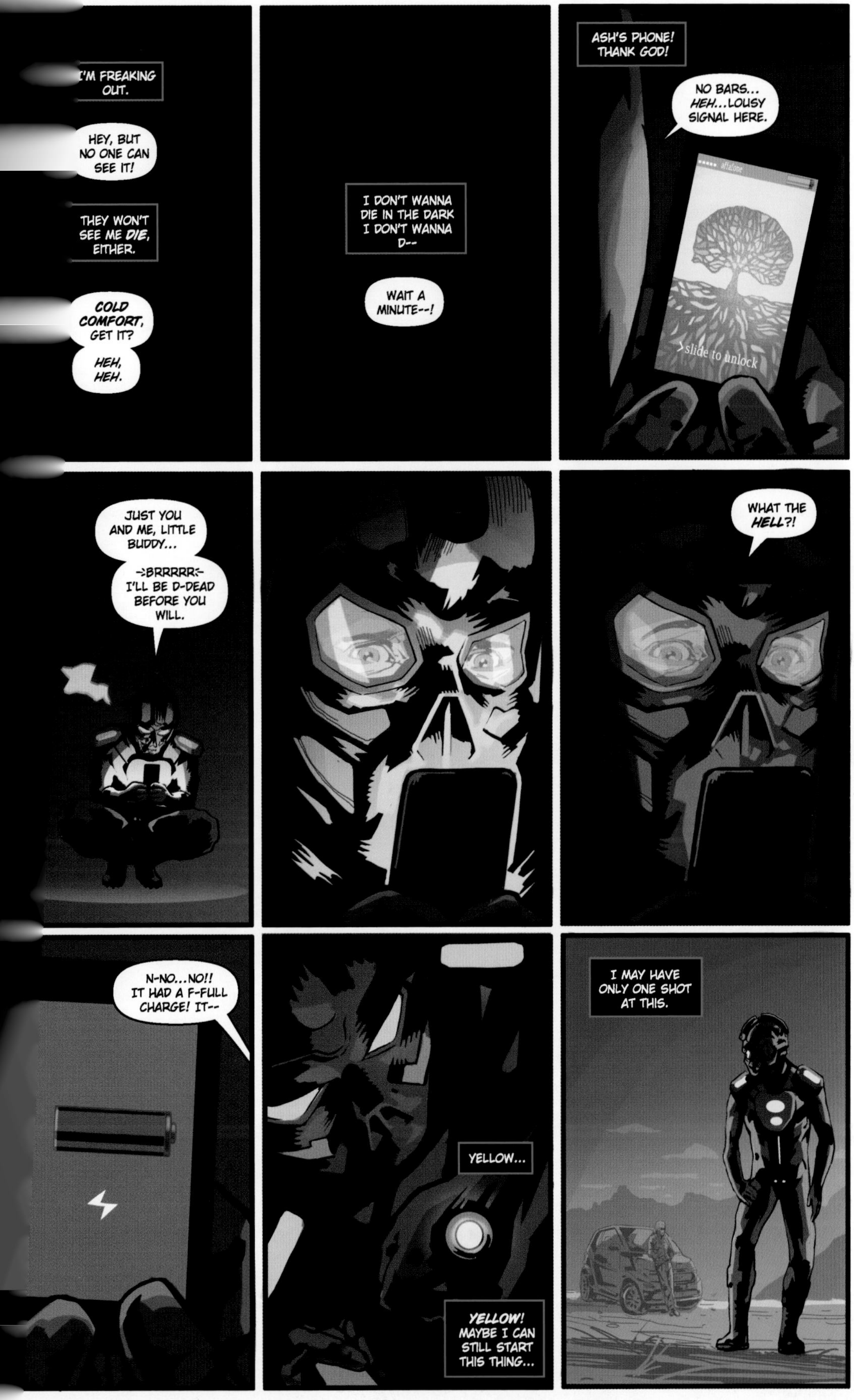
I'M FREAKING OUT.
HEY, BUT NO ONE CAN SEE IT!
THEY WON'T SEE ME *DIE*, EITHER.
COLD COMFORT, GET IT?
HEH, HEH.
I DON'T WANNA DIE IN THE DARK I DON'T WANNA D--
WAIT A MINUTE--!
ASH'S PHONE! THANK GOD!
NO BARS... *HEH*...LOUSY SIGNAL HERE.
aftafone
slide to unlock
JUST YOU AND ME, LITTLE BUDDY...
-BRRRRR- I'LL BE D-DEAD BEFORE YOU WILL.
WHAT THE *HELL*?!
N-NO...NO!! IT HAD A F-FULL CHARGE! IT--
YELLOW...
YELLOW! MAYBE I CAN STILL START THIS THING...
I MAY HAVE ONLY ONE SHOT AT THIS.

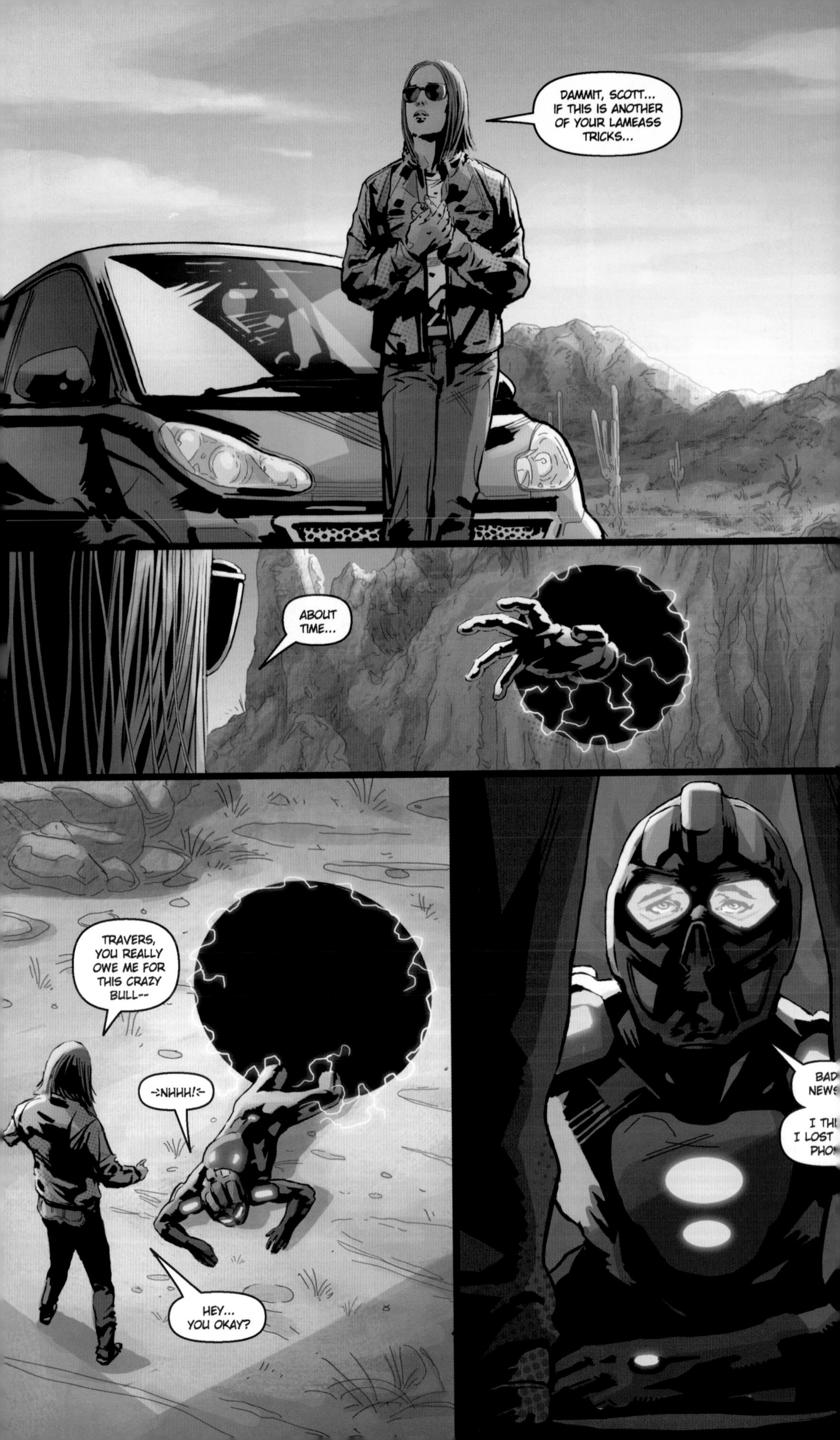
DAMMIT, SCOTT... IF THIS IS ANOTHER OF YOUR LAMEASS TRICKS...
ABOUT TIME...
TRAVERS, YOU REALLY OWE ME FOR THIS CRAZY BULL--
-:NHHH!:-
HEY... YOU OKAY?
I LOST

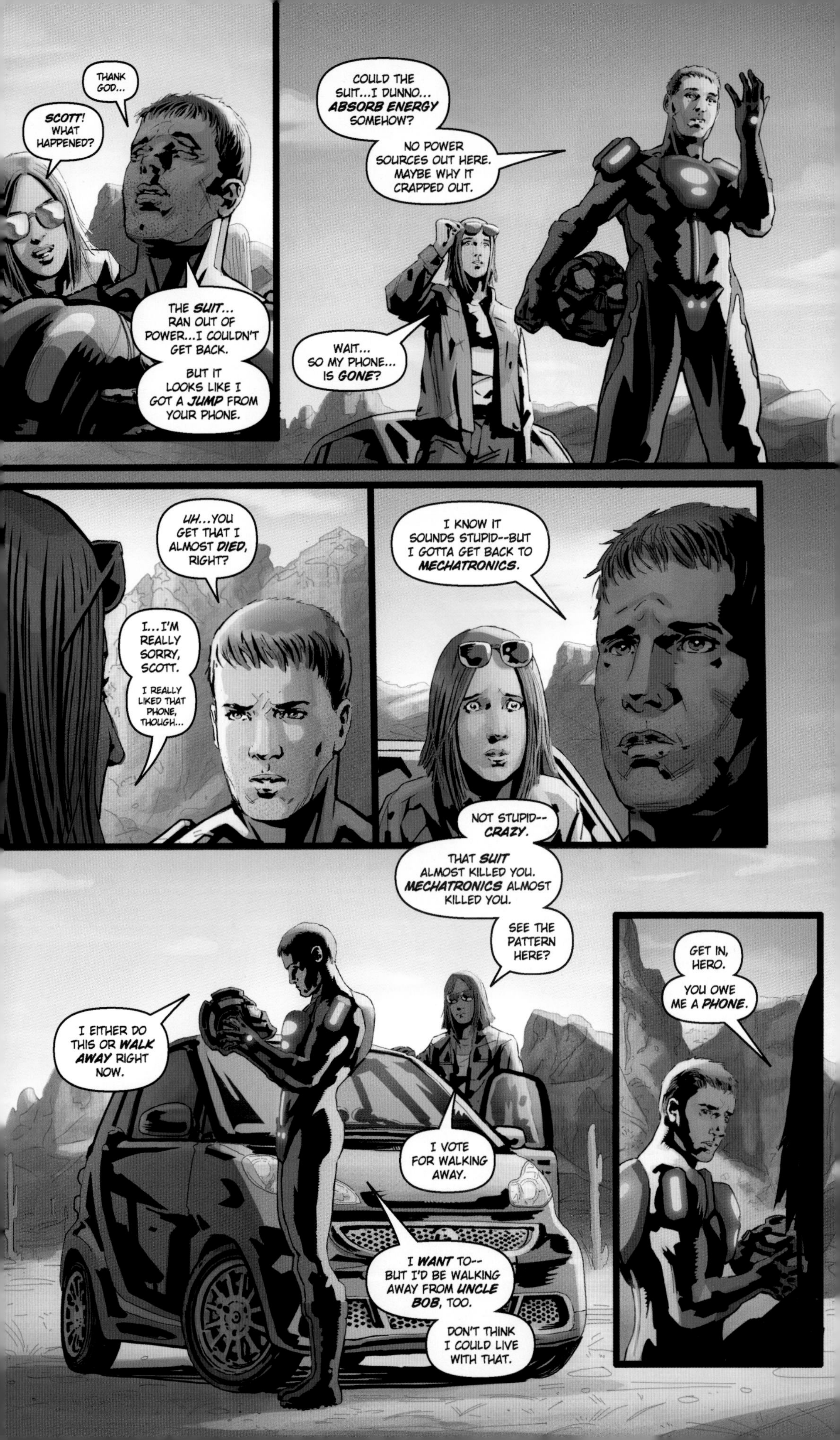
SCOTT! WHAT HAPPENED?
THANK GOD...
THE SUIT... RAN OUT OF POWER...I COULDN'T GET BACK.
BUT IT LOOKS LIKE I GOT A JUMP FROM YOUR PHONE.
COULD THE SUIT...I DUNNO... ABSORB ENERGY SOMEHOW?
NO POWER SOURCES OUT HERE. MAYBE WHY IT CRAPPED OUT.
WAIT... SO MY PHONE... IS GONE?
UH...YOU GET THAT I ALMOST DIED, RIGHT?
I...I'M REALLY SORRY, SCOTT.
I REALLY LIKED THAT PHONE, THOUGH...
I KNOW IT SOUNDS STUPID--BUT I GOTTA GET BACK TO MECHATRONICS.
NOT STUPID-- CRAZY.
THAT SUIT ALMOST KILLED YOU. MECHATRONICS ALMOST KILLED YOU.
SEE THE PATTERN HERE?
I EITHER DO THIS OR WALK AWAY RIGHT NOW.
I VOTE FOR WALKING AWAY.
I WANT TO-- BUT I'D BE WALKING AWAY FROM UNCLE BOB, TOO.
DON'T THINK I COULD LIVE WITH THAT.
GET IN, HERO.
YOU OWE ME A PHONE.

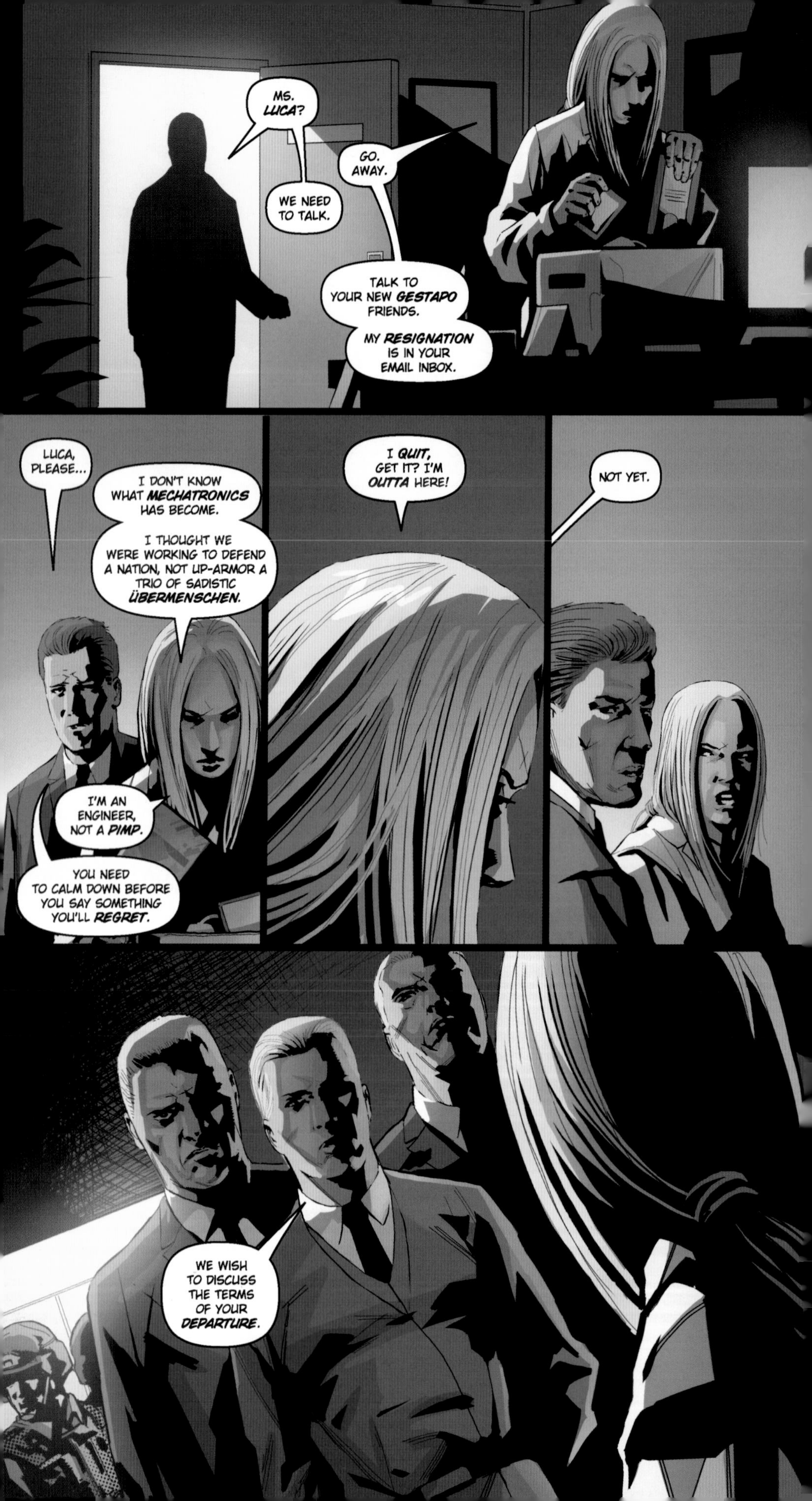
MS. LUCA?
WE NEED TO TALK.
GO. AWAY.
TALK TO YOUR NEW GESTAPO FRIENDS.
MY RESIGNATION IS IN YOUR EMAIL INBOX.
LUCA, PLEASE...
I DON'T KNOW WHAT MECHATRONICS HAS BECOME.
I THOUGHT WE WERE WORKING TO DEFEND A NATION, NOT UP-ARMOR A TRIO OF SADISTIC ÜBERMENSCHEN.
I'M AN ENGINEER, NOT A PIMP.
YOU NEED TO CALM DOWN BEFORE YOU SAY SOMETHING YOU'LL REGRET.
I QUIT, GET IT? I'M OUTTA HERE!
NOT YET.
WE WISH TO DISCUSS THE TERMS OF YOUR DEPARTURE.

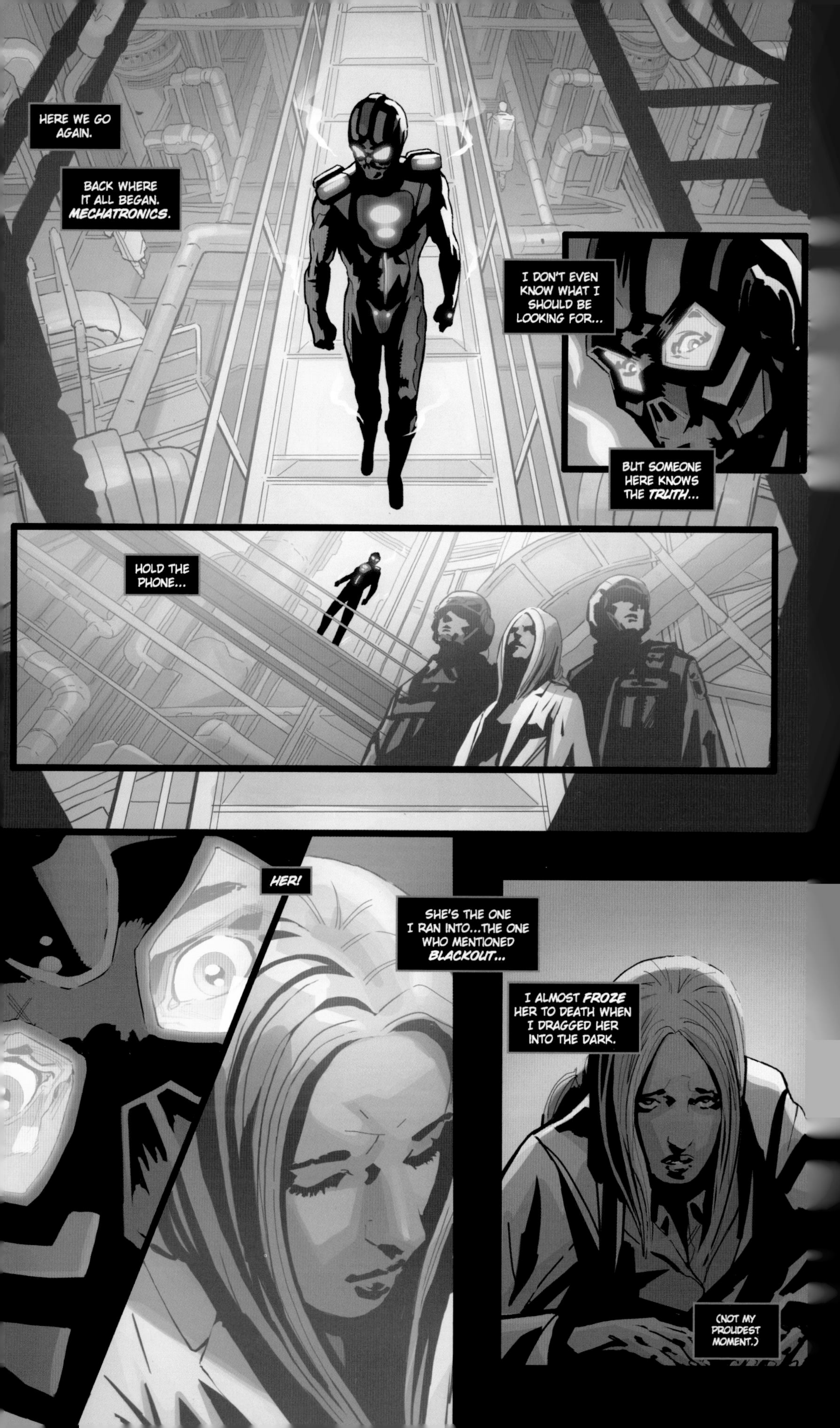
HERE WE GO AGAIN.
BACK WHERE IT ALL BEGAN. *MECHATRONICS*.
I DON'T EVEN KNOW WHAT I SHOULD BE LOOKING FOR...
BUT SOMEONE HERE KNOWS THE *TRUTH*...
HOLD THE PHONE...
HER!
SHE'S THE ONE I RAN INTO...THE ONE WHO MENTIONED *BLACKOUT*...
I ALMOST *FROZE* HER TO DEATH WHEN I DRAGGED HER INTO THE DARK.
(NOT MY PROUDEST MOMENT.)

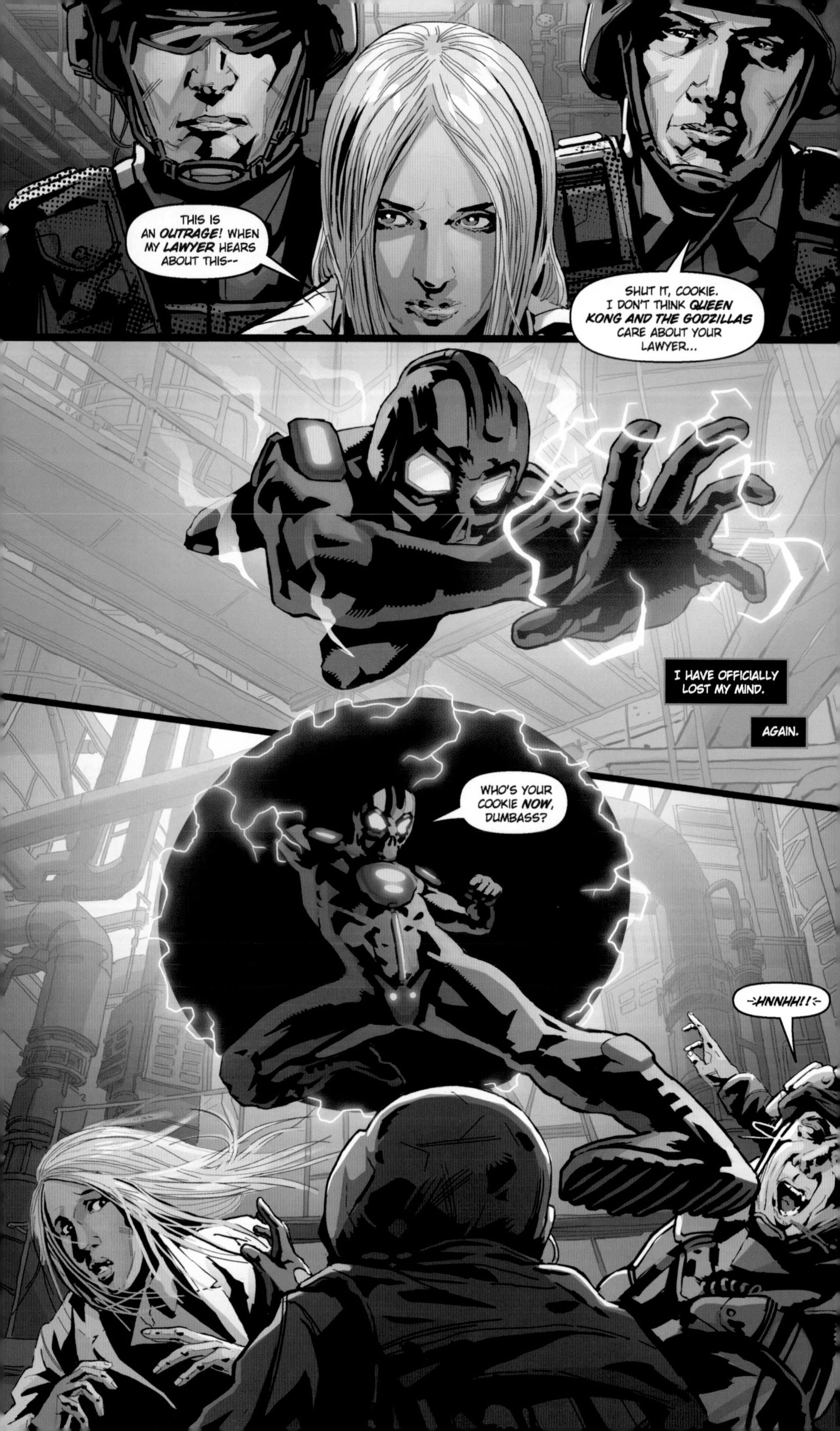
THIS IS AN OUTRAGE! WHEN MY LAWYER HEARS ABOUT THIS--
SHUT IT, COOKIE. I DON'T THINK QUEEN KONG AND THE GODZILLAS CARE ABOUT YOUR LAWYER...
I HAVE OFFICIALLY LOST MY MIND.
AGAIN.
WHO'S YOUR COOKIE NOW, DUMBASS?
-HNNHH!!-

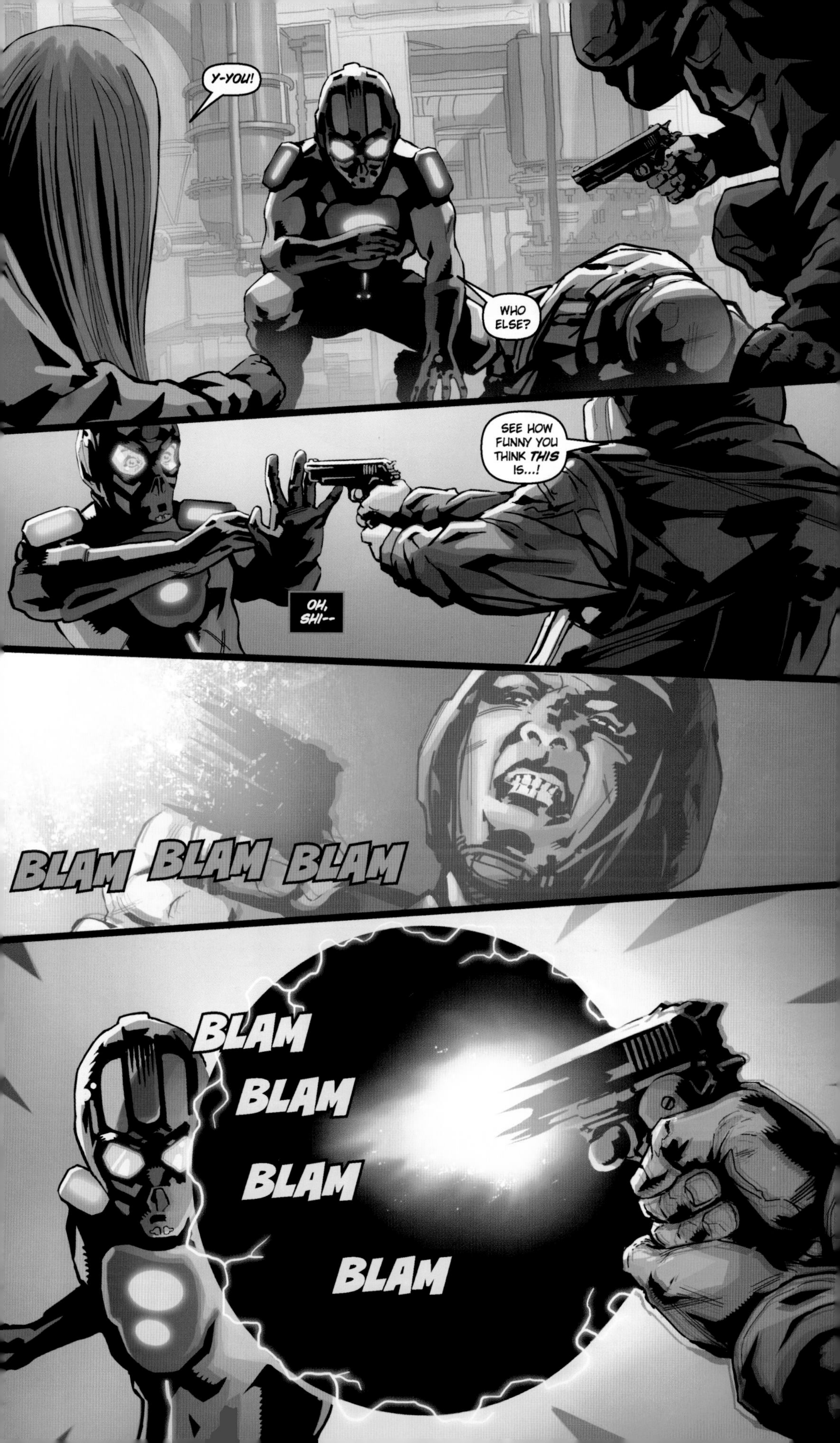
Y-YOU!
WHO ELSE?
SEE HOW FUNNY YOU THINK *THIS* IS...!
OH, SHI--
BLAM BLAM BLAM
BLAM
BLAM
BLAM
BLAM

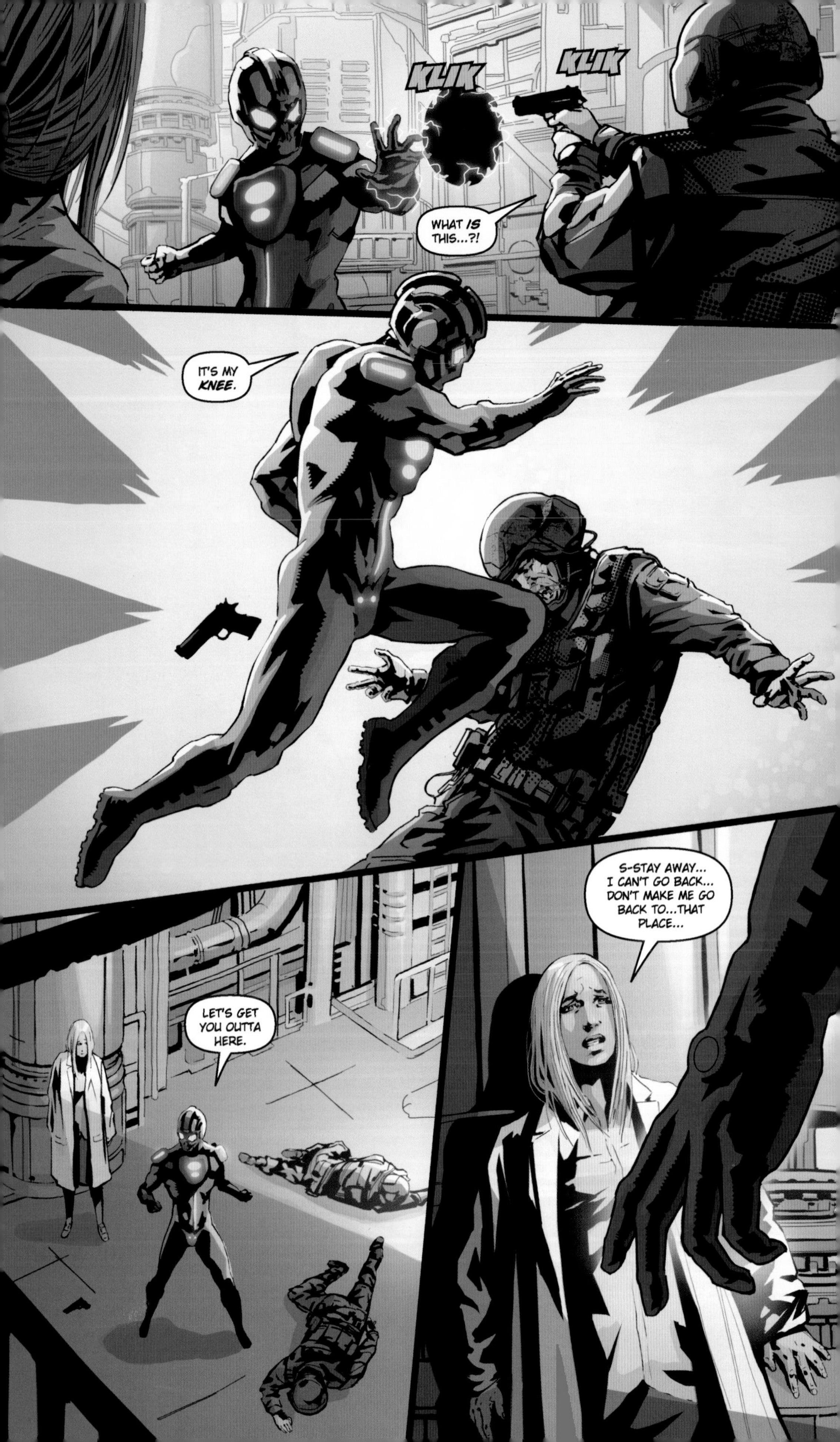
KLIK
KLIK
WHAT IS THIS...?!
IT'S MY KNEE.
S-STAY AWAY... I CAN'T GO BACK... DON'T MAKE ME GO BACK TO...THAT PLACE...
LET'S GET YOU OUTTA HERE.

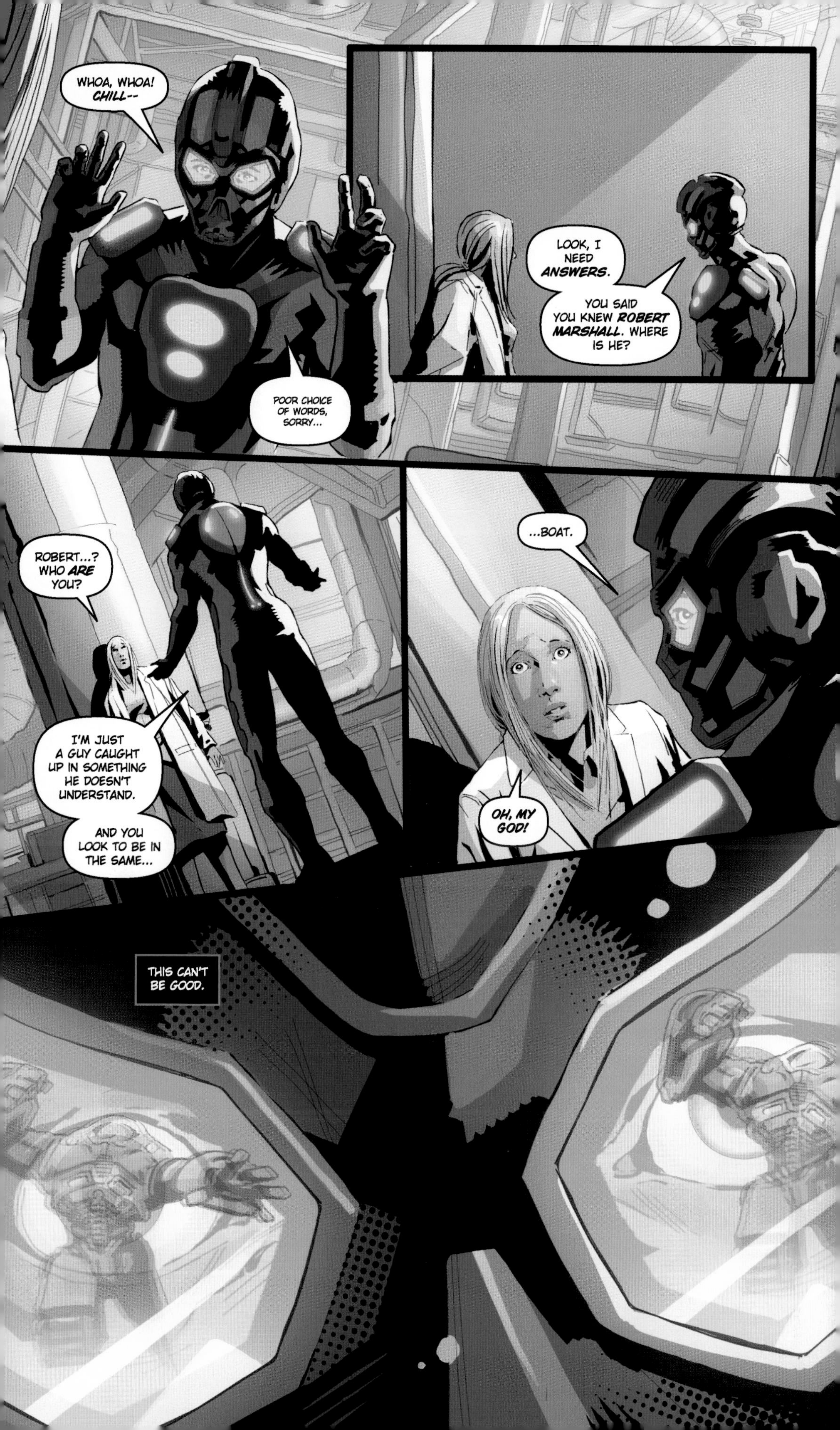
WHOA, WHOA! CHILL--
LOOK, I NEED ANSWERS.
YOU SAID YOU KNEW ROBERT MARSHALL. WHERE IS HE?
POOR CHOICE OF WORDS, SORRY...
ROBERT...? WHO ARE YOU?
I'M JUST A GUY CAUGHT UP IN SOMETHING HE DOESN'T UNDERSTAND.
AND YOU LOOK TO BE IN THE SAME...
...BOAT.
OH, MY GOD!
THIS CAN'T BE GOOD.

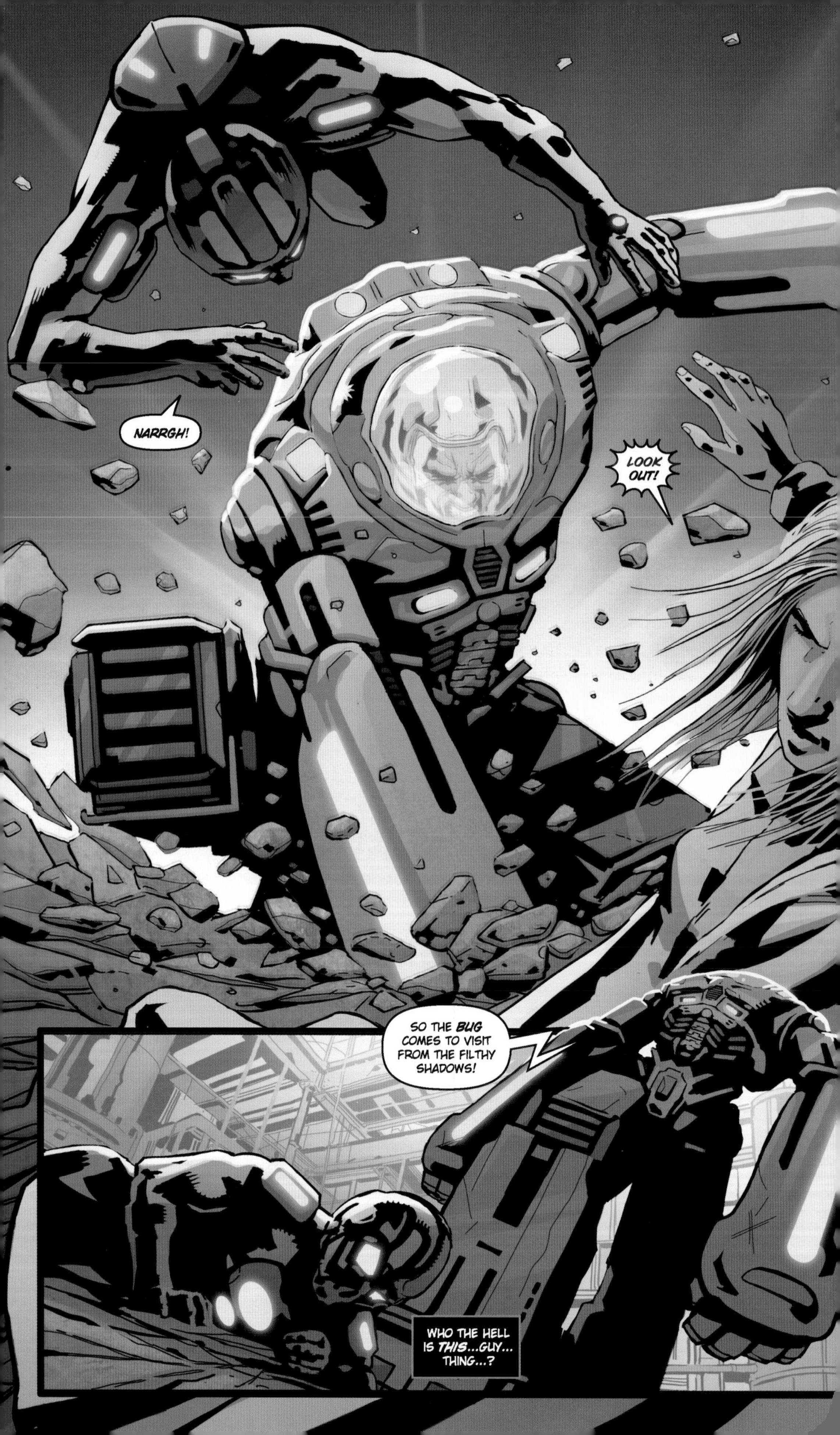
NARRGH!
LOOK OUT!
SO THE BUG COMES TO VISIT FROM THE FILTHY SHADOWS!
WHO THE HELL IS THIS...GUY... THING...?

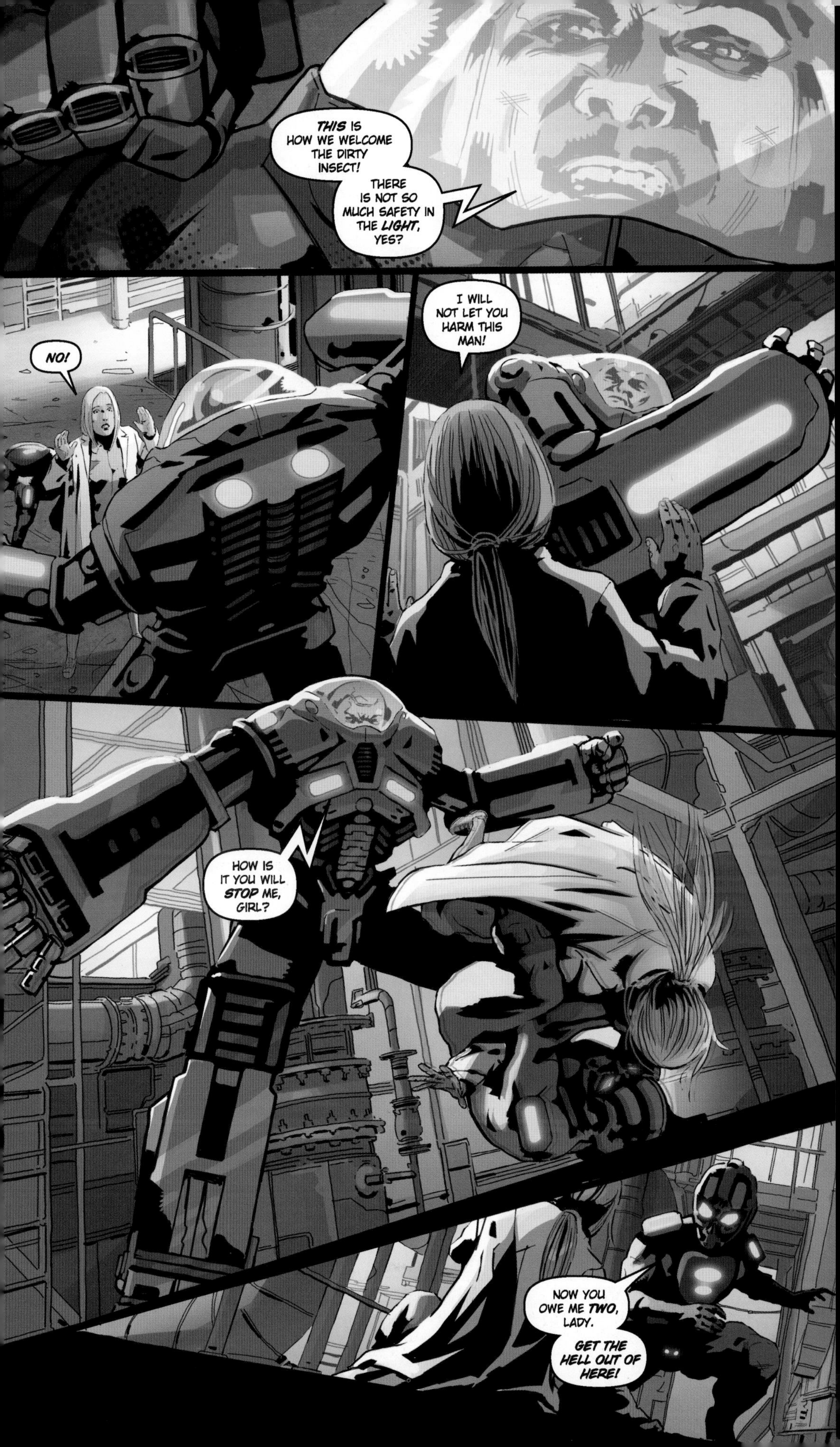
THIS IS HOW WE WELCOME THE DIRTY INSECT!
THERE IS NOT SO MUCH SAFETY IN THE LIGHT, YES?
NO!
I WILL NOT LET YOU HARM THIS MAN!
HOW IS IT YOU WILL STOP ME, GIRL?
NOW YOU OWE ME TWO, LADY.
GET THE HELL OUT OF HERE!

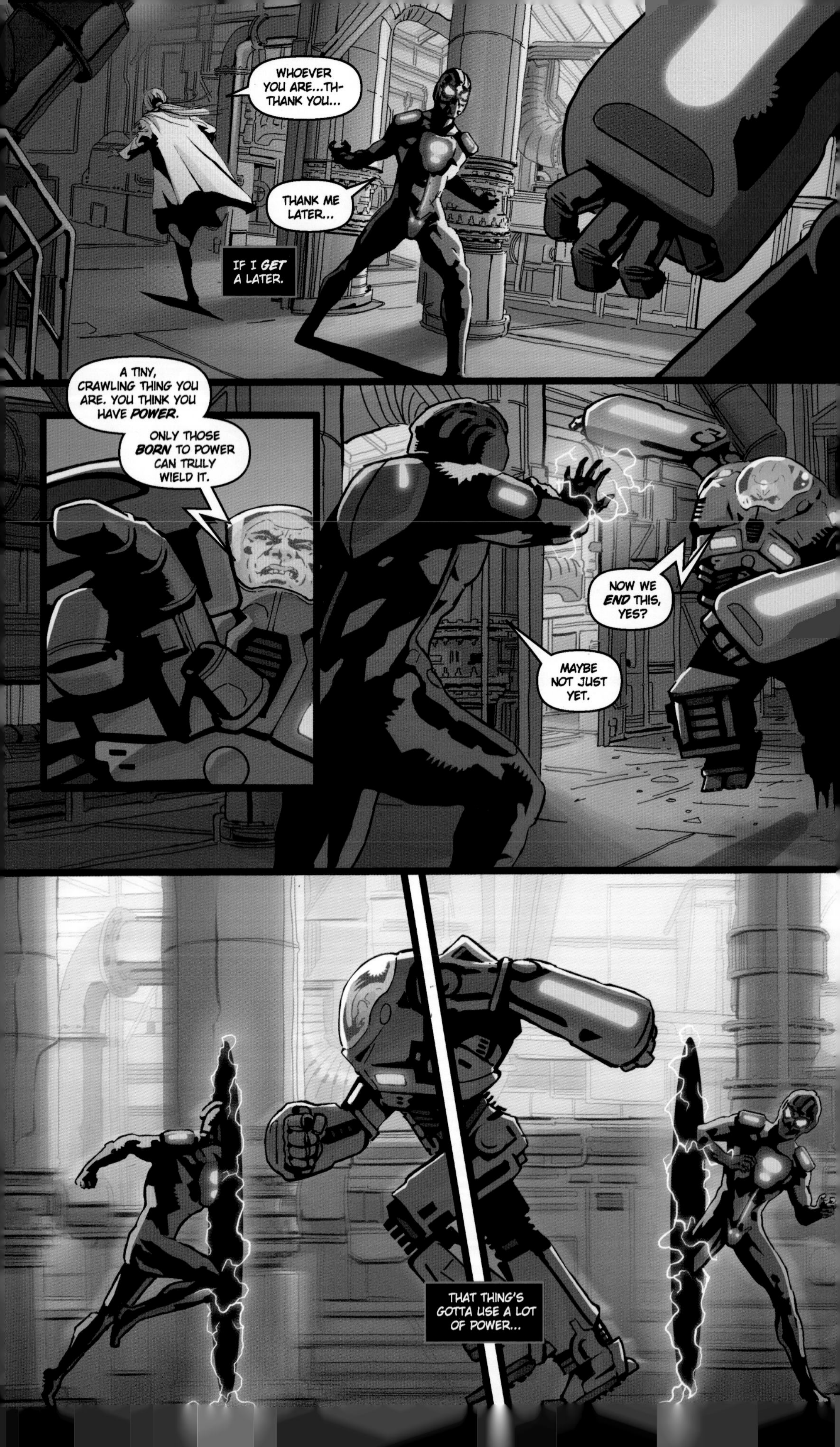
WHOEVER YOU ARE...TH-THANK YOU...
THANK ME LATER...
IF I GET A LATER.
A TINY, CRAWLING THING YOU ARE. YOU THINK YOU HAVE POWER.
ONLY THOSE BORN TO POWER CAN TRULY WIELD IT.
NOW WE END THIS, YES?
MAYBE NOT JUST YET.
THAT THING'S GOTTA USE A LOT OF POWER...

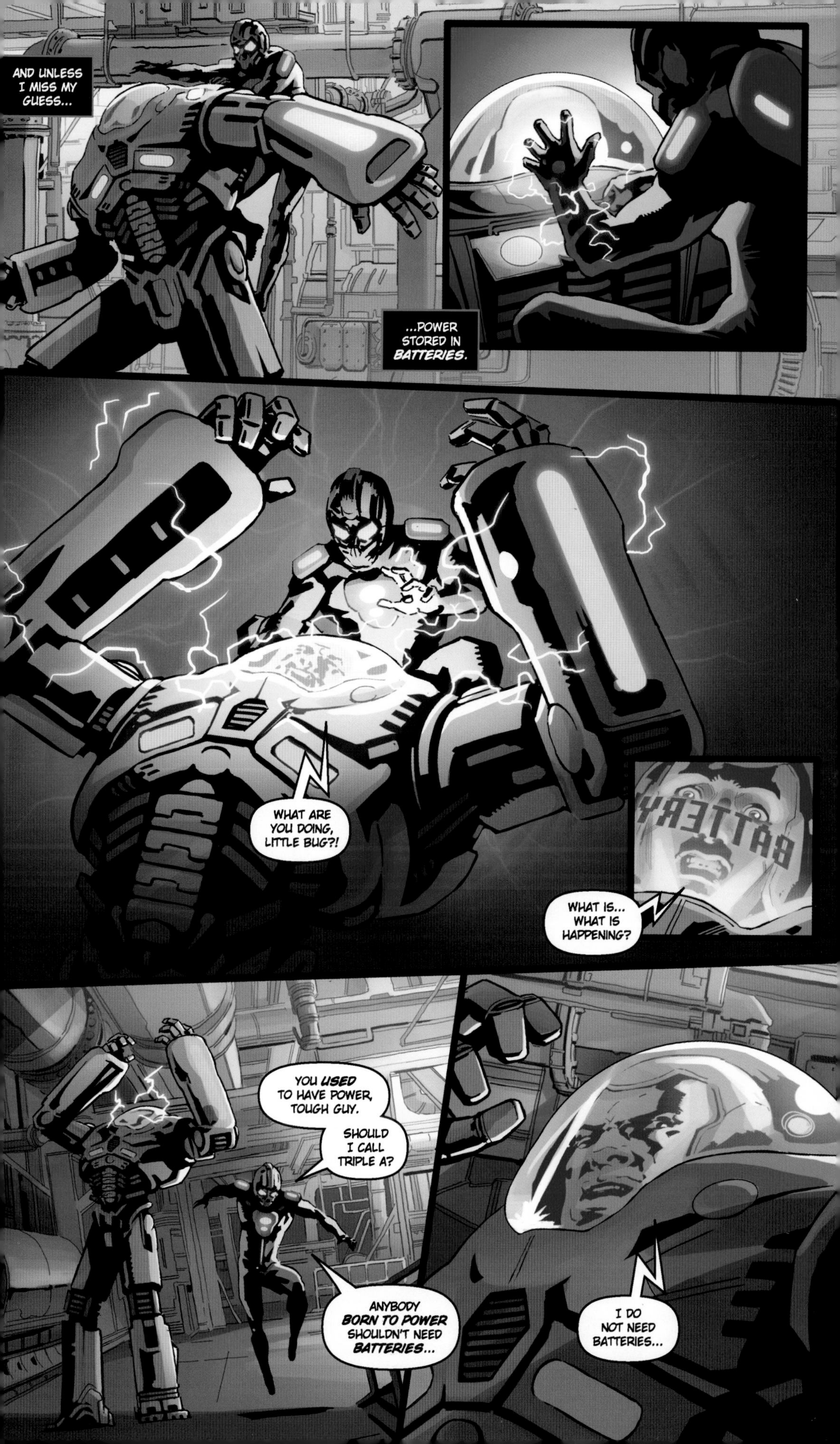

AND UNLESS I MISS MY GUESS...
...POWER STORED IN *BATTERIES.*
WHAT ARE YOU DOING, LITTLE BUG?!
WHAT IS... WHAT IS HAPPENING?
YOU *USED* TO HAVE POWER, TOUGH GUY.
SHOULD I CALL TRIPLE A?
ANYBODY *BORN TO POWER* SHOULDN'T NEED *BATTERIES*...
I DO NOT NEED BATTERIES...

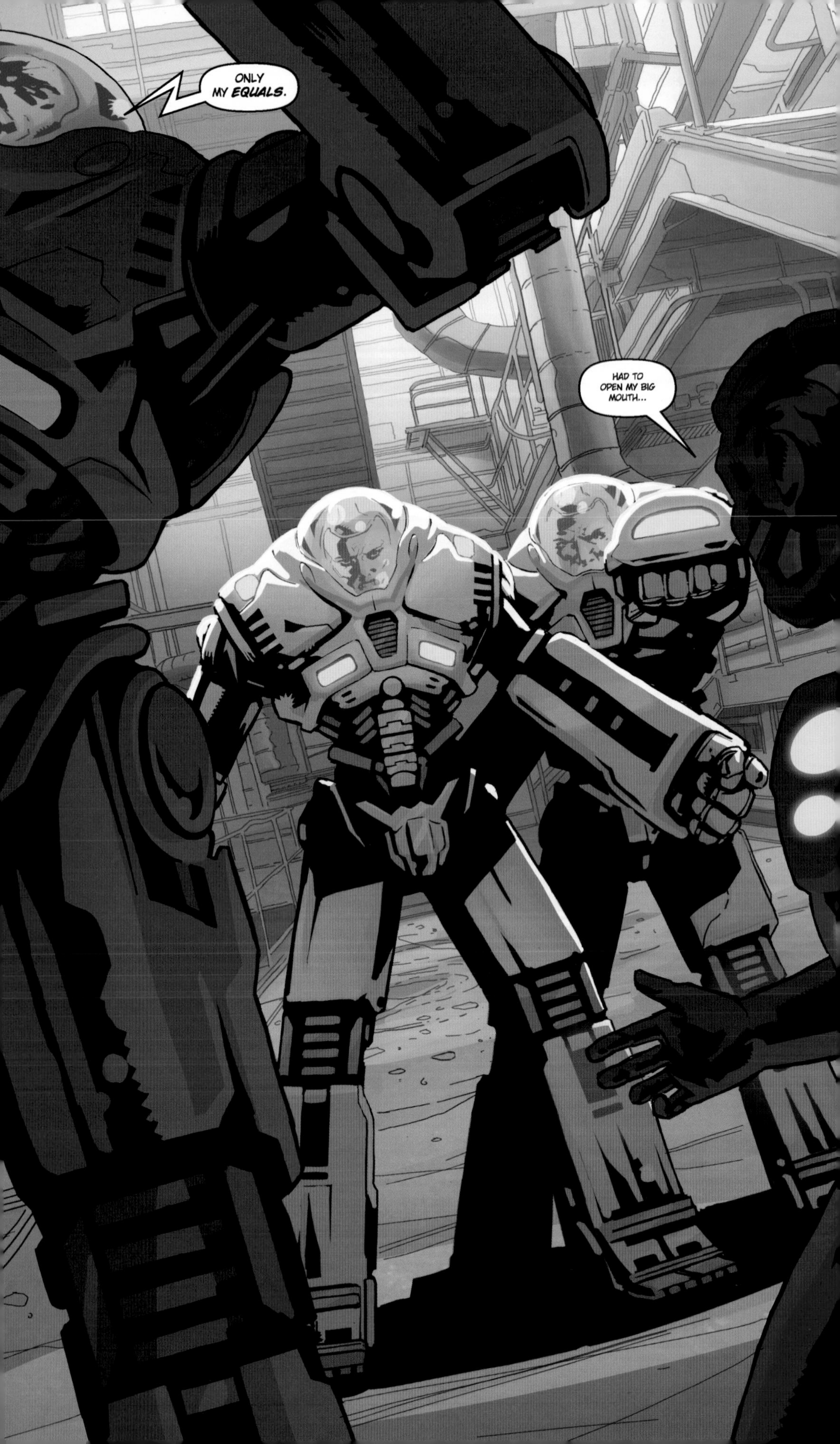
ONLY MY EQUALS.
HAD TO OPEN MY BIG MOUTH...

CHAPTER 4

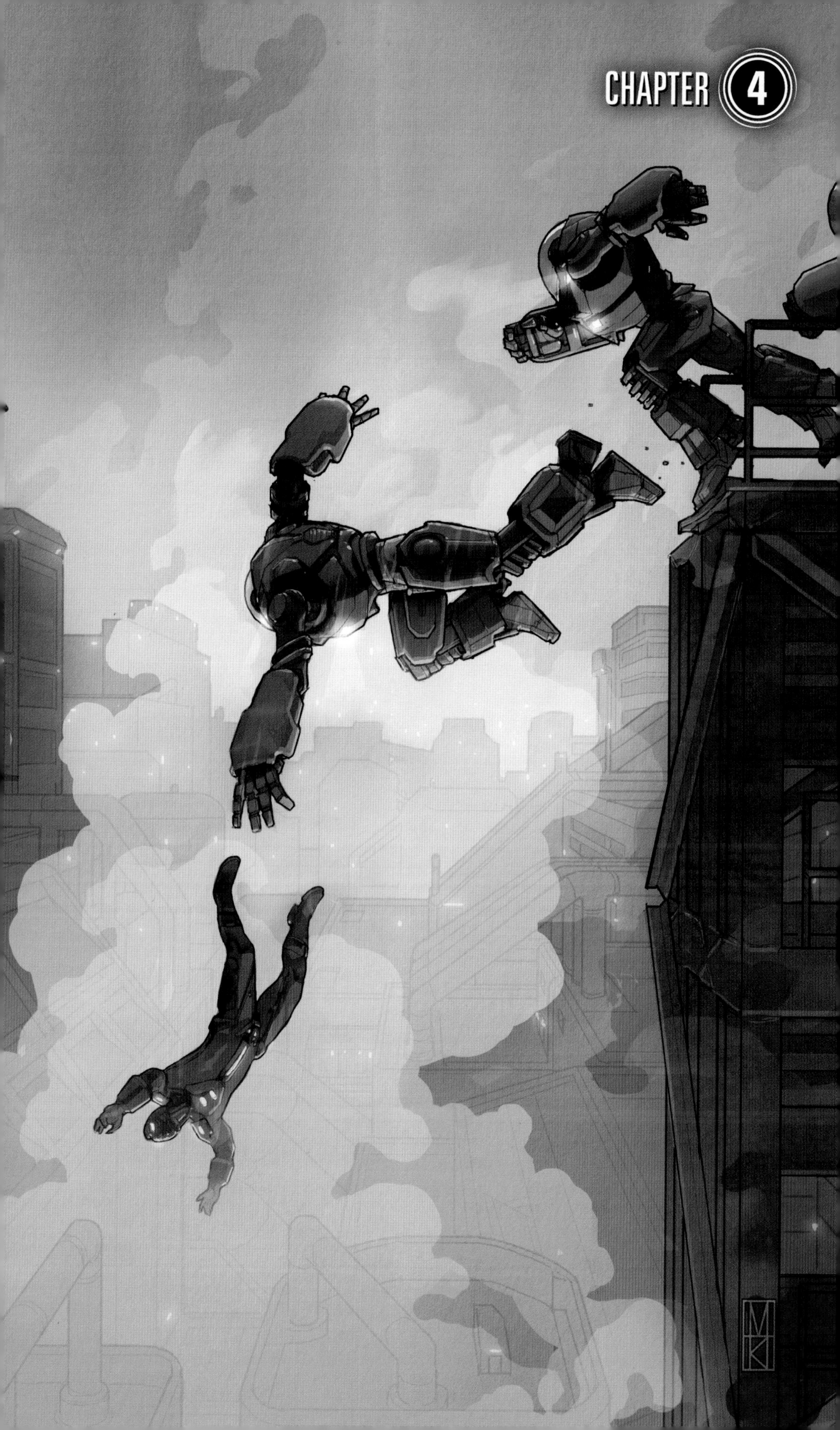

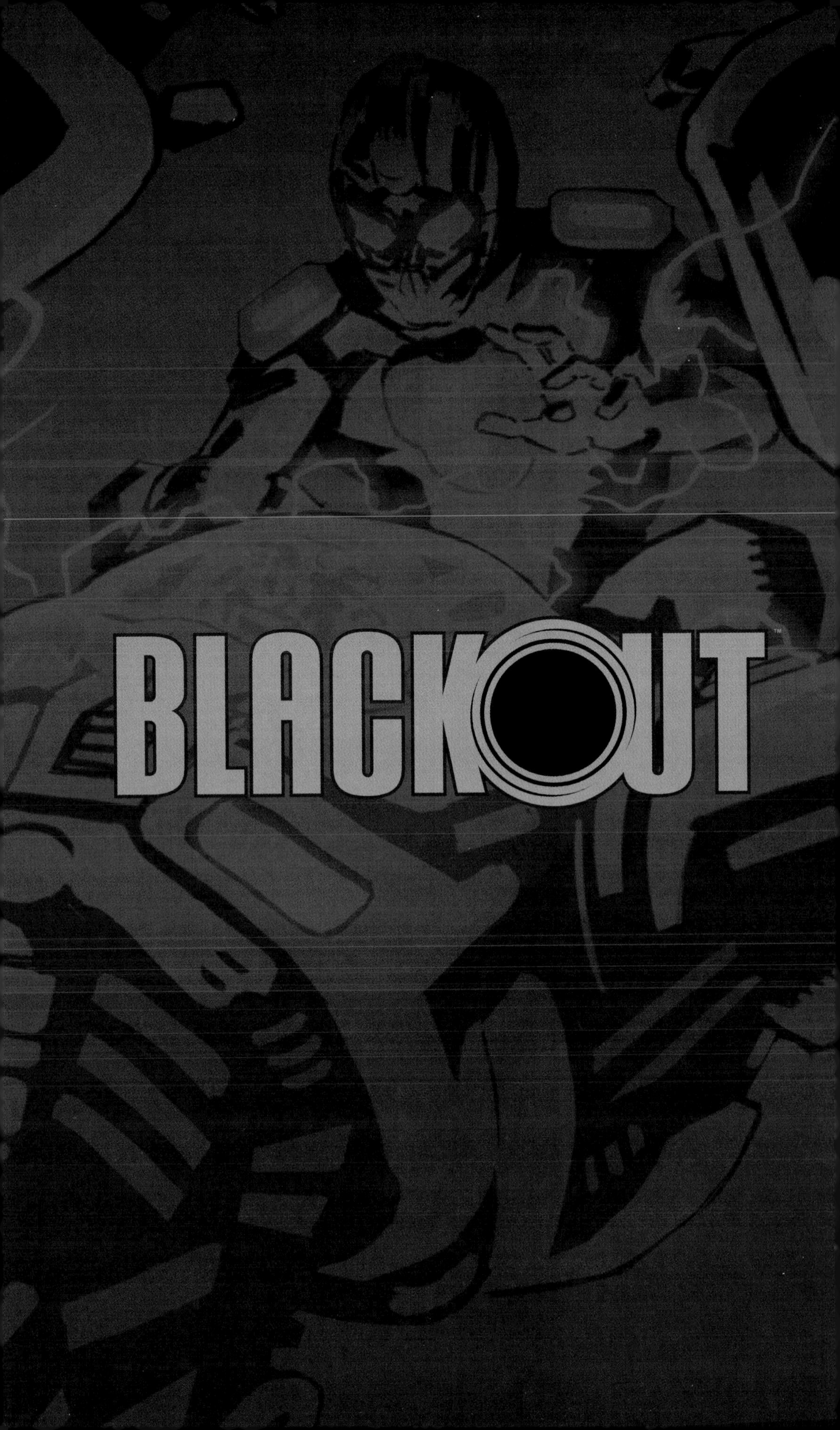
BLACKOUT

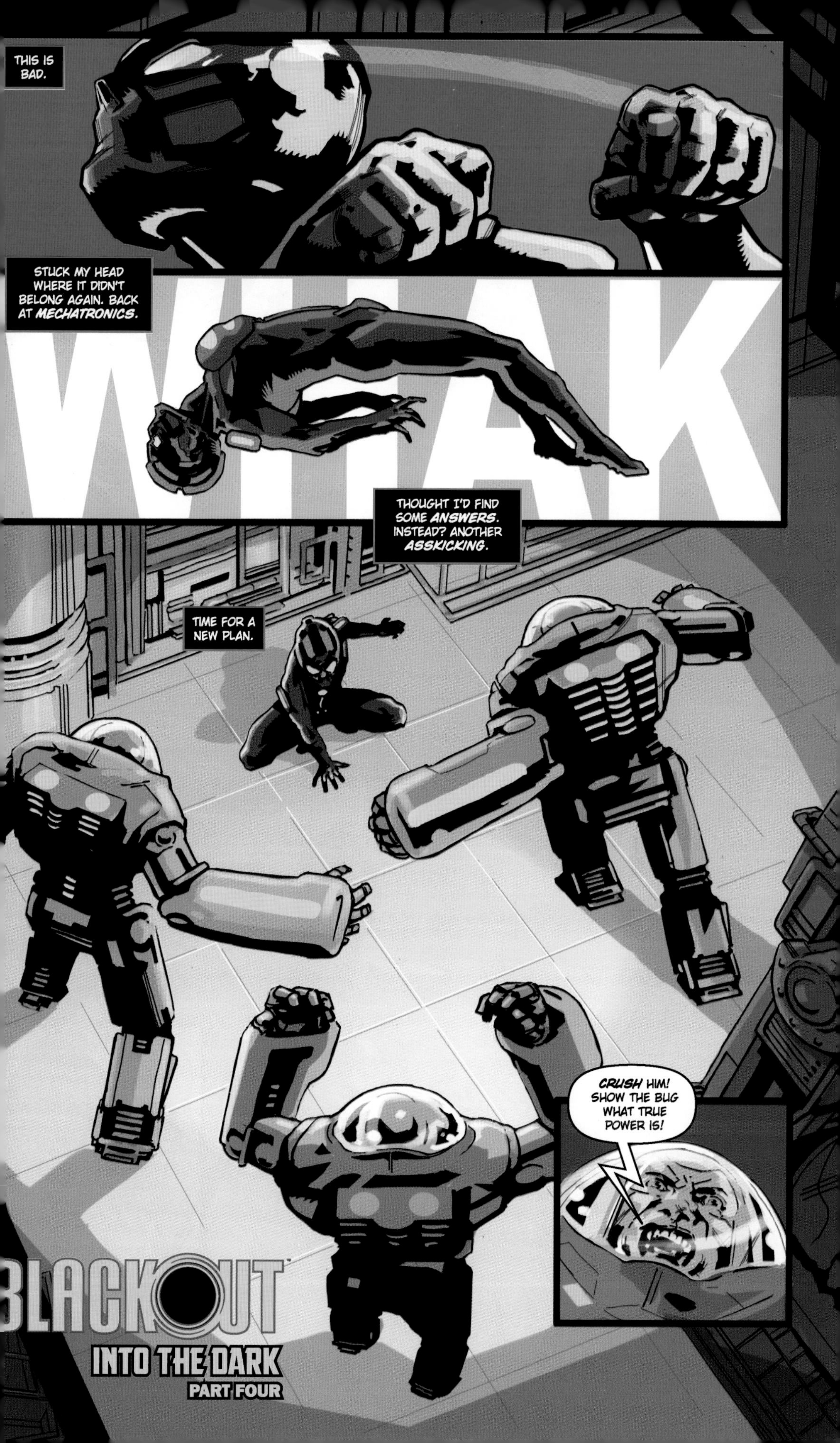

THIS IS BAD.
STUCK MY HEAD WHERE IT DIDN'T BELONG AGAIN. BACK AT MECHATRONICS.
WHAK
THOUGHT I'D FIND SOME ANSWERS. INSTEAD? ANOTHER ASSKICKING.
TIME FOR A NEW PLAN.
CRUSH HIM! SHOW THE BUG WHAT TRUE POWER IS!
BLACKOUT
INTO THE DARK
PART FOUR

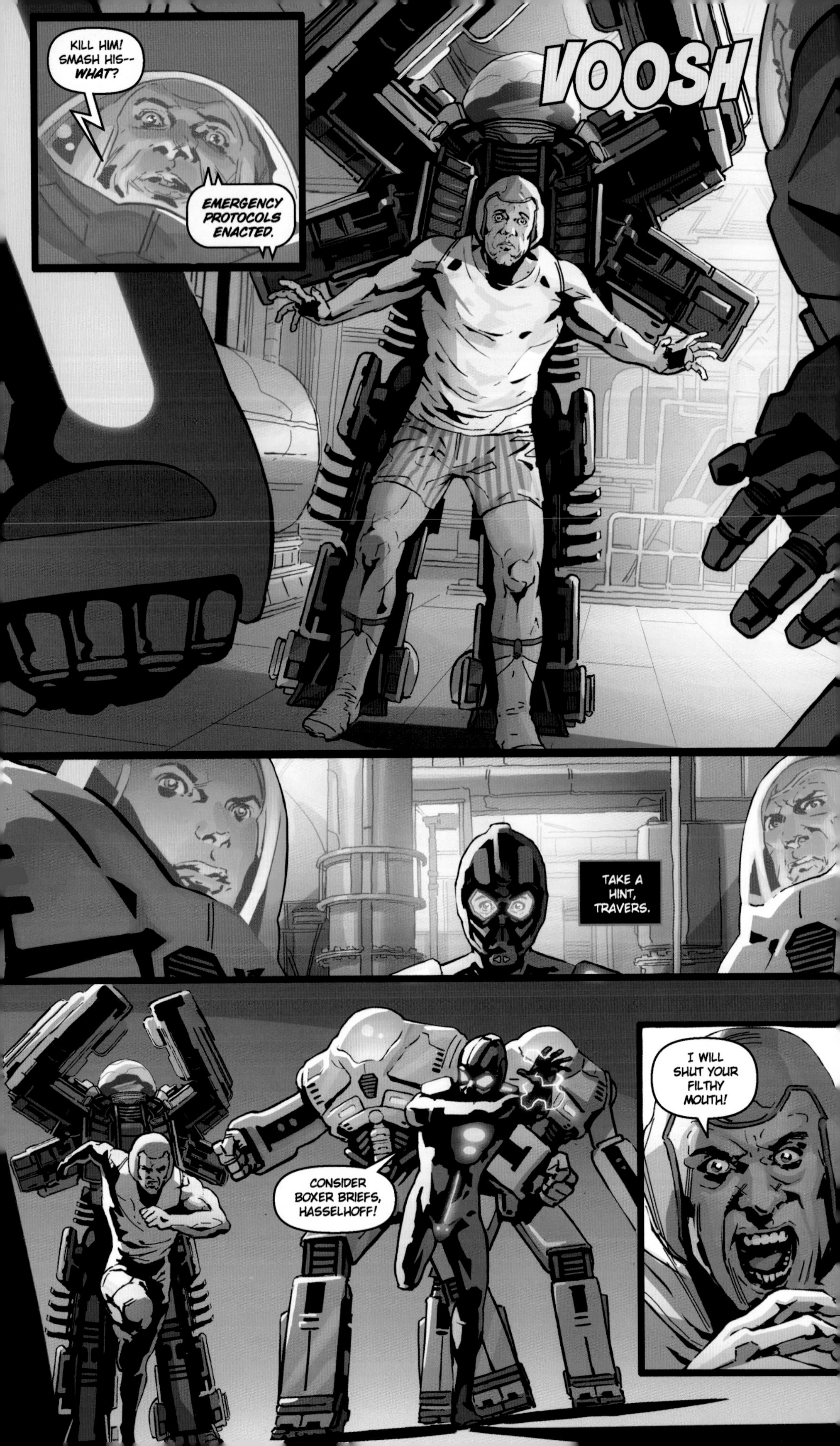
KILL HIM! SMASH HIS-- WHAT?
EMERGENCY PROTOCOLS ENACTED.
VOOSH
TAKE A HINT, TRAVERS.
CONSIDER BOXER BRIEFS, HASSELHOFF!
I WILL SHUT YOUR FILTHY MOUTH!

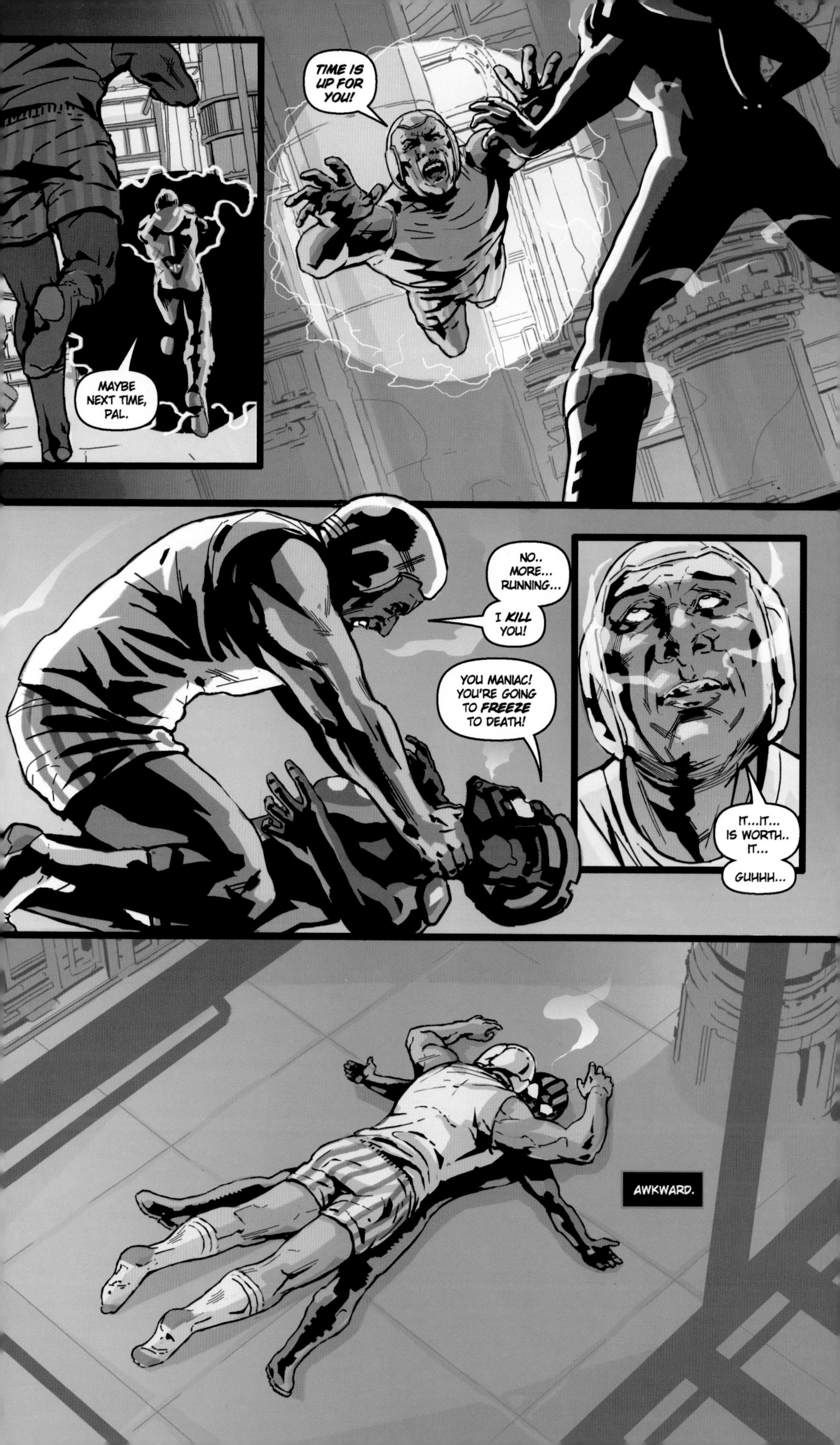
MAYBE NEXT TIME, PAL.
TIME IS UP FOR YOU!
NO.. MORE... RUNNING...
I KILL YOU!
YOU MANIAC! YOU'RE GOING TO FREEZE TO DEATH!
IT...IT... IS WORTH.. IT...
GUHHH...
AWKWARD.

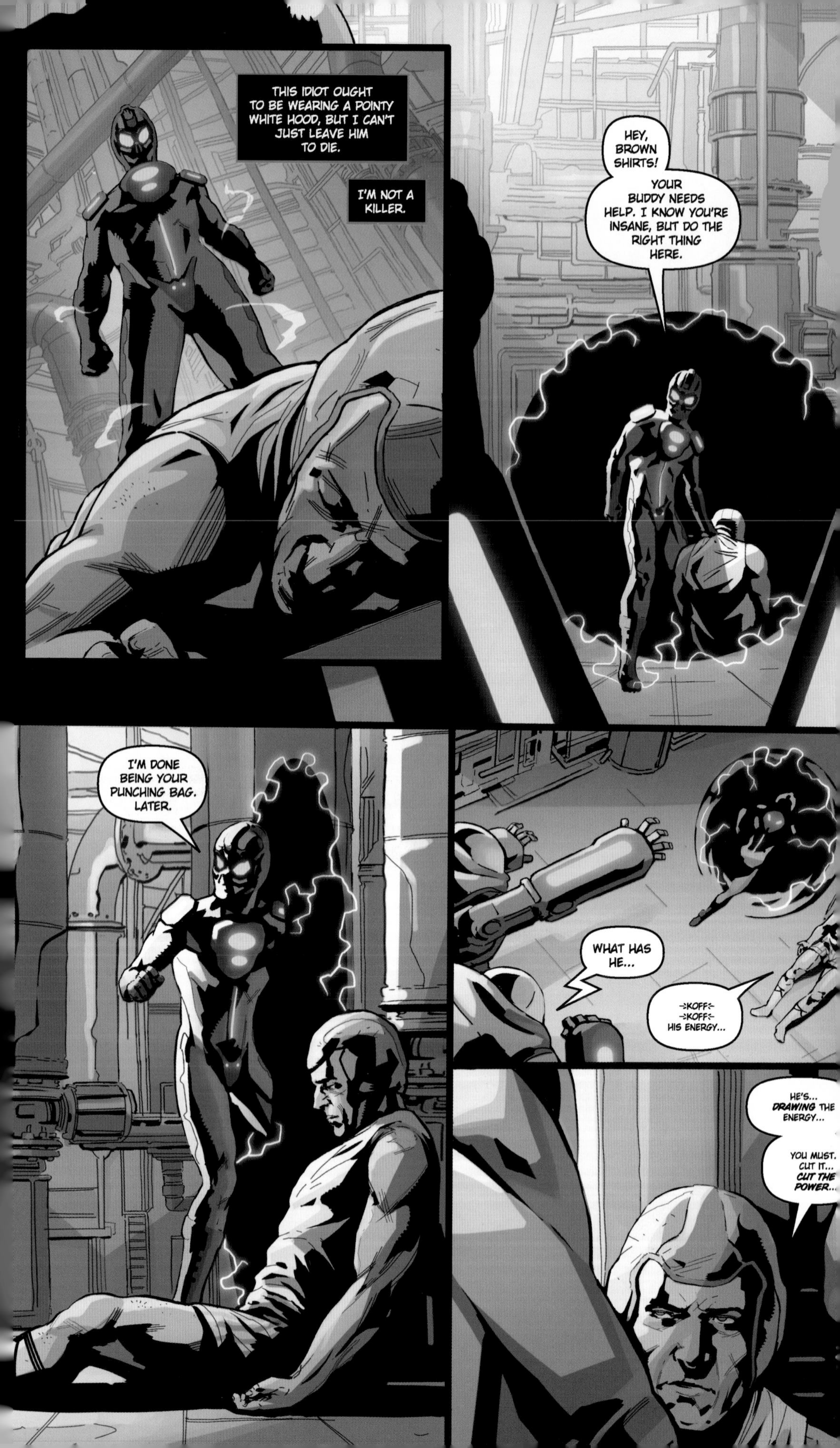
THIS IDIOT OUGHT TO BE WEARING A POINTY WHITE HOOD, BUT I CAN'T JUST LEAVE HIM TO DIE.
I'M NOT A KILLER.
HEY, BROWN SHIRTS!
YOUR BUDDY NEEDS HELP. I KNOW YOU'RE INSANE, BUT DO THE RIGHT THING HERE.
I'M DONE BEING YOUR PUNCHING BAG. LATER.
WHAT HAS HE...
-KOFF- -KOFF- HIS ENERGY...
HE'S... DRAWING THE ENERGY...
YOU MUST. CUT IT... CUT THE POWER...

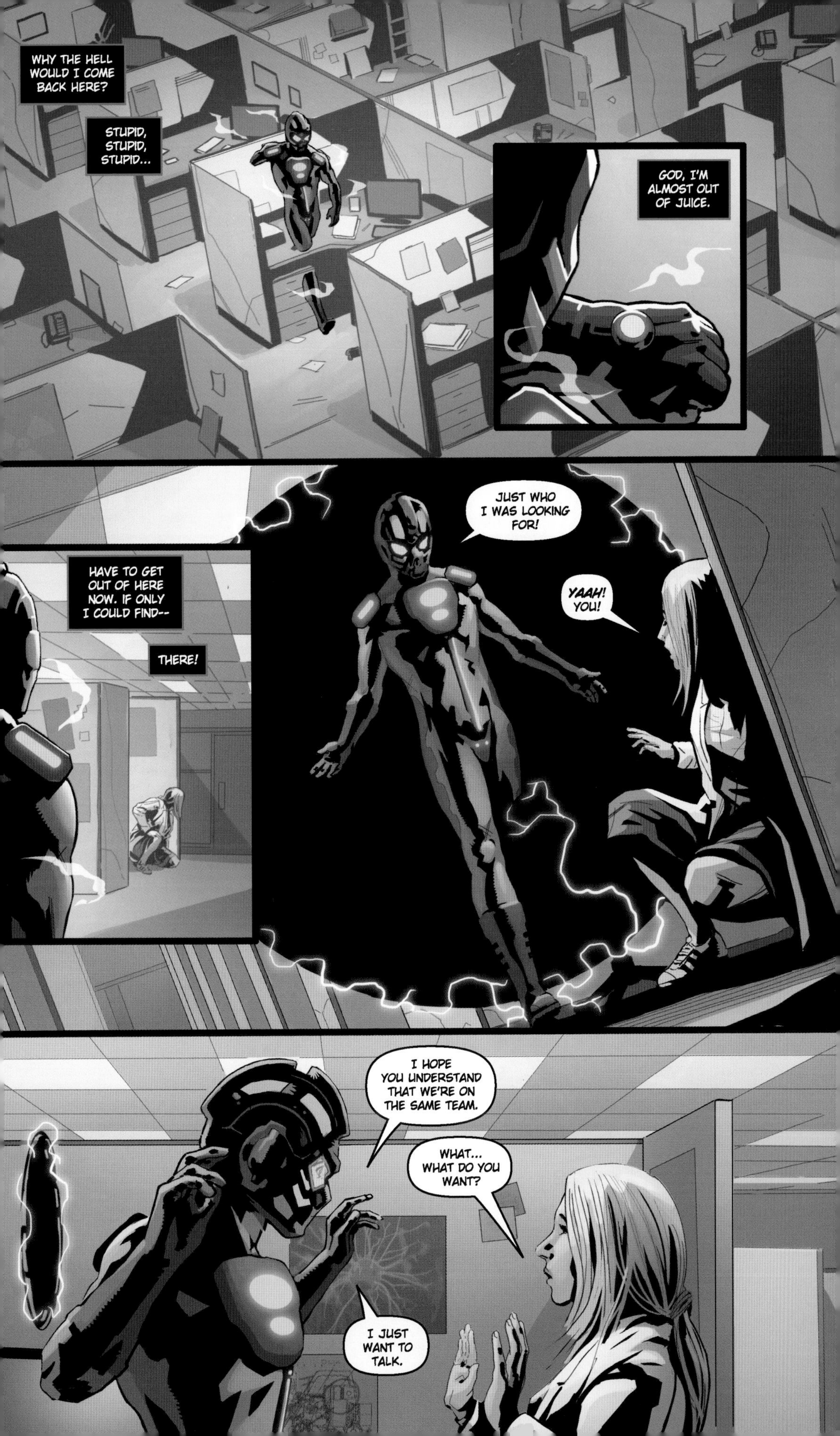
WHY THE HELL WOULD I COME BACK HERE?
STUPID, STUPID, STUPID...
GOD, I'M ALMOST OUT OF JUICE.
HAVE TO GET OUT OF HERE NOW. IF ONLY I COULD FIND--
THERE!
JUST WHO I WAS LOOKING FOR!
YAAH! YOU!
I HOPE YOU UNDERSTAND THAT WE'RE ON THE SAME TEAM.
WHAT... WHAT DO YOU WANT?
I JUST WANT TO TALK.

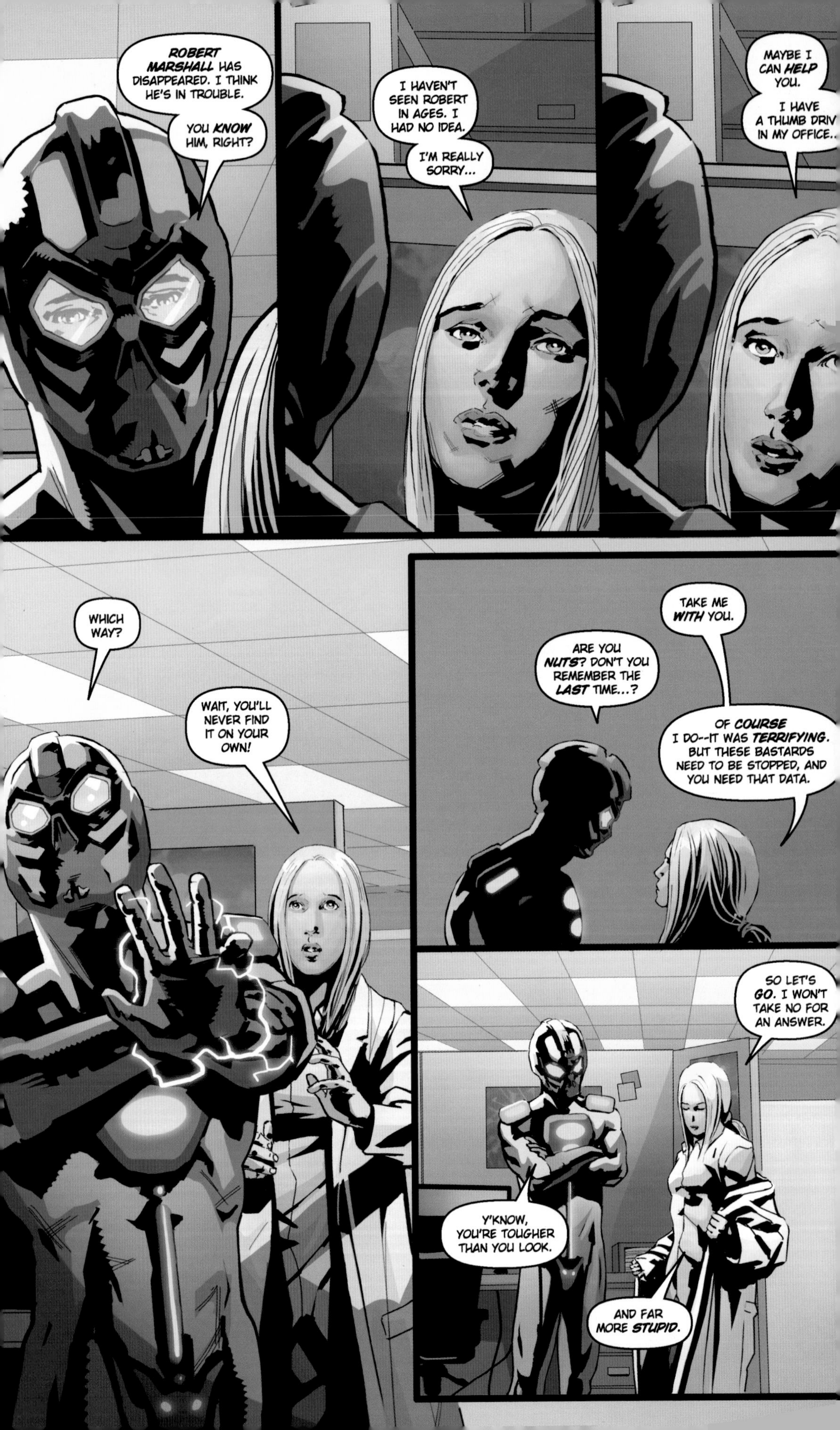
ROBERT MARSHALL HAS DISAPPEARED. I THINK HE'S IN TROUBLE.
YOU KNOW HIM, RIGHT?
I HAVEN'T SEEN ROBERT IN AGES. I HAD NO IDEA.
I'M REALLY SORRY...
MAYBE I CAN HELP YOU.
I HAVE A THUMB DRIV IN MY OFFICE..
WHICH WAY?
WAIT, YOU'LL NEVER FIND IT ON YOUR OWN!
TAKE ME WITH YOU.
ARE YOU NUTS? DON'T YOU REMEMBER THE LAST TIME...?
OF COURSE I DO--IT WAS TERRIFYING. BUT THESE BASTARDS NEED TO BE STOPPED, AND YOU NEED THAT DATA.
SO LET'S GO. I WON'T TAKE NO FOR AN ANSWER.
Y'KNOW, YOU'RE TOUGHER THAN YOU LOOK.
AND FAR MORE STUPID.

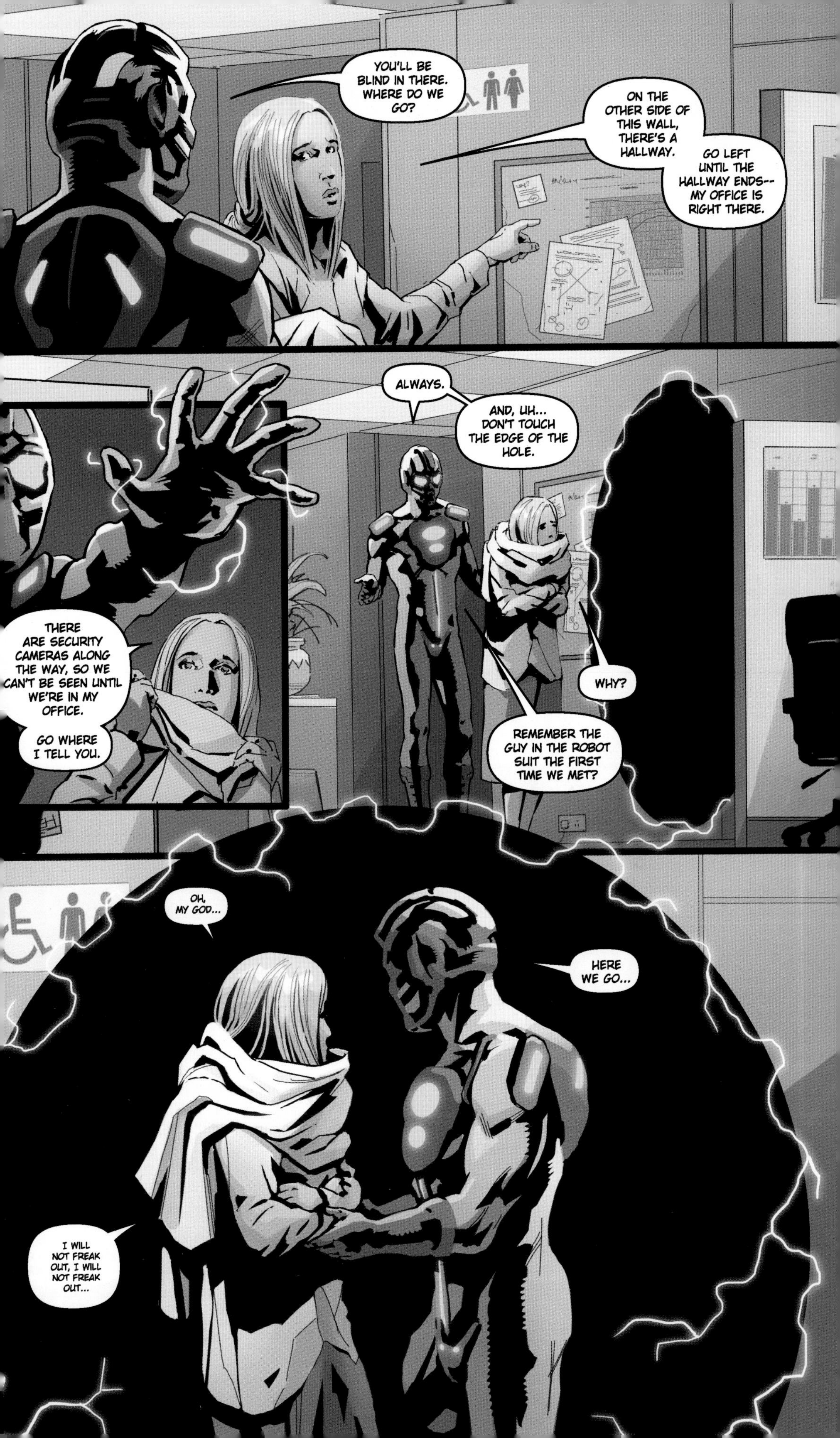
YOU'LL BE BLIND IN THERE. WHERE DO WE GO?
ON THE OTHER SIDE OF THIS WALL, THERE'S A HALLWAY.
GO LEFT UNTIL THE HALLWAY ENDS-- MY OFFICE IS RIGHT THERE.
THERE ARE SECURITY CAMERAS ALONG THE WAY, SO WE CAN'T BE SEEN UNTIL WE'RE IN MY OFFICE.
GO WHERE I TELL YOU.
ALWAYS.
AND, UH... DON'T TOUCH THE EDGE OF THE HOLE.
WHY?
REMEMBER THE GUY IN THE ROBOT SUIT THE FIRST TIME WE MET?
OH, MY GOD...
HERE WE GO...
I WILL NOT FREAK OUT, I WILL NOT FREAK OUT...

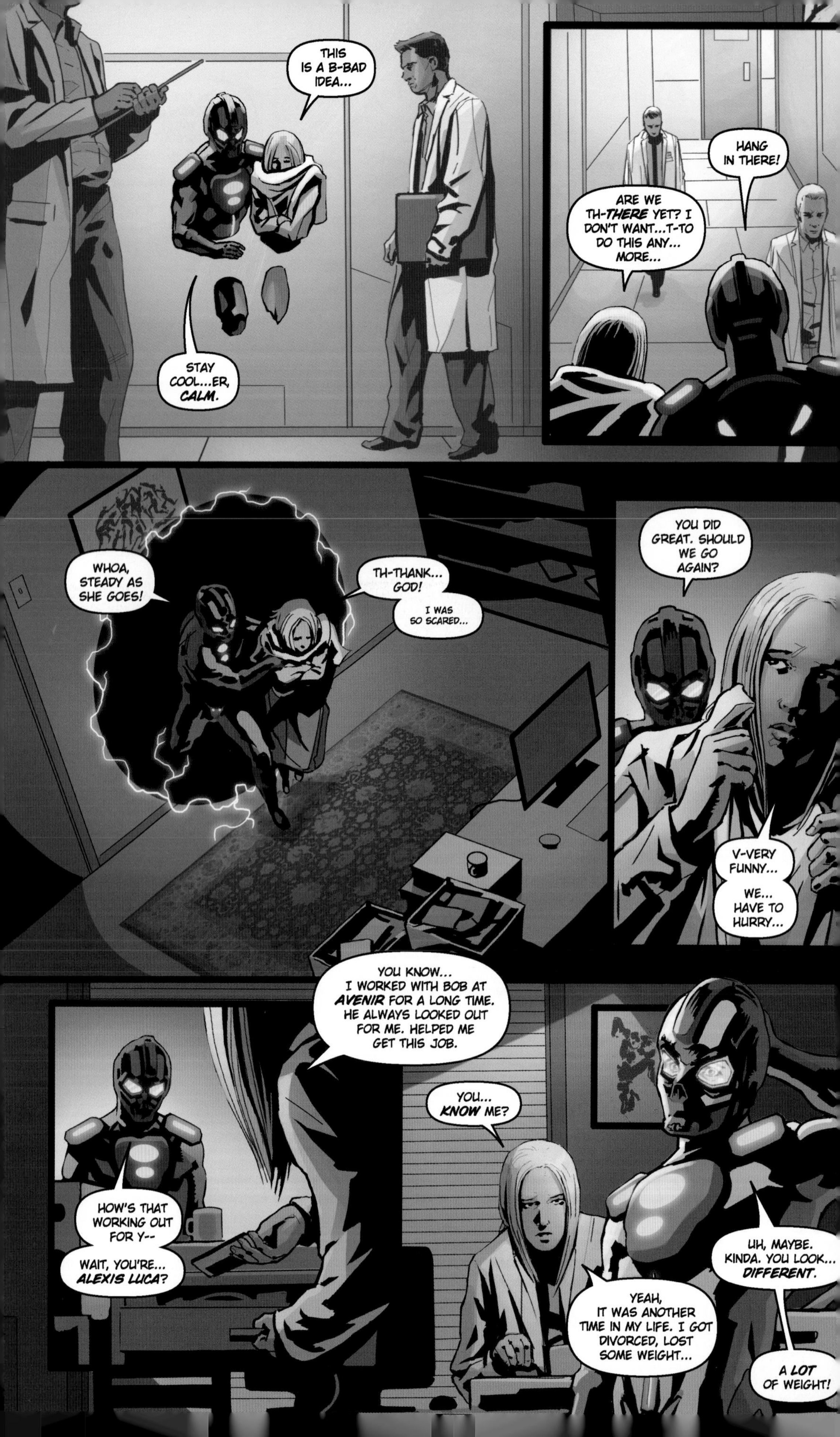
THIS IS A B-BAD IDEA...
STAY COOL...ER, CALM.
HANG IN THERE!
ARE WE TH-THERE YET? I DON'T WANT...T-TO DO THIS ANY... MORE...
WHOA, STEADY AS SHE GOES!
TH-THANK... GOD!
I WAS SO SCARED...
YOU DID GREAT. SHOULD WE GO AGAIN?
V-VERY FUNNY...
WE... HAVE TO HURRY...
YOU KNOW... I WORKED WITH BOB AT AVENIR FOR A LONG TIME. HE ALWAYS LOOKED OUT FOR ME. HELPED ME GET THIS JOB.
HOW'S THAT WORKING OUT FOR Y--
WAIT, YOU'RE... ALEXIS LUCA?
YOU... KNOW ME?
UH, MAYBE. KINDA. YOU LOOK... DIFFERENT.
YEAH, IT WAS ANOTHER TIME IN MY LIFE. I GOT DIVORCED, LOST SOME WEIGHT...
A LOT OF WEIGHT!

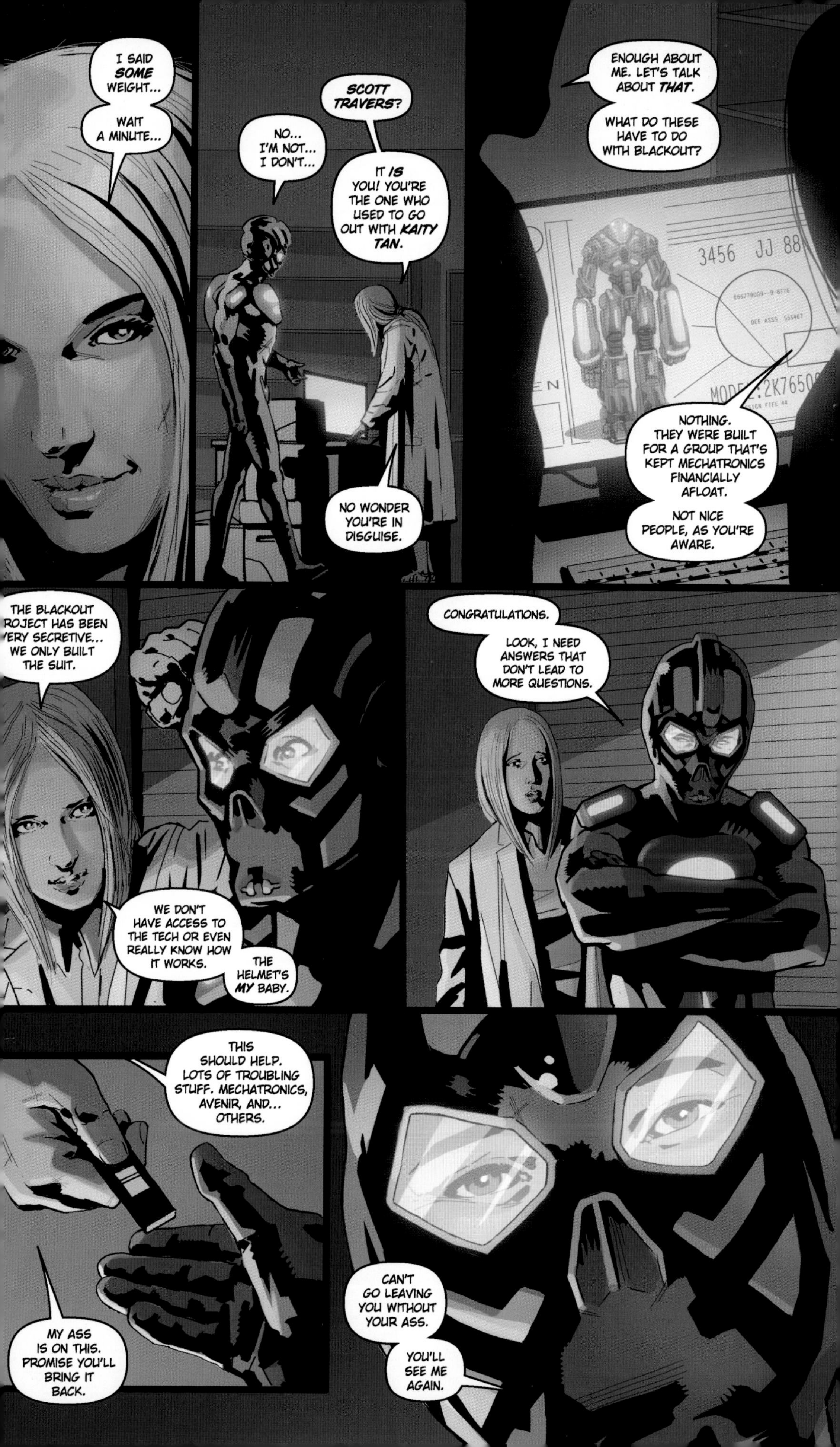
I SAID SOME WEIGHT...
WAIT A MINUTE...
NO... I'M NOT... I DON'T...
SCOTT TRAVERS?
IT IS YOU! YOU'RE THE ONE WHO USED TO GO OUT WITH KAITY TAN.
NO WONDER YOU'RE IN DISGUISE.
ENOUGH ABOUT ME. LET'S TALK ABOUT THAT.
WHAT DO THESE HAVE TO DO WITH BLACKOUT?
3456 JJ 88
NOTHING. THEY WERE BUILT FOR A GROUP THAT'S KEPT MECHATRONICS FINANCIALLY AFLOAT.
NOT NICE PEOPLE, AS YOU'RE AWARE.
THE BLACKOUT ROJECT HAS BEEN ERY SECRETIVE... WE ONLY BUILT THE SUIT.
WE DON'T HAVE ACCESS TO THE TECH OR EVEN REALLY KNOW HOW IT WORKS.
THE HELMET'S MY BABY.
CONGRATULATIONS.
LOOK, I NEED ANSWERS THAT DON'T LEAD TO MORE QUESTIONS.
THIS SHOULD HELP. LOTS OF TROUBLING STUFF. MECHATRONICS, AVENIR, AND... OTHERS.
MY ASS IS ON THIS. PROMISE YOU'LL BRING IT BACK.
CAN'T GO LEAVING YOU WITHOUT YOUR ASS.
YOU'LL SEE ME AGAIN.

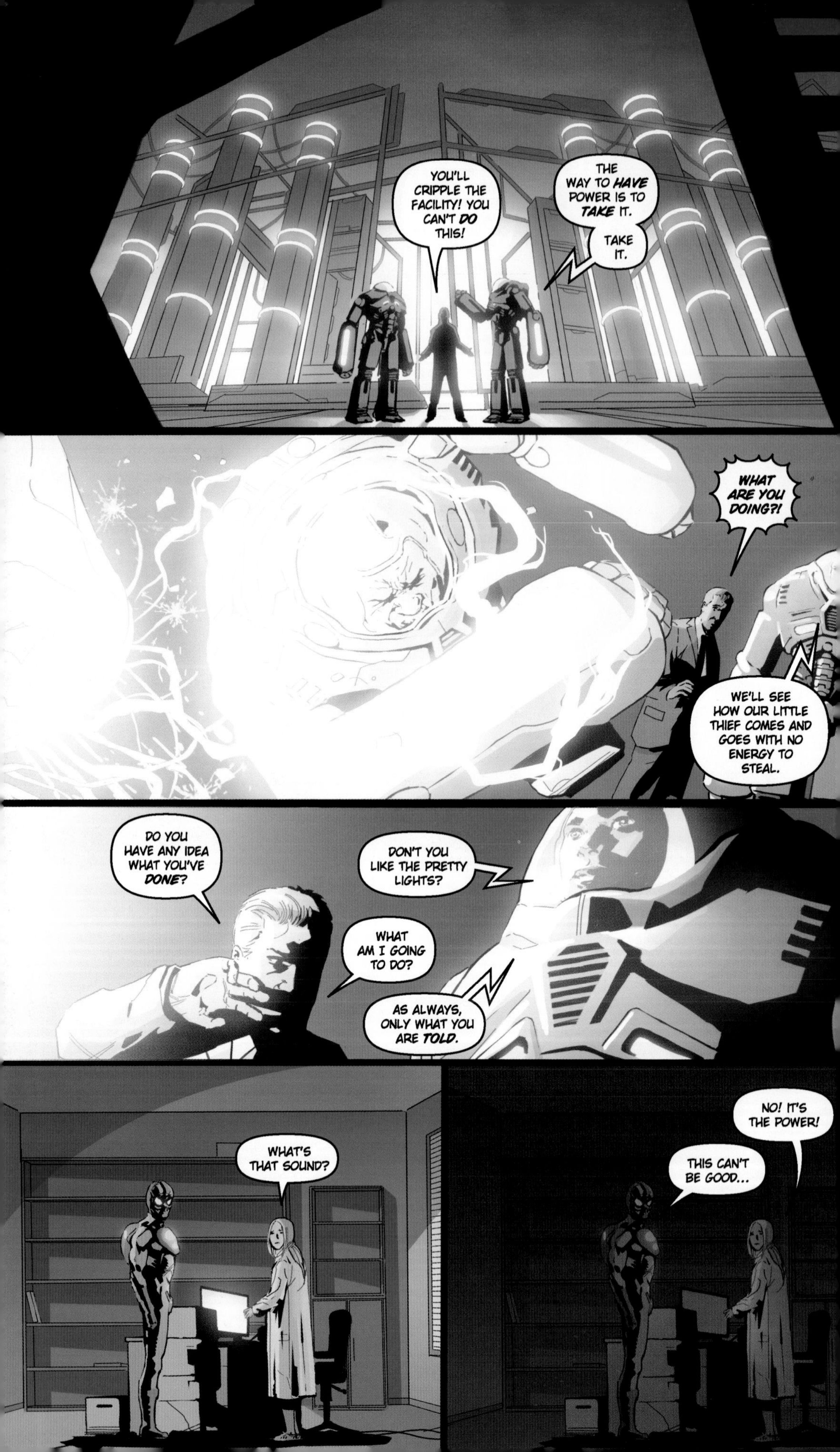
YOU'LL CRIPPLE THE FACILITY! YOU CAN'T DO THIS!
THE WAY TO HAVE POWER IS TO TAKE IT.
TAKE IT.
WHAT ARE YOU DOING?!
WE'LL SEE HOW OUR LITTLE THIEF COMES AND GOES WITH NO ENERGY TO STEAL.
DO YOU HAVE ANY IDEA WHAT YOU'VE DONE?
DON'T YOU LIKE THE PRETTY LIGHTS?
WHAT AM I GOING TO DO?
AS ALWAYS, ONLY WHAT YOU ARE TOLD.
WHAT'S THAT SOUND?
NO! IT'S THE POWER!
THIS CAN'T BE GOOD...

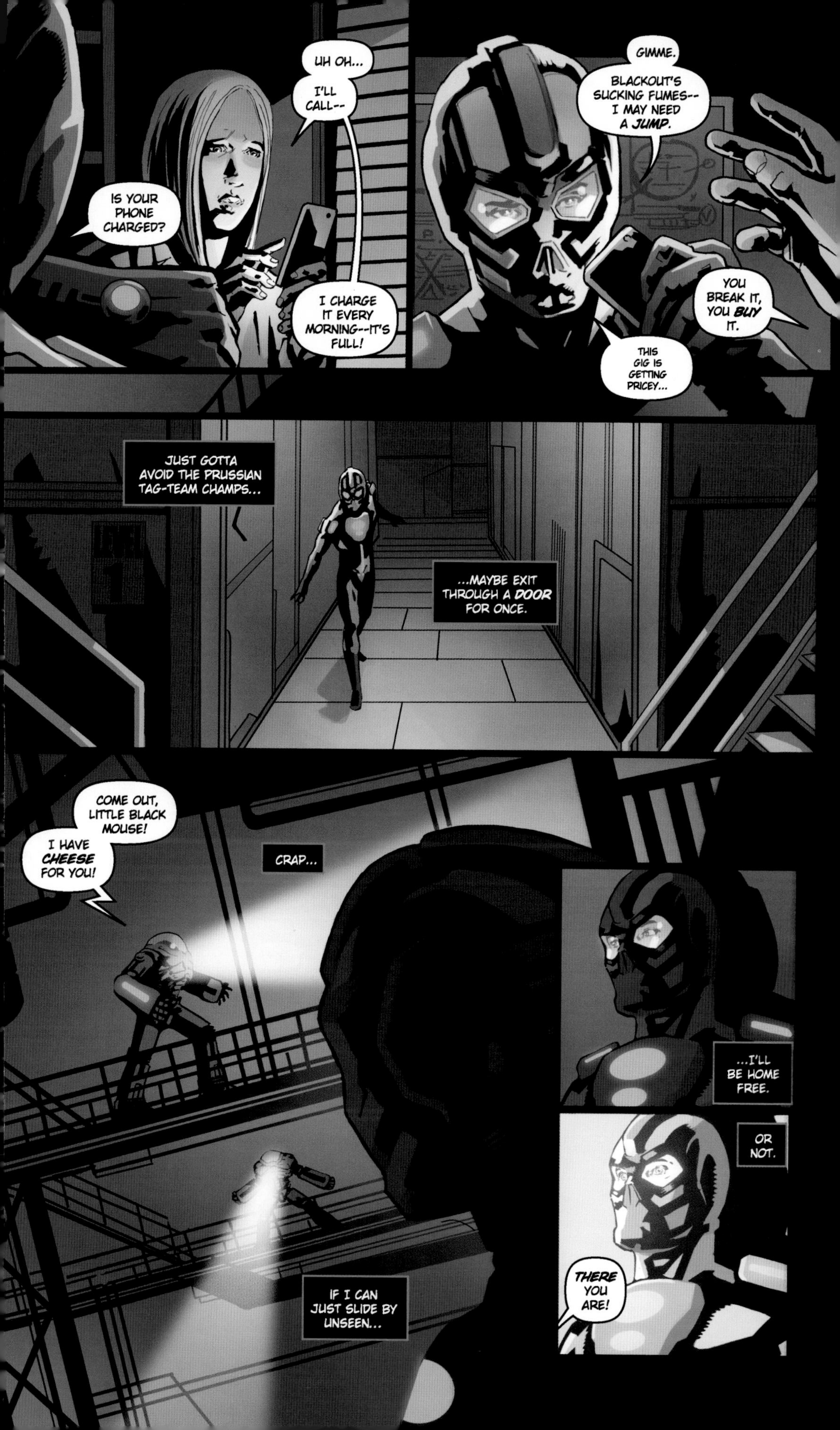
UH OH...
I'LL CALL--
IS YOUR PHONE CHARGED?
I CHARGE IT EVERY MORNING--IT'S FULL!
GIMME.
BLACKOUT'S SUCKING FUMES-- I MAY NEED A JUMP.
YOU BREAK IT, YOU BUY IT.
THIS GIG IS GETTING PRICEY...
JUST GOTTA AVOID THE PRUSSIAN TAG-TEAM CHAMPS...
...MAYBE EXIT THROUGH A DOOR FOR ONCE.
COME OUT, LITTLE BLACK MOUSE!
I HAVE CHEESE FOR YOU!
CRAP...
IF I CAN JUST SLIDE BY UNSEEN...
...I'LL BE HOME FREE.
OR NOT.
THERE YOU ARE!

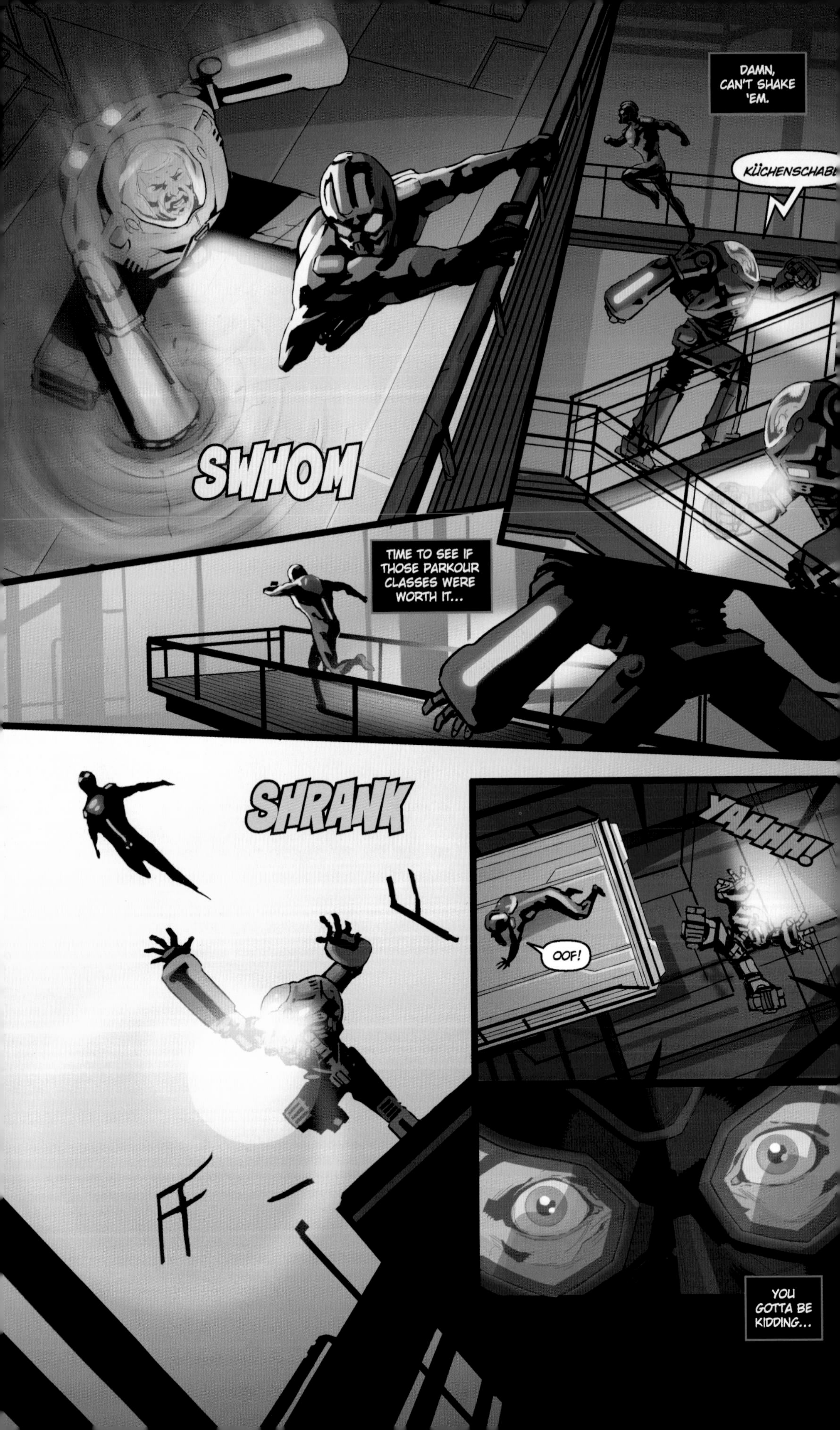

DAMN, CAN'T SHAKE 'EM.
KÜCHENSCHABE
SWHOM
TIME TO SEE IF THOSE PARKOUR CLASSES WERE WORTH IT...
SHRANK
YAHHH!
OOF!
YOU GOTTA BE KIDDING...

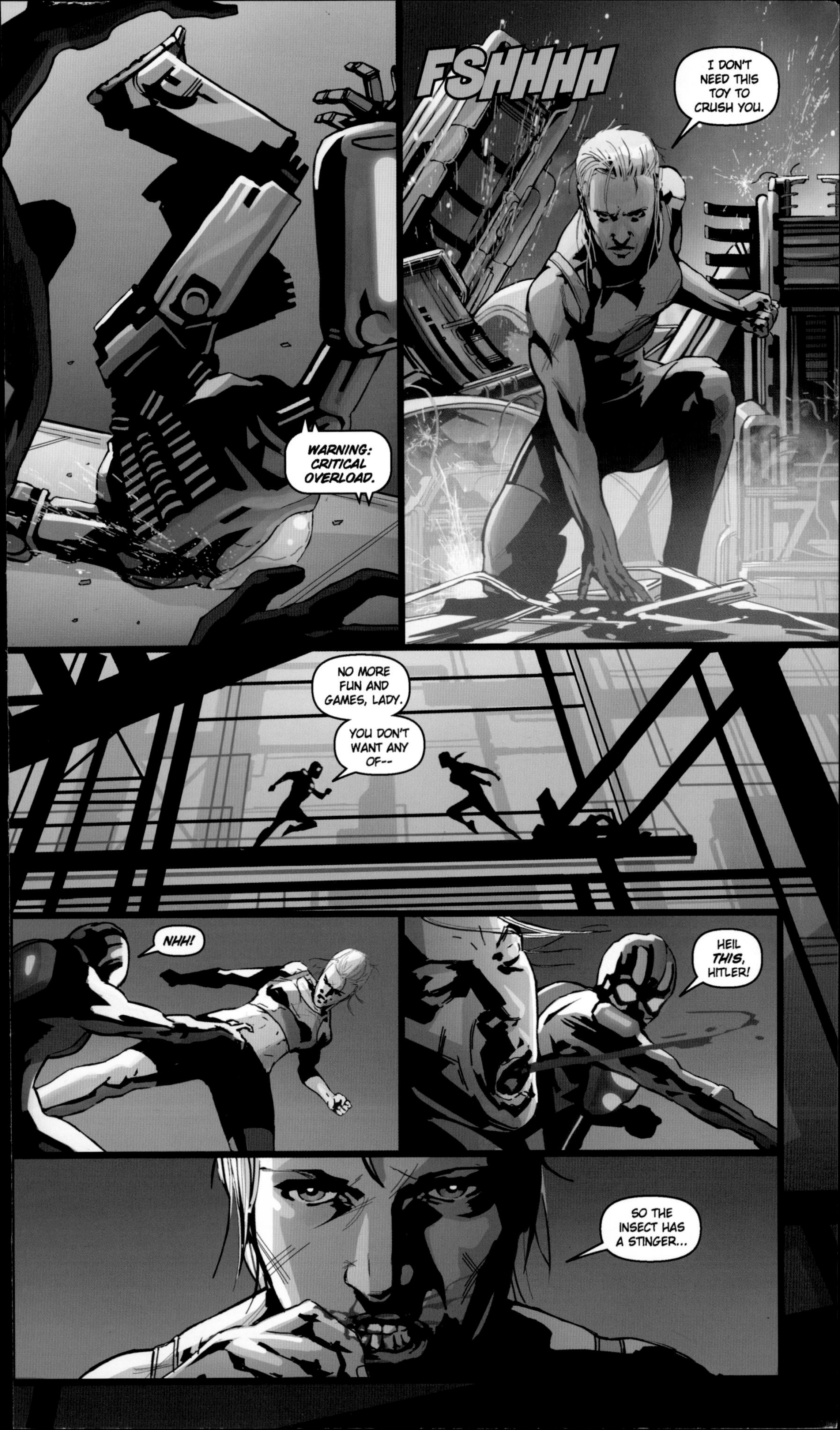
WARNING: CRITICAL OVERLOAD.
FSHHHH
I DON'T NEED THIS TOY TO CRUSH YOU.
NO MORE FUN AND GAMES, LADY.
YOU DON'T WANT ANY OF--
NHH!
HEIL THIS, HITLER!
SO THE INSECT HAS A STINGER...

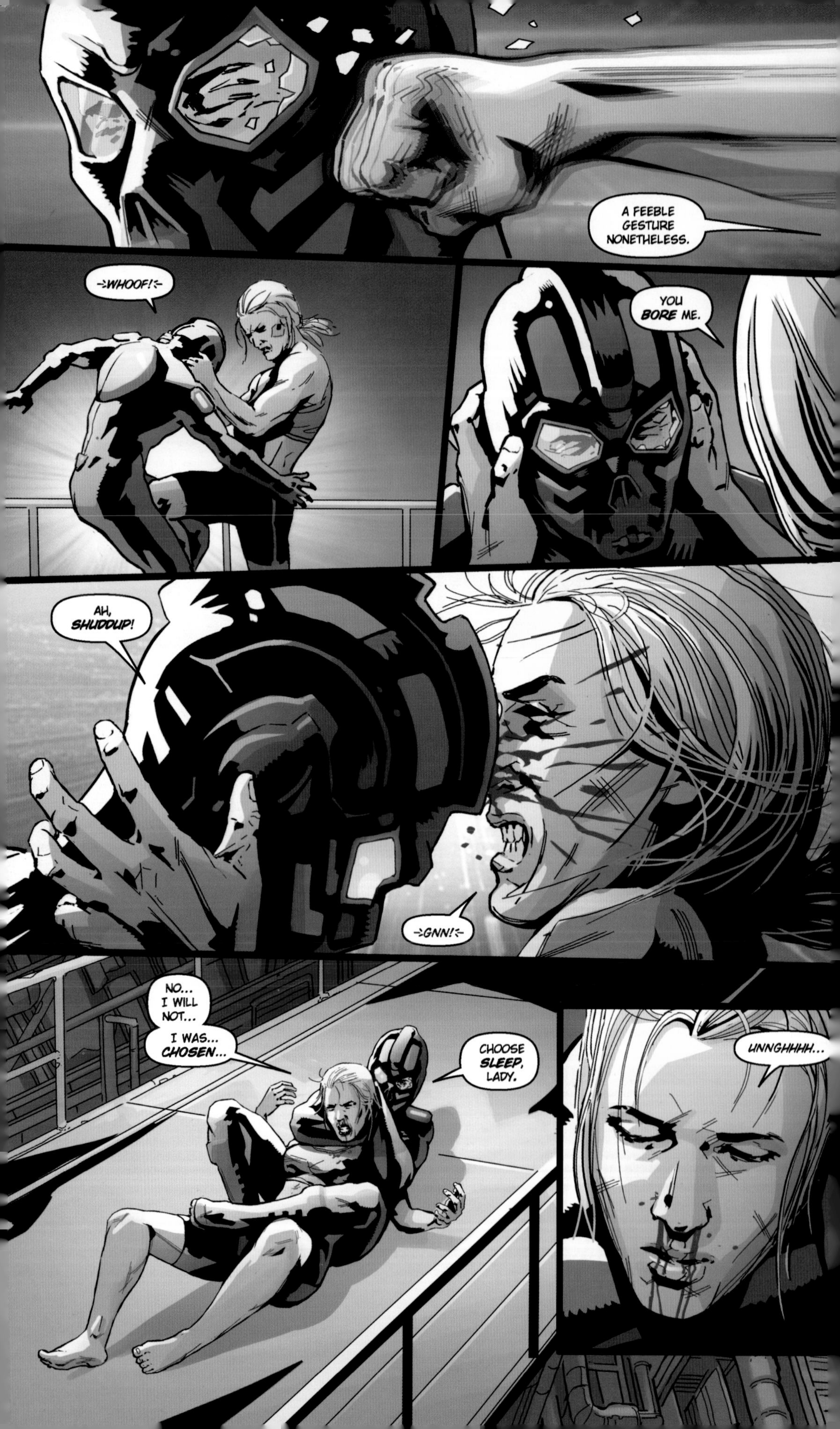

A FEEBLE GESTURE NONETHELESS.
-WHOOF!-
YOU BORE ME.
AH, SHUDDUP!
-GNN!-
NO... I WILL NOT...
I WAS... CHOSEN...
CHOOSE SLEEP, LADY.
UNNGHHHH...

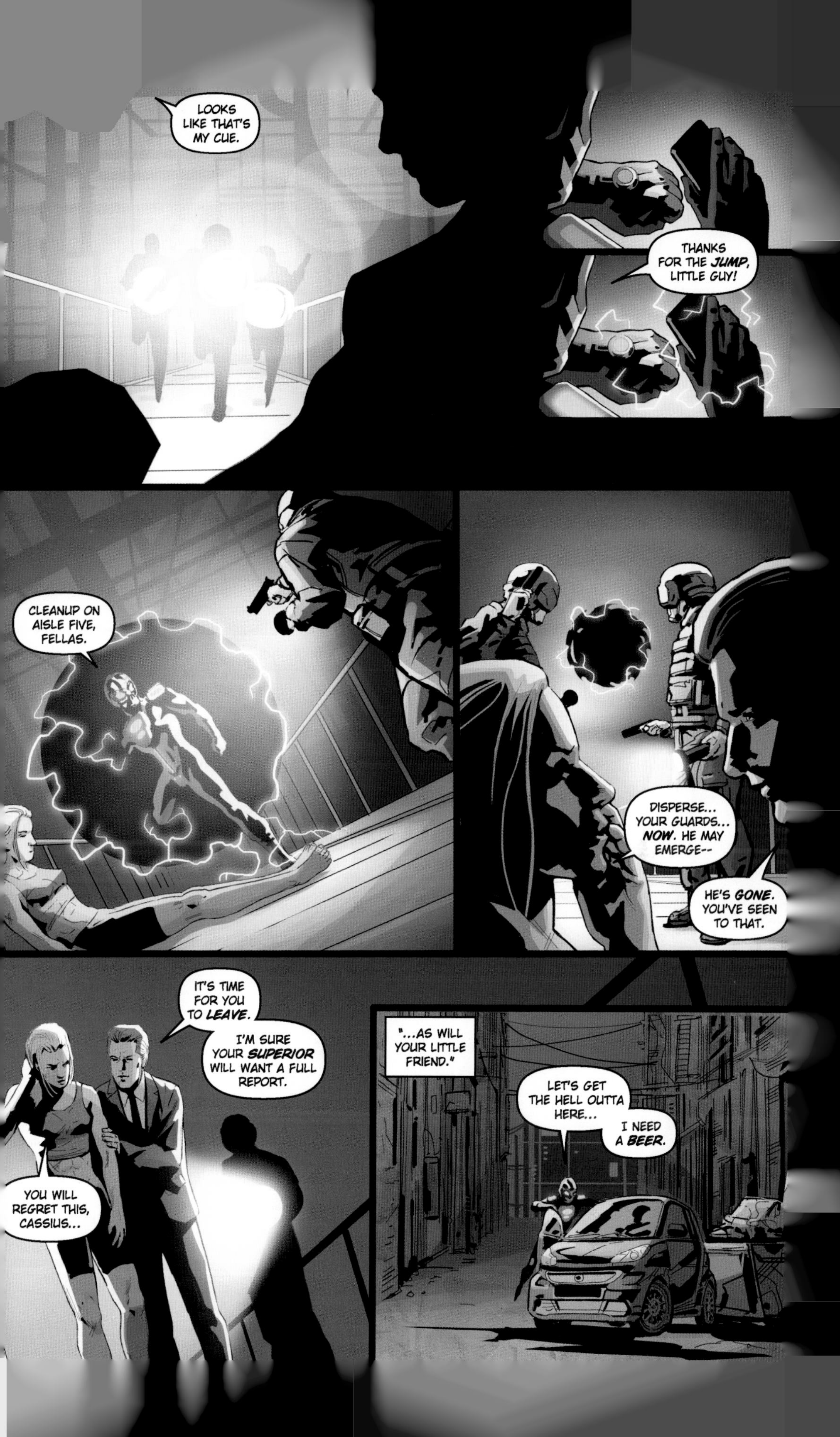
LOOKS LIKE THAT'S MY CUE.
THANKS FOR THE JUMP, LITTLE GUY!
CLEANUP ON AISLE FIVE, FELLAS.
DISPERSE... YOUR GUARDS... NOW. HE MAY EMERGE--
HE'S GONE. YOU'VE SEEN TO THAT.
IT'S TIME FOR YOU TO LEAVE.
I'M SURE YOUR SUPERIOR WILL WANT A FULL REPORT.
YOU WILL REGRET THIS, CASSIUS...
"...AS WILL YOUR LITTLE FRIEND."
LET'S GET THE HELL OUTTA HERE...
I NEED A BEER.

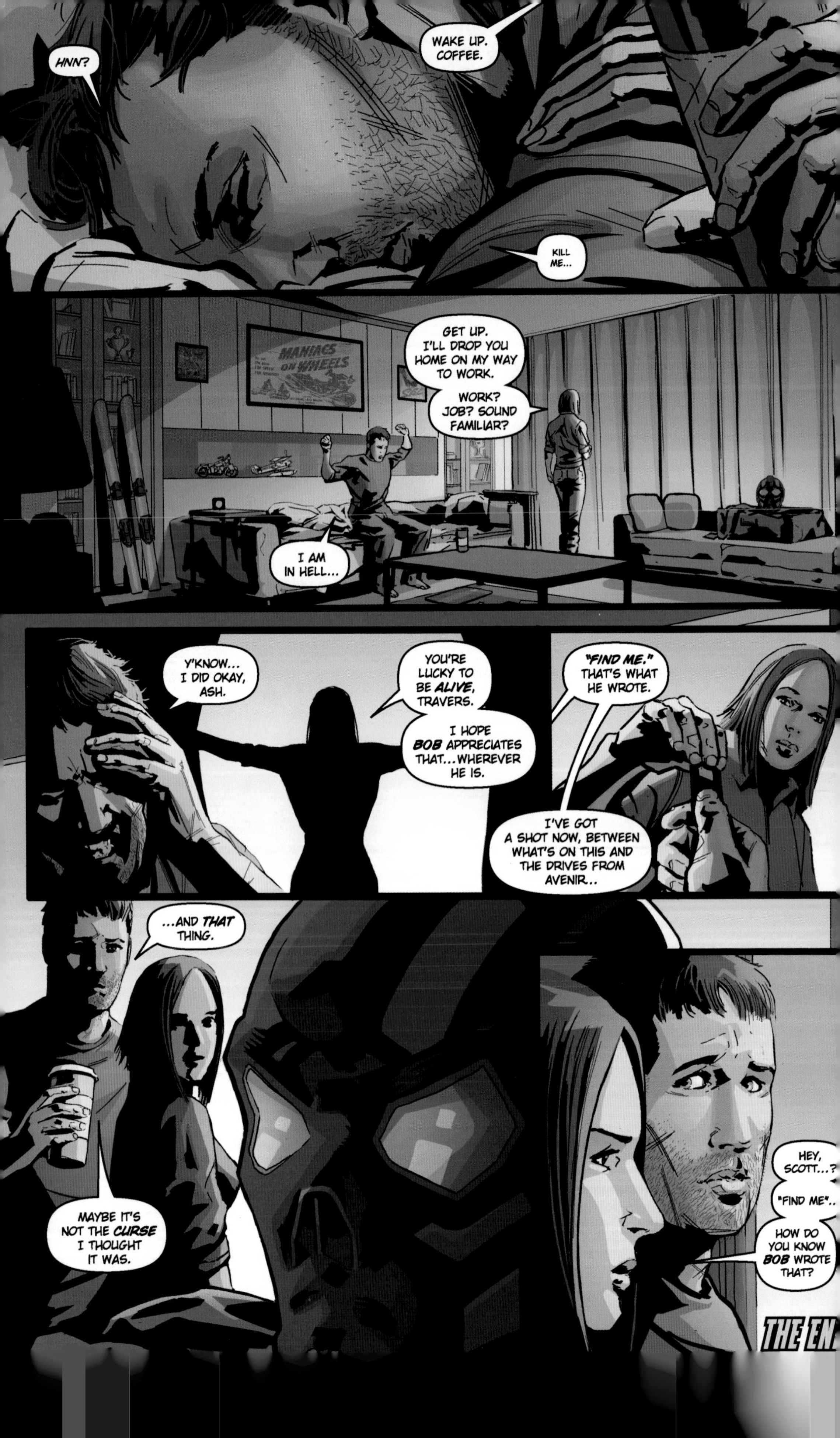

HNN?
WAKE UP. COFFEE.
KILL ME...
GET UP. I'LL DROP YOU HOME ON MY WAY TO WORK.
WORK? JOB? SOUND FAMILIAR?
I AM IN HELL...
Y'KNOW... I DID OKAY, ASH.
YOU'RE LUCKY TO BE ALIVE, TRAVERS.
I HOPE BOB APPRECIATES THAT...WHEREVER HE IS.
"FIND ME." THAT'S WHAT HE WROTE.
I'VE GOT A SHOT NOW, BETWEEN WHAT'S ON THIS AND THE DRIVES FROM AVENIR..
...AND THAT THING.
MAYBE IT'S NOT THE CURSE I THOUGHT IT WAS.
HEY, SCOTT...?
"FIND ME"..
HOW DO YOU KNOW BOB WROTE THAT?
THE EN

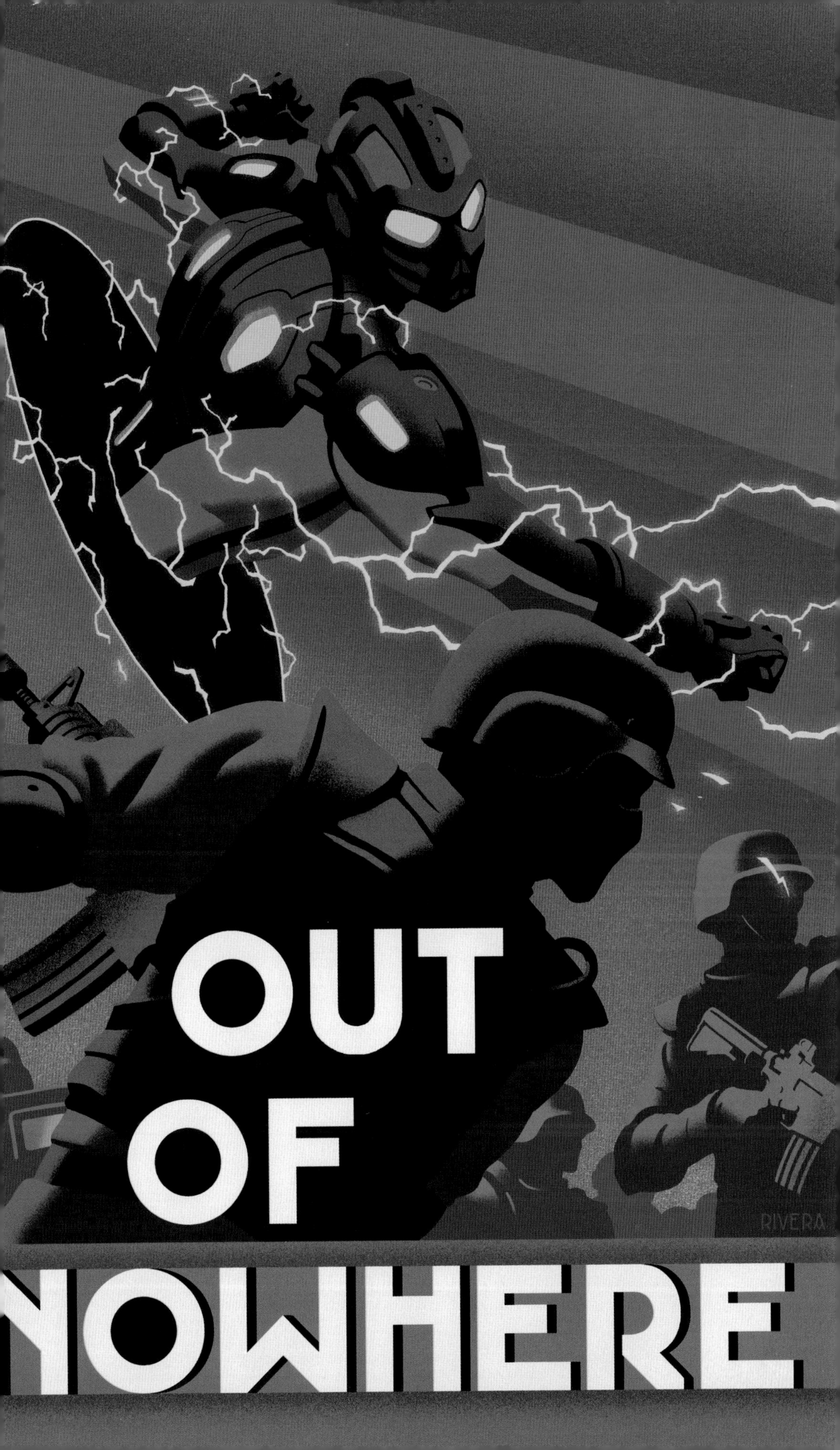
OUT
OF
NOWHERE
RIVERA

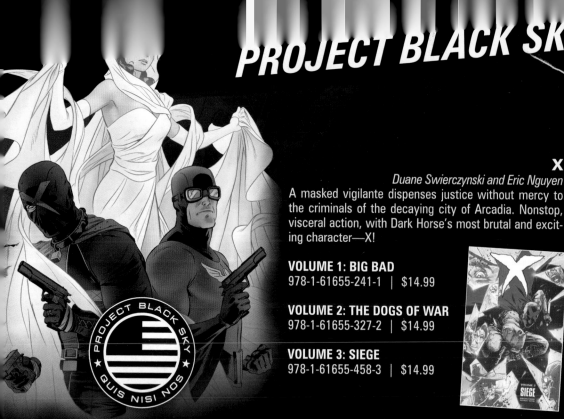

PROJECT BLACK SK

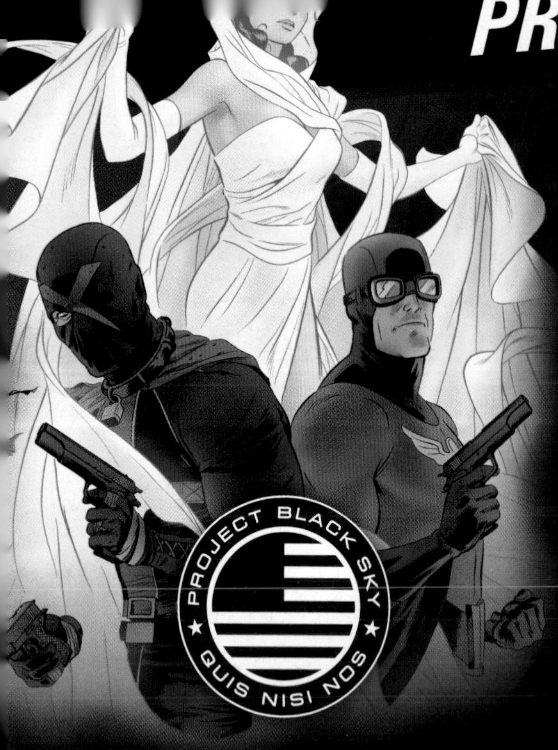
PROJECT BLACK SKY
QUIS NISI NOS

X

Duane Swierczynski and Eric Nguyen

A masked vigilante dispenses justice without mercy to the criminals of the decaying city of Arcadia. Nonstop, visceral action, with Dark Horse's most brutal and exciting character—X!

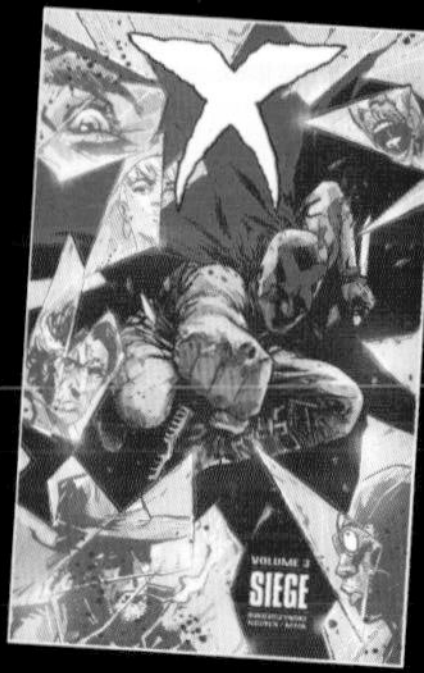
X
SIEGE

VOLUME 1: BIG BAD
978-1-61655-241-1 | $14.99

VOLUME 2: THE DOGS OF WAR
978-1-61655-327-2 | $14.99

VOLUME 3: SIEGE
978-1-61655-458-3 | $14.99

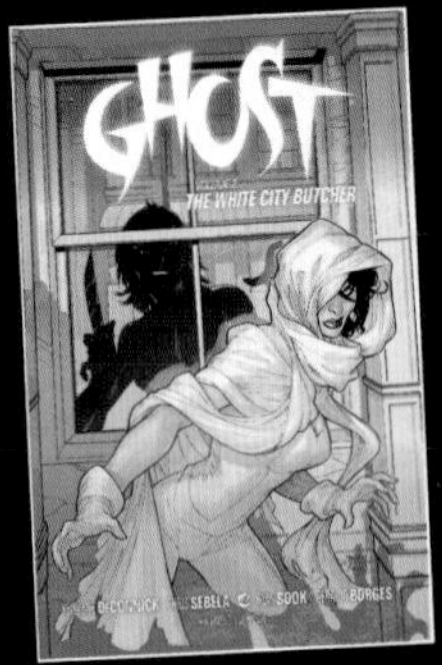
GHOST
THE WHITE CITY BUTCHER

GHOST

Kelly Sue DeConnick, Chris Sebela, Alex Ross, Ryan Sook, and others

Paranormal investigators accidentally summon a ghostly woman. The search for her identity uncovers a deadly alliance between political corruption and demonic science! In the middle stands a woman trapped between two worlds!

VOLUME 1: IN THE SMOKE AND DIN
978-1-61655-121-6 | $14.99

VOLUME 2: THE WHITE CITY BUTCHER
978-1-61655-420-0 | $14.99

CAPTAIN MIDNIGHT

Joshua Williamson, Fernando Dagnino, Eduardo Francisco, and others

In the forties, he was an American hero, a daredevil fighter pilot, a technological genius . . . a superhero. Since he rifled out of the Bermuda Triangle and into the present day, Captain Midnight has been labeled a threat to homeland security. Can Captain Midnight survive in the modern world, with the US government on his heels and an old enemy out for revenge?

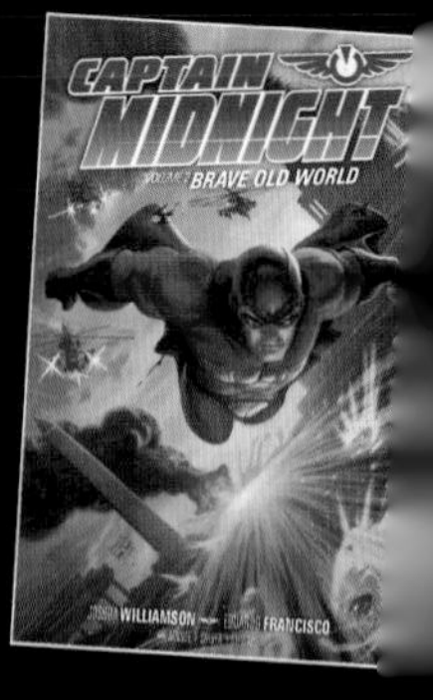
CAPTAIN MIDNIGHT
BRAVE OLD WORLD
WILLIAMSON
FRANCISCO

VOLUME 1: ON THE RUN
978-1-61655-229-9 | $14.99

VOLUME 2: BRAVE OLD WORLD
978-1-61655-230-5 | $14.99

VOLUME 3: FOR A BETTER TOMORROW
978-1-61655-231-2 | $14.99